S0-AXJ-086

Mountain of Gold

Mountain of Gold

The Story of the Chinese in America

卍 卍 卍 卍 卍 卍

BETTY LEE SUNG

THE MACMILLAN COMPANY, NEW YORK, N.Y.

Library of Congress Catalog Card Number: 67-21422
Second Printing 1970
The Macmillan Company
866 Third Avenue, New York, N.Y. 10022
Collier-Macmillan Canada Ltd., Toronto, Ontario
Printed in the United States of America

The author is grateful for the permission given by:
Pardee Lowe to use extensive portions of his book, *Father and Glorious Descendant*, published by Little, Brown and Company, Inc. 1943, pp. 143–146;
Alfred A. Knopf, Inc. to use excerpts from *The Big Four* by Oscar Lewis, copyright 1938.
Beulah Ong Kwoh to quote from her Master's Thesis, "The Occupational Status of the American-born Chinese College Graduates."

To

Tina

Victor

Cynthia

Alan

Acknowledgments

How can I thank all the people who have helped me, encouraged me, and given me information for this book? It would take columns to list the names of the hundreds whom I have spoken to or interviewed—who took time out of their busy schedules to tell me about their personal experiences, to send me pertinent material, or to refer me to other people.

I have never ceased to marvel at the friendliness and willingness of people to help an earnest writer. Were it not for Mort Presting of Funk and Wagnalls and for Charles Jones, director of the New York Foundation, who spent hours with me giving me editorial guidance, I would never have had the courage to begin.

For scholarly direction, I am indebted to Professor Joseph Gittler, formerly chairman of the Institute of Minority Relations at the University of Rochester and presently dean of Yeshiva University; Professor Davis McEntire of the University of California; Dr. Paul K. T. Sih, director of the Asian Institute of St. John's University; Dr. Chih Meng of the China Institute; and Dr. Francis L. K. Hsu, chairman of the Department of Anthropology at Northwestern University.

For the use of many of his news stories, I am indebted to William Yukon Chang, editor of the *Chinese American Times*.

For government statistics on immigration, I express my gratitude to Mrs. Helen Eckerson, chief of the statistics branch of the Immigration and Naturalization Service.

To all the librarians (especially those at the Queens Borough Public Library, the New York Public Library, the Great Neck, N.Y., Library, and the Library of Congress) whom I pestered unmercifully and who so graciously searched for and interloaned material for me, I say thank you and thank you again.

To all the writers and scholars whose works I consulted or referred to, and to those who so graciously permitted me to quote from their writings, I acknowledge my debt.

And to my children, who shared and spared their Mommy during the writing of this book, I dedicate this work.

Contents

1

Introduction

I WAS an angry young woman! Of course racial pride played a part in my indignation, but that the popular image of the Chinese in the United States was so grossly distorted made me all the more furious.

It all began with a weekly program that I wrote for the Voice of America, beamed to listeners throughout the Far East. Titled "Chinese Activities," its intent was to report on the daily lives and happenings of the Chinese in the United States. "What," thought the editorial staff, "would interest the Chinese in China and Southeast Asia more than learning about how their compatriots lived and were treated in a country that represented to them the 'Mountain of Gold,' the 'Land of the Beautiful,'[1] and presently archenemy of the Chinese Communists?"

The editors were right. The program found a very receptive audience, and it ran for years as a weekly feature. In trying to find material for my scripts, I scouted some of the best-stocked libraries in the country. There was almost no reliable published material to speak of. What little there was, was woefully inadequate or hopelessly outdated. But most shocking was what I did find—it literally set my hair on end.

Over and over again I found the same adjectives, the same characteristics, the same stereotyped labels ascribed to the Chinese: opium dens, tong wars, coolie labor, yellow peril, highbinders, hatchetmen,

[1] A literal translation of the Chinese characters for the United States is "Land of the Beautiful," but among the Chinese in the United States, the vernacular term for this country is *Gum Shan* or "Mountain of Gold." The name originated with the earliest immigrants who came to mine gold in the hills of California.

laundries, waiters, houseboys, slave wages, unassimilable aliens, and so on *ad nauseam*.

Were these my people? If so, I did not recognize them. Were these labels true of them in the past? If so, how long ago and from what perspective? How come the Chinese had never presented their side of the story? True, the Chinese have enjoyed a good press of late, but newspaper stories are transitory. Most puzzling is that amidst the intense interest in minority groups in recent years and the publication explosion of books and articles on race relations, the image of the Chinese in the United States has not been brought up to date.

From 1909, when Professor Mary Coolidge's book, *Chinese Immigration*, was published, to 1960, when Professor Rose Hum Lee's book, *The Chinese in the United States of America*, was imported from Hong Kong, no serious work about this neglected minority appeared in the United States. Some attempts have been made by American publishers since then to fill in the void, but I was utterly dismayed when new books published in the sixties harped upon the same worn-out themes a century old.

A learned tome put out by a university press dealt exclusively with the period of intense agitation against Chinese labor one hundred years ago. The author relied almost exclusively for his information on the newspapers in California at that time, and to say that they were biased is to be somewhat charitable.

Another volume published in 1962 dealt exclusively with tong wars and hatchetmen in San Francisco. And it is a wonder to me why the author of yet a third volume which came out in 1965 could not find more up-to-date photographs of the Chinese than those depicting his fellow countrymen with pigtails and in opium dens.

It seems to me that there is a fixation about the Chinese that demands the sensational, the lurid, the peculiarities, and the mysteries of this national group to the exclusion of fact. A case in point is the characterization of Fu Manchu originated by Sax Rohmer in the 1920's. For three decades, the escapades and adventures of this wizard of crime have entertained millions. With each episode, the image of the Chinese as devious and cunning, but most of all as evil, is impressed upon the American mind. Yet there has been a conspicuous absence of Chinese hauled before law-enforcement agencies.

Restrictionists and race purists have consistently played upon the fears of the American people by conjuring up pictures of hordes of Chinese coolies inundating the country if the severest exclusion laws were not enacted. Yet in 1888, when the Scott Act, harshest of all the exclusion laws against the Chinese, was passed, only ten Chinese persons entered the United States the preceding year. This, so the saying goes, was draining the pond to catch the minnow.

Tong wars, opium dens, highbinders, and Chinese houseboys went the way of the cowboy-and-Indian skirmishes on the Western frontier, but they are still favorite themes on television and in the movies.

Chinese-Americans sometimes swallow the stereotyped image of themselves conjured up by the public. They look upon themselves as insignificant, as handicapped and discriminated against. They develop an inferiority complex and are afraid to project themselves. Yet in this book you will read about some Chinese who have made significant contributions to American science, literature, and the arts.

Because of these misconceptions and because there was so little published material, I started to dig for the facts myself. It was not easy. I discovered that the mistaken image and the paucity of information about the Chinese in the United States were not entirely due to indifference or apathy on the part of the American public. The Chinese in the United States are equally at fault.

They were decidedly reluctant and averse to giving out any information they thought would appear in print. The general feeling among them is that the less the Americans know about the Chinese, the better. The trait comes from a cultural tradition and from fear that such information may be used against them. It had not occurred to them to dispute or attempt to disprove or improve their public image.

They do not realize that such reticence is self-damaging. Nor does it facilitate their acceptance and standing among the American people. Under favorable circumstances all is well, but in times of crises and hardship, people look for targets upon which to vent their pent-up emotions. They look for scapegoats to place the blame. Never willing to admit their true purpose, they may mask their motives in a moralistic crusade. If the Chinese are made to appear base and evil, any action against them will be readily condoned. The physical characteristics of the Chinese set them apart, making them easily identifiable targets. A little oil on the fire enhances the flame.

A nation is at a disadvantage when it is ignorant about a segment of its population. The Chinese constitute only a small percentage of that population, but it is a segment that now assumes a unique position.

The United States has always identified itself with Europe to the exclusion of the rest of the world. Now with the awakening of Asia, Africa, and Latin America, the United States finds itself ill-equipped and unprepared to cope with the situation. It does not have enough people who understand the languages of these lands. It is puzzled by attitudes and values that depart from its own. It is hurt by rejection of what it considers sincere offers of aid. And it is helpless and impatient in the face of an intransigence that it cannot comprehend.

It is almost appalling to think how little the American people know about China—a country with more than a quarter of the world's population and with a sixth of its arable land surface. When I attended the University of Illinois, one two-credit-hour course was offered in Asian history, but the professor was drafted from another discipline to teach a subject that he knew very little about. I was shocked one day to discover that his lectures were taken almost word for word from the *Encyclopedia Britannica.*

In 1957, a survey conducted by the Chinese Advisory Committee on Cultural Relations in America found that only a negligible number of courses on China were offered in American institutions of higher learning. Of the more than 1,800 institutions, only 219 offered any course touching on China or Chinese culture in any way. The survey revealed that for the entire country, a mere 123 students were then majoring in studies on China.

Again in 1957, the Foreign Service of the United States sent out a questionnaire to all of its foreign service officers asking them to list the languages in which they were fluent or in which they had a working knowledge. Only three men in the entire Foreign Service listed Chinese.

At the junior high and high school level, French, Spanish, German, and Latin are common electives in the New York City school system, but in the entire public school system in the city, only one school offers a course in beginning Chinese—and this lone course was initiated in 1964.

George A. Kennedy, having foreseen the postwar role of China, founded the Yale Institute of Far Eastern Languages in 1943. It was a pioneer. Harvard's East Asian Research Center was not established until 1957. It took Sputnik and an atomic bomb—the first detonated by China—to prod American leaders into realizing that China could not be ignored. A crash program under the National Defense Educational Act provided top priority federal grants and scholarships for studies of China. In 1966, about 60 U.S. colleges and universities offered degree programs in Chinese with approximately 2,500 students registered. This is a substantial increase from 123, but the number is puny in comparison with the need. Let me tell you a story, a first-hand account related to me by a war correspondent who covered the long, drawn-out negotiations with Communist China in the Korean armistice talks.

During this humiliating chapter in American history, the United States was maneuvered into an impossible position by the Chinese Communists. In the prisoner-of-war camps the American captors were subjected to the whims and dictates of the captured. Chinese prisoners of war were herded into compounds where the capturing troops, for all their guns and weapons, dared not venture.

Each day, food was shoved into the compounds with long sticks. The leaders immediately cornered the food and apportioned it out to those who obeyed their dictates. The compounds were ruled within by trained cadres who allowed themselves to be captured for the express purpose of organizing the prisoners into insurgents. These leaders spoke excellent English while their captors spoke no Chinese. *The American Armed Forces were compelled to rely upon the enemy for communication with the prisoners of war, and thus were completely at their mercy.*

Amidst the smoldering prisoner-of-war camps was a Chinese-American sergeant attached to the U.S. forces. When it was discovered that he could speak Chinese, his services were in incessant demand. Like a lone doctor in the midst of a raging epidemic, the sergeant was on call twenty-four hours a day.

An urgent call was put through to Washington to send out more interpreters. As my war correspondent friend related, among the first to arrive was a student of Chinese fresh out of Yale. He was commissioned immediately and sent to Panmunjom. Arriving in splendid regalia, with the oak leaves of a major on his shoulders, he was called for his first assignment. As the prisoners of war poured out their invectives in torrents, the major stood dumbstruck. He understood not one syllable that was uttered. The Chinese he had learned at Yale was the pure Mandarin dialect, the language of officials and scholars. These POW's were farmers, laborers, common folk from every province in the vast expanse of China. They spoke their local variations of the Mandarin dialect, which in a broad general term is called the "common dialect." A person well grounded in his Mandarin would understand the common dialect and vice versa. But one whose knowledge of Chinese was shallow would find the variations totally incomprehensible.

Since the Korean War, Sino-American relations have worsened. Anger and hatred against the United States are being pounded and instilled into Chinese minds to replace the deep affection and warm friendship that the Chinese people once held for the United States. The American people are hurt and puzzled that their former good friend has become their enemy. At the same time, they have no idea how to go about winning back China's friendship, for they do not know enough about China. Nor are there enough leaders trained in the language and familiar with Chinese customs and thought to lead the American people toward a better rapport with China.

Another two decades have gone by. The United States is still bogged down in Asia, and it finds itself even deeper in the mire. Instead of Korea, the battleground has shifted to Vietnam. Perhaps after that, it will shift to India, but the real protagonist is China. Unless Sino-American differences are resolved, world tension will remain at high pitch.

Bound up in this struggle between the United States and China is the battle for the support of the overseas Chinese in Southeast Asia, an area rich in the primary resources of the world. It may come as a surprise and revelation that the total overseas Chinese population is quite large. It numbers about 13.5 million, which is equal to the entire population of countries as vast as Canada or Australia. Chinese are found in almost every nook on the globe, but by and large, they are heavily concentrated in Southeast Asia. In this area they are pillars of economic and political strength.

The ties of common ancestry bind the overseas Chinese together. As I mentioned previously, my program on the Chinese in the United States found a receptive audience among Chinese everywhere. This is human nature, for undoubtedly Americans would be equally interested in finding out how American expatriates are faring in China.

Historically, ill treatment of the overseas Chinese has been a sore bone of contention among a nationally aroused Chinese populace. In years past, the governments of China were indifferent or were too weak to protect the interests of Chinese subjects abroad. Peking could capture the hearts of the overseas Chinese instantly if she were provided with the opportunity to take a strong stand against the discrimination and abuse suffered by the Chinese living abroad. How the Chinese in the United States are treated should prove of special interest.

In this fracture of Sino-American relations, I submit that the Chinese-Americans could serve as interpreters of the Oriental mind. To a large extent, they are already fulfilling this role. Most of the instructors at the Army Language School in Monterey, California, are Chinese. The budding courses in Chinese history, philosophy, art, and language in American universities and colleges are being taught by a distinguished group of more than 1,450 professors and instructors of Chinese ancestry. Many of the learned tomes recently published on China were authored by Chinese-Americans. These are the people who are initiating a belated but concentrated effort toward a better understanding of China.

The position of the Chinese in the United States is tied in not only with the international situation, but with the domestic issue of race relations as well. Although the struggle is primarily between Negroes and whites, comparisons can be made with the Chinese experiences, and it should be noted that the Chinese have benefited from the Negro's struggle.

Because of readily identifiable physical distinctness, which will always set them apart as hyphenated Americans, the term "Chinese in the United States" as used in this book includes not only the recent immigrants but also the American-born Chinese, whose roots have been imbedded in American soil for nearly one hundred years.

Since 1949 the homogeneity of the group has been disturbed. Economic betterment, once the most compelling reason for emigration from China, gave way to ideological and political reasons for leaving the motherland. A large number of the recent immigrants may be classified under the heading of refugee. Of these refugees, a large number were students who came to the United States for their higher education. With the Communists in control of the mainland, many of these students were reluctant to return to their homeland upon completion of their studies. They were allowed to remain in the United States. Most of these students have already found their niches in American society, both economically and socially. They have become American citizens. Because of their excellent education and scholastic background, they are a group that any nation would be proud to claim.

Others in the refugee class are former officials of the Nationalist government, the monied class, or intelligentsia who sought sanctuary from Communist persecution. These form a motley group and, along with the former students, must be differentiated from the more homogeneous immigrant Chinese and their families. The main dialect of the refugee class is Mandarin while the vernacular for the immigrant group is Cantonese or Toishanese. Since Mandarin is incomprehensible to the Cantonese and vice versa, and since their backgrounds are so dissimilar, the two groups have not merged.

In a larger sense, the refugee class is part of the Chinese population in the United States, but their numbers are comparatively small, and their sojourn in this country has been of short duration. Yet, if they have taken out American citizenship, they are properly Chinese-Americans. But when I speak of the Chinese in the United States, I refer mainly to the larger numbers who emigrated from China or whose ancestors emigrated from China to seek their livelihood in this country, except when I speak specifically about the refugee class.

Because I deplore exploitation of the sensational, the exotic, the stereotyped image of the Chinese, I do not mean to imply that this book is a refutation or whitewash. Nor is it a public relations scheme. I have tried to present the facts, and the facts speak for themselves.

The Chinese population in the United States according to the 1960 census was 237,000. By 1970, this figure should exceed 300,000. The group is not large when compared with total U.S. population. In fact, three stadiums as large as the Rose Bowl in Pasadena, California, could seat all the Chinese now in this country and still not be filled to capacity. But the rate of increase within the group itself is high. It will nearly triple in size in the twenty years between 1950 and 1970. The repercussions of this expansion will be marked both within the group and in relationship to the larger society.

Along with the rapid growth in population during this time, the Chinese have enjoyed an unprecedented degree of acceptance among the American people. This once static and insignificant minority is undergoing dynamic transformation. In this book we will be looking back into history and the years that have passed, but hopefully we may also catch a glimpse of the future.

2

The Fountainhead

EMIGRATION requires powerful motivation. Creatures of habit and tradition, men are inclined to stay where they are and endure what they must, rather than strike out for uncertainty and the unknown. That the pioneer Chinese emigrant ventured across 7,000 miles of ocean from his staid and stable society to the wild unruly West of the American continent is the outcome of strong conflicting forces.

In the 1840's, when the first Chinese had already set sail for the shores of the "Mountain of Gold," he knew that if he was caught, his head would be severed from his body by one stroke of the executioner's axe. For the *Laws and Precedents of the Ching Dynasty, Volume 20* stated:

> When officials, whether soldiers or civil servants, illegally go out to sea, to trade or to settle on islands there to live and farm, they shall be considered as conniving with rebels, and if caught shall receive the death penalty. Magistrates found conniving in such an offense on the part of others likewise shall receive the death penalty. . . . Any official responsible for the arrest of ten illegal emigrants shall be accorded one merit toward his promotion; if of one hundred such culprits, his reward shall be promotion to the next higher rank. . . .

China's repressive policy on emigration was not relaxed until 1860, long after thousands of Chinese had risked the wrath of the Emperor and the perils of the sea to seek their fortunes in the land where the streets were rumored to be paved with gold. Another thirty-four years elapsed before the death penalty against emigration was formally abrogated by imperial decree.

As if a death sentence was not enough, other deterrents faced the would-be emigrant. Confucian teachings—the foundation of Chinese culture—placed filial piety at the top of the list of virtues. For a son to leave his ancestral home and aged parents for any protracted length of time was unfilial behavior, a cardinal sin.

Monetary considerations were also paramount. Passage to the United States was no mean sum for these emigrants to raise while shipowners took advantage of the gold cry to enrich themselves with human cargoes between Canton and San Francisco. But those who had gone before sent back word and money for relatives to come.

It took rare courage, grim determination, and a venturesome spirit for these men to circumvent the law, to buck society, and to leave home and loved ones for unknown destinations in the hopes of bettering their fortunes.

Strange though it may seem, only Toishan, a tiny district of Kwangtung in southern China, responded to the news of the discovery of gold in California. The news had filtered down the eastern coast of China by the ships that put into port, but it made no impact elsewhere. Family ties were too strong, the risks too great. The people were resigned to toil and deprivation. It remained for the Toishanese and those in the immediate vicinity to take that first step and set in motion a steady stream of emigration.

The Toishanese came originally from pioneering stock. The Middle Kingdom, as the Chinese call their country, had its origin along the banks of the Yellow River, far to the north. Gradually, China's borders were pushed south by the adventuresome, the exiles, the discontented, until they could push no further. The barrier of the sea stopped them, so they stayed to till the rocky mountainsides and scrape a meager living from their constant toil. As the sea hemmed them in, they could only suppress the surging of their adventuresome blood. But this same blood flowed on in the veins of their offspring to manifest its true quality as soon as opportunity arose.

There has been no precise count, but reliable estimates place 60 percent of the Chinese immigrants in this country as hailing from this one district, Toishan[1] alone, and a good proportion of the remaining

[1] Sometimes romanized Tai-shan or Hoishan. Prior to 1914, this district was known as Sunning or Hsin-ning.

40 percent as originating from the surrounding vicinity of that same district. These neighboring places are: Hsin-hui, Hoi-ping, Yan-ping, Nan-hoi, Pan-yu, Hsun-tak, Canton, Hok-san, Tung-kwan, Chung-shan, Pao-an, Chin-hoi, Hakka, and Hong Kong. In recent years, political refugees and student groups have diluted this homogeneity, but only to a slight degree. The forebears of the majority of Chinese in this country originated from the general area of Toishan.

That the Toishanese outnumber emigrants from other parts of China is confirmed by three substantiating facts:

One, the constitution of the Chinese Benevolent Association of New York City, former quasi-official but now self-styled governing organization of the Chinese community, specifies that its chairmanship and executive officers must alternate between a governing board from the district of Toishan and a board representing all other places in China combined. The purpose of this stipulation, no doubt, was to make sure that the Toishanese are proportionately represented according to their numbers in the powerful and influential postitions as leaders of this once over-all governing body.

Two, in San Francisco, another major center of Chinese population in the United States, the Chinese Six Companies, equivalent of the Chinese Benevolent Associations in other cities, elects its officers on a similar basis. The Chinese Six Companies derives its name from the six regions whose emigrants make up practically the entire Chinese population in the United States. These six regions include all the districts and cities mentioned above. As members from Toishan far outnumber the others combined, the chairmanship of the Chinese Six Companies goes to a Toishanese every other term. The other five regions must be content with rotating among themselves the alternating term. In other words, the chairmanship goes from Region A to Toishan to Region B and then back to Toishan again.

Three, Gabriel Lasker, in a study of physical differentiation between China-born and native-born Chinese, incidentally gave us a statistical substantiation of the overwhelming majority of Toishanese among the Chinese in New York City. One of the questions put to his subjects was: What part of China do you come from? The tabulated results are given in Table 2–1.

TABLE 2-1
Origin of Chinese Immigrants in New York City

Place	*No. of Immigrants*
Sze Yup (4 Counties)	
Hsin-hui	32
Toishan	216
Hoi-ping	26
Yan-ping	4
Sam Yup (3 Counties including Canton)	
Nan-hoi	2
Pan-yu	4
Hsun-tak	1
Canton City	24
Other Cantonese*	
Hok-shan	11
Tung-kwan	4
Chung-shan	18
Pao-an	20
Chin-hoi	4
"Near Canton"	14
Hakka	4
Hong Kong	4
Total	388

* Popular term for people from province of Kwangtung

SOURCE: Gabriel Ward Lasker, unpublished doctoral dissertation, "Physical Characteristics of the Chinese, A Study of Physical Differences and Development Among the Chinese at Home and Abroad" (Harvard University, 1945), p. 44.

To understand why, in the face of such overwhelming deterrents, the Toishanese—while few from other parts of China—emigrated to the United States, it is necessary to go back to this fountainhead of the immigrant flow. What is Toishan like? What are her resources, her industries, the occupations of her people? What are some of the customs and habits of this region? What caused her sons to leave for distant shores?

Toishan is one of 98 districts in the province of Kwangtung. It is a small political subdivision equivalent to an American county. Only 3,200 kilometers in area, it supports a present population of 680,000.[2]

Situated at 22° 15′ latitude and 112° 45′ longitude, Toishan is near the major cities of Canton, which lies to her northeast, and Hong Kong to her southeast. In this semi-tropical zone, the climate is hot and humid most of the year, ideal for agricultural purposes were it not for the rocky terrain, which gives the district its name. A glance at a topographical map of Kwangtung shows that Toishan rises like a mountain island to a height of 800 to 1,000 feet while the surrounding regions drop like a cliff to sea level. The name, Toishan itself, is an accurate description of the place. Toi means plateau or elevated. Shan means mountain. Toishan together means Plateau Mountain or Elevated Mountain. Whichever you choose, the place is mountainous, rocky, and almost barren. Her agricultural output can feed her population for only four months out of the year. Because rice, the money crop and main staple of the southern Chinese, grows only in low, flooded, level ground, Toishan is literally left high and dry.

Hemmed in by mountain terrain, besieged by the ever-present threat of starvation, and pressured by masses of swarming population all grasping at a food supply that could sustain only a third of them, the Toishanese were forced to look for nonagricultural means of subsistence. But China was an agrarian society—sustenance came only from the land. There was little industry to speak of and human labor was too plentiful and much too cheap to exchange for a decent livelihood.

Many Toishanese turned to trade, acting as middlemen between buyers and sellers. And as salesmen and merchants, they traveled to the big cities and coastal ports, where they came into frequent contact with the white man and the huge sailing vessels with their cargoes of goods. The harbor nearest to Toishan is Hong Kong, which had been ceded to Great Britain after the Opium War in 1842, and which the British quickly made the major port of the entire Southeast Asian region.

Proximity and contact made the Toishanese more receptive to the news about the discovery of gold in California in 1845. Having dealt

[2] *Kwangtung Travel Guide* (in Chinese). The figures were based on a census taken by the Chinese Communist Government in 1953.

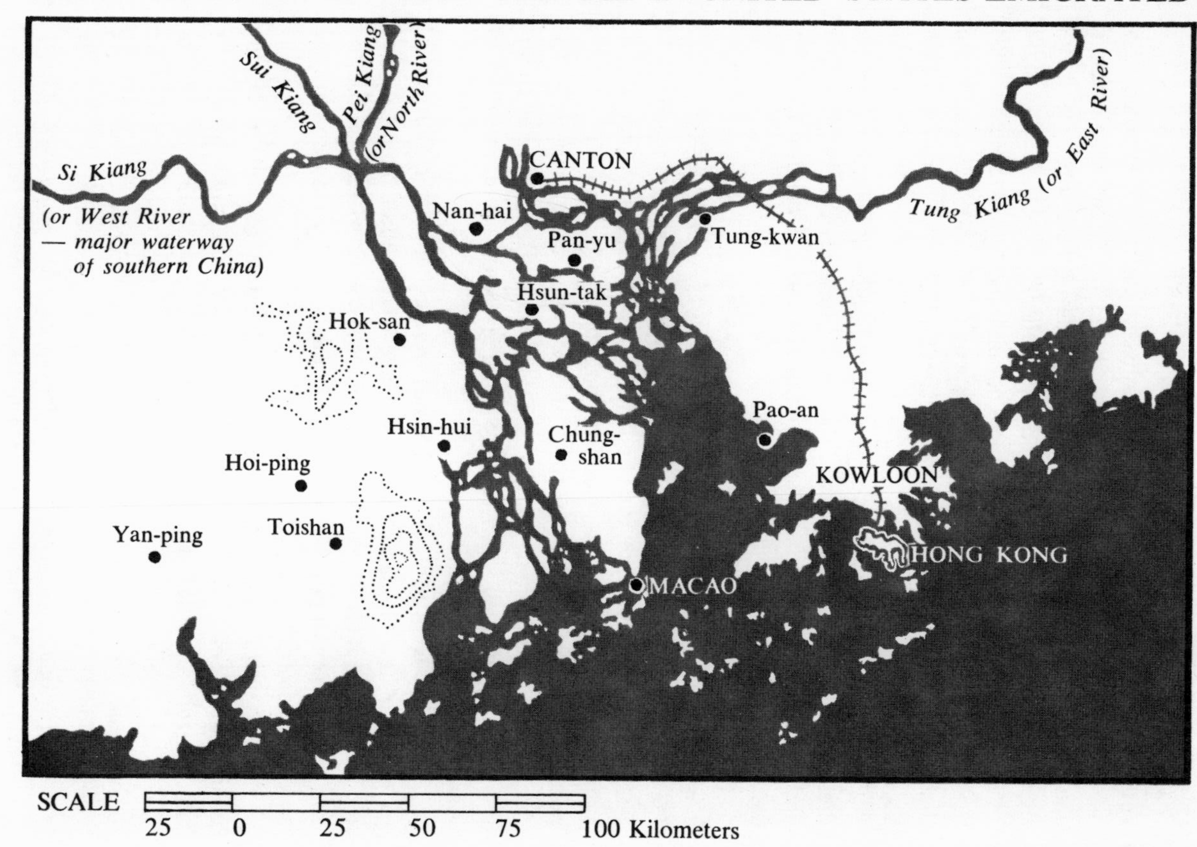
AREA FROM WHICH MOST CHINESE IN UNITED STATES EMIGRATED
Sui Kiang
Pei Kiang
(or North River)
Si Kiang
(or West River
— major waterway
of southern China)
CANTON
Tung Kiang (or East River)
Nan-hai
Pan-yu
Tung-kwan
Hsun-tak
Hok-san
Pao-an
Hsin-hui
Chung-
shan
Hoi-ping
KOWLOON
Yan-ping
Toishan
HONG KONG
MACAO
SCALE
25
0
25
50
75
100 Kilometers

Figure 2–A

with the white man in their business transactions, the Toishanese did not find the idea of sailing in one of the ships to the white man's country so forbidding or preposterous. Besides, greater obstacles have succumbed to man's lust and greed for wealth.

Thus goaded by his circumstance, conditioned by his contacts with the white man, and lured by the prospect of getting rich quick, the first of the Toishanese bought passage and set sail for California shores.

Obviously the first arrivals were not disappointed. Eager to impress their families and acquaintances, they sent home packets of gold dust and gold nuggets. The news spread rapidly and the clamor to go to the Mountain of Gold began.

The United States continued to prove itself the Mountain of Gold even when the veins of that precious metal gave out in California (see page 29), for a steady stream of remittances enhanced by a favorable rate of exchange flowed home. Special prestige and social standing soon attached to families with husbands, sons, or fathers abroad. Families worked, scraped, and schemed to raise passage for one of their men to go to the United States, and girls considered themselves lucky if they married into families with some member in America.

Those who went to the United States were called "Gum Shan Hok" or guests of the Golden Mountain. Their wives didn't have to go to the fields and their sons and daughters were sent to school, for the remittances sent home enabled the families to live in comparative ease and comfort.

Like an intravenous injection, the remittances also sustained the economy of Toishan. So, in spite of her poor soil, made poorer by the natural calamities of floods and typhoons and depleted after centuries of intensive cultivation, Toishan became one of the most prosperous districts in China. It was often referred to as "Little Canton" after the bustling commercial port of southern China. In the town proper, the streets of Toishan were wide and paved, illuminated with electric lights at night. Impressive modern buildings lined the busy streets. On market days, the town was jammed with people from nearby villages who came to town to do their shopping or selling.

Nature had also been penurious in endowing Toishan with any natural outlet, but this problem was also solved by overseas remittances. Railway mileage was and is a scarcity in China, but Toishan once boasted of her own railroad[3] radiating north, south, and east, connecting her with the more usual mode of transportation—water. A good system of motor roads complemented her railroads to give her easy access to adjacent territories and the sea.

In education, Toishan stood near the top, if not the top, for a political subdivision of its kind in China. In 1940, there were 7 high schools, 2 normal schools, 2 trade schools, 167 consolidated schools, and 834 grade schools.[4] In 1953, the Communist government asserted that Toishan had 30 high schools or normal schools and that 85 percent of the children of school age attended classes. No other district in Kwangtung Province could claim the same educational facilities.

The school buildings helped beautify the town. Toi-chung, an outstanding high school, stood on the top of a hill. Its modern architecture, its rolling campus, and its groups of uniformed young students gave the place a dignified academic air, quite comparable to the atmosphere of an American college campus.

Most of the normal and high schools in Toishan had buildings and campuses that any school would be proud to claim. These school buildings were largely built in the 1930's. During the Japanese occupation, however, many of these spacious and lovely buildings were used for troop quarters and defaced.

The District Government Building was a green and white office building approached by a wide avenue. Not far to the right was a white marble library with facilities for exhibitions, for recreation, and of course for reading and borrowing books and periodicals.

Many other buildings worth mentioning were landmarks of the town: the railway station, the movie house, the YMCA, and a modern white marble hospital. These may sound commonplace to Americans accustomed to these facilities, but compared with the facilities in other small towns in China, these edifices gave Toishan special distinction.

[3] This railroad was completely destroyed by Japanese bombs during World War II.

[4] Han-Wen Li, *Districts of Kwangtung Province,* Sept. 1940. (in Chinese)

The schools were built and maintained by contributions from the Chinese abroad. Every time a new civic project needed funds, someone was dispatched to make the rounds of the Chinese overseas. It was a five-dollar contribution from the laundryman in his little shop, a fifteen-dollar contribution from the man who runs that chop suey place, a two-dollar contribution from the clerk in the grocery store that built the schools, the hospital, the library. Everyone gave. Seldom did they refuse. Although their government once looked upon them as disloyal subjects, and the land that gave them birth denied them a decent existence, these emigrants held no grudges. In fact, their love for their hometown and country was so strong that the fruits of their labor and hardships went in large measure to transforming this mountainous, rocky area into one of the first-rate towns of China.

The town itself was comparatively small in area, for most of the people lived in suburban villages. The villages were almost uniformly alike: gray brick houses set in rows four to six feet apart. A group of these houses made up one village whose members in all probability were related in some way or another. Members of the same village invariably shared the same family name.

The family name is an interesting characteristic of the Chinese people. There are but 438 surnames in China. That is why so many Chinese have the name of Wong, Moy, Lee, or Chan. There are millions of Lees, some related to each other but most not. Yet, it is taboo for a couple with the same surname to marry, for it would be considered incest.

The Chinese family was one of the most closely knit units in the world. Often, several generations of the male side lived under the same roof. A daughter who was married off, once she crossed her husband's threshold, became part of the husband's family. Almost all ties were severed with her own family except for visits on special occasions. A man was obligated to support his brother's widow and children, but not his sister should she become widowed. Her husband's family was responsible and the lines of responsibility were clear-cut.

In any event, the family looked after its own, as there were no insurance benefits, orphanages, old folks' homes, or poor houses. Insurance or social security operates on the principle of spreading the risks. Since the Chinese family is invariably large, providing a bulwark in numbers, and family property is common property, each member is entitled to his share of the contents of the rice pot. More than rice is shared by the family that lives and works as a unit. One member's disgrace is a disgrace to all. One member's honor is an honor to all.

Toishan has its own dialect, different from Cantonese and radically different from Mandarin. But while it is a local dialect in China, it is the main tongue of the Chinese in this country. In any business dealings with the Chinese in the United States, not to speak or understand Toishanese can be a handicap. Even those who speak Mandarin or other dialects fluently are sometimes ridiculed by the Toishanese as being unable to speak Chinese.

Spiritually, the Toishanese do not adhere to any one religion unless ancestor worship is labeled as such. However, ancestor worship is not a religion in the true sense of the word. Confucius taught his people to honor their parents. In no other country in the world did parents and elders enjoy such respect, such veneration, such consideration. This held true in life as well as in death. That was why memorial plaques with the names of deceased ancestors were set up in prominent places in the home. During holidays or festive occasions, incense was burned and food dutifully offered in front of the plaques in memory of those departed.

In spite of the poor soil and mountainous topography of Toishan, the village people were mainly farmers. The hills were terraced and planted with sweet potatoes, peanuts, and vegetables. And where the ground could be leveled and flooded, rice was grown. Each family tended a vegetable patch and kept a brood of chickens. Since the economy was supplemented by overseas remittances, and the population did not entirely depend upon the land for existence, there was little of that grim battle between man and nature found in other parts of China.

Since 1951, when Communist China entered the Korean War, the United States Foreign Assets Control Board forbade any further remittances to mainland China. Of course this worked severe hardship upon the families dependent upon this source of income. Regularly, the sons and fathers had sent money home for the support of their families, and more often than not, this support extended to brothers, nephews, uncles and aunts, and even distant relatives. Now the flow of remittances has dried up.

According to the *China Year Book*, immediately after the termination of World War II in 1946, the overseas Chinese sent through the Toishan Branch of the Bank of China a sum of $14,000,000 in Chinese currency. The uncertainty caused by the political atmosphere in 1947 caused the remittances to take a plunge to $1,900,000. When the Communists occupied Kwangtung in 1948, the total year's remittances came to $50,000, and during the first six months of 1949, after the Communists entered Toishan, only $8,900 was remitted.

How Toishan has been able to adjust to this situation we do not know. Reliable information from mainland China is not available. Kinsmen dare not write to their relatives in the United States for fear of being associated with "imperialistic America." The Chinese in the United States do not write home for fear that they will endanger their kinsmen in China. Fortunately, a great number of families were united with their menfolk in the United States as a result of the liberalized immigration policies following World War II. But Toishan, which had been so long dependent upon overseas remittances for the major part of her revenue and income, must have undergone thrashing throes of readjustment.

Because of the political tension between the United States and Red China, the Chinese in the United States have also had to undergo reorientation in outlook and thinking. No longer is Toishan or China their home. Once the tie was cut, the Chinese sought for themselves a new niche in American life. The story of their search is the theme of this book.

3

The Pioneer Chinese

SURPRISINGLY, the very first Chinese to set foot on United States soil were not adventurers or laborers in search of gold but students in search of knowledge. In 1847, a year before the glitter of that metallic substance caught the eye of John Marshall on the south bank of the American River, an American missionary, the Reverend S. R. Brown, had brought with him three Chinese boys to the United States to study at the Monson Academy in Massachusetts. One of them was Yung Wing, who later graduated from Yale and who attained high office in the Chinese government. He was successful in persuading the Emperor to send other students to the United States for specialized training and education, almost all of whom eventually rendered distinguished service to their country, then emerging from her self-isolation.

Historian J. O'Meara said the first Chinese to arrive on the West Coast were merchants with beautiful silks, tea, and *objets d'art*.[1] The first Chinese immigrants, according to H. H. Bancroft, were two men and a woman who arrived aboard the *Bard Eagle* in 1848. The two men went directly to the mines and the woman went to work in the home of a missionary named Charles Gillespie, who had also come on the same boat from Hong Kong.[2]

Under ordinary circumstances, the number of Chinese who would venture beyond their native shores across 7,000 miles of ocean would have been inconsequential. The deterrents were too many. But when merchant ships put into Canton with exaggerated tales of the gold discovery in California, mountains crumbled, oceans dried up,

[1] J. O'Meara, "The Chinese in Early Days," *Overland Monthly*, n.s.v. 3 (1884).
[2] H. H. Bancroft, *History of California*, (San Francisco, The San Francisco History Co., 1884–1890), Vol. III, p. 336.

distances shrank, and dangers were shrugged off for men of ambition quick to take advantage of a situation that promised fortunes in nothing less than gold. By 1851, in a matter of three years, there were 25,000 Chinese in California.

Fatt Hing was one of these 25,000. His story is typical of the pioneer Chinese, many who came with him and many who came after him.

As a lad of nineteen, Fatt Hing had already seen and heard and learned more about the world than most of the men in his village, who had seldom set foot beyond the nearest town square. For Fatt Hing was a fish peddler who went frequently from Toishan to Kwanghai on the coast to buy his fish to sell at the market.

Down by the wharves, where the fishing boats came in, Fatt Hing had often seen foreign ships with their sails fluttering in the wind. He had seen hairy white men on the decks, and he had often wondered and dreamed about the lands they came from. Fatt Hing had been fortunate in that he had been to school, although this schooling lasted no more than two years. In this short period of time, he had gained an awareness that China was not the center of the universe and that foreign white devils with guns and boats had been pushing China around.

One morning there was a great deal of commotion and excitement on the wharves. Elbowing his way to the center of the crowd, Fatt Hing caught snatches of the cause of the commotion amidst the shouting and the pushing. By putting together a word here and a word there, he surmised that there were mountains of gold for the picking, somewhere beyond the oceans.

In the gray dawn of early mornings following, Fatt Hing's ears strained to catch every word pertaining to the Mountain of Gold on the wharves. His mind was already made up. How to get there was the question he sought to answer.

Fatt Hing was cautious. He confided in no one, for he did not wish to alarm his parents. True, they were not solely dependent upon him for support. He had two older brothers, but his parents would forbid him to go and he did not want to upset them. By the time Fatt Hing had gathered enough information to learn that he could buy passage on one of the huge foreign ships, he was shocked into a cold sweat to discover that the magistrate's soldiers had arrested many of the less discreet who had tried to board a ship. Belatedly, they had learned that it was a crime punishable by capital punishment for a subject of the Emperor to emigrate from his homeland.

Many more months of cautious probing rewarded Fatt Hing with the knowledge that the garrison leader could be bribed. It took longer to persuade his parents to let him go. By that time, reports were filtering back that the Mountain of Gold was no myth and that the gold was free to any who would come and mine it. Then there was no holding Fatt Hing back. His father sold the water buffalo and Fatt Hing's mother pawned her earrings for his passage. Together they bade their son a tearful farewell, and he was smuggled on board a Spanish ship bound for California.

After he was secreted on board, Fatt Hing discovered to his surprise that the entire hold was filled with young men like himself. They slept, sat, ate, and waited on straw mats on the floor. The air in the hold was stifling and foul, putrid from the vomiting of those who had yet to acquire their sea legs. Most of the time, the wind-swept decks were much too cold for the thin cotton or flax garments which Fatt Hing and his fellow passengers wore. Besides, most of the deck was roped off, absolutely forbidden grounds to the human cargo. Fatt Hing spent many days and nights with his nose pressed against a crack in the board covering the hold. Those days and nights were given to a lot of thinking with misgivings about the step that he had taken.

The uncertainties of what they were headed for and the rigors of the trip drew the men together. None actually knew anything beyond what he had learned through hearsay gathered surreptitiously from the grapevine. Yet they had committed themselves totally to embarkation for lands unknown. None had expected the trip to take more than three months. Ten days—twenty days—a month on ship, some had anticipated. Each day after that added to their apprehensions and fear.

Fatt Hing recognized no familiar face when he came aboard. As his surname was Chin, he quickly sought out others with the same name, for presumably a Chin was related to another Chin regardless of how many generations back they may have shared a common ancestor. Those without name relations sought out others from the same vicinity or district. It was imperative to their sense of security to know that they belonged to a group. Had they remained in China and been thrown together under different circumstances, their relationship most likely would have been characterized by surface formality demanded by social conventions. Here in the stifling hold of a Spanish ship, an invisible bond welded the men together so that Fatt Hing felt closer to these men than he had ever felt toward his own brothers.

The fears of some that they had been hoodwinked and were being transported to a foreign land to be sold as slaves proved unfounded. Toward dusk on the ninety-fifth day, the hills of San Francisco rose over the horizon. The captain ordered the holds opened and the men swarmed out onto the decks. None slept that night as they watched the ship inch in toward the harbor.

When the ship docked the next day, a delegation of Chinese was on hand to greet the new arrivals. "Come with us," said the spokesman for the group, "and we will take you to the Chinese Street."

After the new arrivals were fed and refreshed with cups of strong hot tea, the leader spoke again.

"I am Wong Wing Dock, chairman of the Six Companies," he said. "We came as you came on board one of those ships, and we came for the same purpose—to seek gold. When we set foot on these shores, however, there were no Chinese faces to greet us, for we were among the first to arrive. Weak and wearied from our long journey, we were bewildered and lost. We did not know where to turn for shelter or food. Fortunately, there were enough of us so that some set to putting up these houses while others looked for food. We followed the white men into the hills and found out how they sifted the sands for gold and we did the same.

"One valuable lesson we have learned and which you will soon appreciate is that we must stick together and help one another, even though we are not kin. That is why we have formed this organization called the Six Companies representing the six districts which most of us come from. Our compatriots have honored me by choosing me chairman.

"You will always find food and shelter here among us. Any needed supplies can be purchased from the shops on this street. No doubt you will want to send a letter home to let your families know of your safe arrival. Elder brother Leong is a learned man, and he will help you write your letters.

"When you have earned money from your diggings or from your wages, you will pay dues into the company fund. This fund helps us to maintain the company headquarters and helps us set up an orderly system to take care of our own.

"We are Chinese in a land of foreigners. Their ways are different from our ways. Their language is different from our language. Most of them are loud and rough. We are accustomed to an orderly society, but it seems as if they are not bound by any rules of conduct. It is best, if possible, to avoid any contact with them.

"Try not to provoke the foreigners. But you will find that they like to provoke us. We are comfortable in our loose cotton jackets and trousers and we are used to going barefooted. They like to wear rough coarse clothing with high-laced boots. They cut their hair short and let the hair grow on their faces. We wear our hair long and braided and we shave the hair from our faces. Since we all want to return to our homeland, we cannot cut off our queues.[3]

"Be patient and maintain your dignity. If you are lucky you may not have to stay here long. Some of us and many white men have made rich finds. They need workers to help them. As new arrivals you may want to work for these men, or you may choose to prospect on your own.

"You will need a pick, a shovel and a few supplies," continued Chairman Wong. "You may take what you need from our headquarters now, and the sum will be entered in the company books against your name."

As soon as Chairman Wong had finished speaking, some of the men hastily asked where they should go for their pick and shovel. Though the strangeness of their environment was disconcerting, and though they were weak from their confinement in the ship's hold, they were impatient to be off into the hills.

[3] The queue was a symbol of subjugation forced upon the Chinese by the ruling Manchus. The Chinese hated the queue but were compelled to wear it. In 1911, with the overthrow of the Manchus, the Chinese were liberated from this loathsome reminder of subjugation and immediately cut off their queues.

Fatt Hing held back. As one of the younger men, he did not want to push ahead of his elders, but he also wanted time to think. "What do I know about mining?" he pondered. "Where should I start looking? Perhaps it would be better if I hired myself out until I get to know more about this new land."

The thoughts of Fatt Hing's shipmates ran in the same vein. Chairman Wong had received many requests for Chinese workers and he knew exactly where to send them. The terms were generous. Each worker was to receive half of the gold he mined.

Early next morning, the men set out on foot for the hills. When they arrived at their destination, Fatt Hing saw that hundreds of his fellow countrymen who had come previously had set up camp. It was comforting for him to know that he would be among his own people—people who spoke his own language and observed his own customs—though he was thousands of miles away from home.

Dig and sift, dig and sift. Fatt Hing and his fellow workers pecked at the mountainsides, in the ravines and gulches, working loose the earth and washing out the fine gold particles which sank to the bottom of the pan. It seemed as if other miners had worked the claim before, taking out the larger pieces while scorning the fine gold particles which required more laborious work. To Fatt Hing, however, the glitter of the gold dust in the loose earth drove him to work with unrelenting fury. "Truly, these are mountains of gold," he cried. "I must write my brothers and my cousins and tell them to come."

Thus each boatload brought more Chinese and more. Brothers sent for brothers and even distant kin so that Chinese immigration snowballed. No sooner had a ship disgorged its passengers than they were off to the mines. Although Canton, China, was 7,000 miles and a three months' journey away, it was a less hazardous and quicker trip than the overland route across the American continent or the boat trip around Cape Horn. From Canton also came lumber for the houses, cottons and silks, and even bundles of clean laundry which had been sent clear across the Pacific for washing.

In 1850, the new state legislature, casting about for a source of revenue, passed a Foreign Miners' License Law imposing $20.00 per month on all foreign miners. Instead of bringing into the state treasury the expected revenue, the law had the effect of depopulating the miners' camps. By the time the legislators realized that the tax was a mistake and repealed it a year later, many Chinese miners had quit the hills and swarmed into San Francisco. Quick to grasp at the excellent opportunities for making money in the city, the Chinese took to carpentering, washing and ironing, and operating restaurants and hotels. Everywhere, the Chinese were considered indispensable and were praised for their industry and efficiency. Noting these virtues, Mary Coolidge wrote:

> The editor of the Pacific News remarked upon their industry, quietness, cheerfulness and cleanliness of their personal habits. Whatever the white man scorned to do, the Chinaman took up; whatever the white men did, the Chinese could learn to do; he was a gapfiller, doing what no one else would do, or what remained undone, adapting himself to the white man's tastes and slipping away, unprotestingly to other tasks when the white man wanted his job.[4]

When California was admitted as the thirty-first state to the Union, the Chinese took a prominent part in the ceremonies and the parade. The *Alta California*, a San Francisco newspaper, said: "The China Boys will yet vote at the same polls, study at the same schools, and bow at the same altar as our countrymen."

Governor McDougal recommended in 1852 a system of land grants to induce the further immigration and settlement of the Chinese, whom he called "one of the most worthy of our newly adopted citizens."[5]

Renewed agitation by late-arriving Americans who complained that foreigners were carrying off millions in American wealth resulted in the repassage of a foreign miners' tax, set this time at $4.00 per month. Although the levy was intended against all foreigners, it amounted to a tax almost exclusively against the Chinese. Though Irish outnumbered the Chinese and the Germans were a close third, the Chinese *looked* more foreign. Besides, the Chinese always paid up, and it was easier for the tax collector to collect from a willing

[4] Mary Coolidge, *Chinese Immigration* (New York, Henry Holt & Co., 1909), pp. 34–37.
[5] *Ibid.*

payer. It was estimated that the Chinese paid 85 percent of the revenue from the miners' tax, an amount approximating five million dollars during the time the law was in force. This tax was later declared unconstitutional, but none of it was refunded.[6]

Nearly two years went by for Fatt Hing, and his little hoard of gold had increased steadily. He had continued to work for others, hiring himself out when he heard of a particularly rich find. He had gone into San Francisco on a few occasions to write a letter and send some money home, or to meet his brothers when they arrived. Otherwise, he had worked unremittingly. But the claim he now worked was yielding less each day, and he found himself thinking more and more about his parents and home. Finally he decided that he would take his gold and return to China.

Before he set sail, he cleared his account with the Six Companies and was delegated by Chairman Wong to see that the bones of several of his compatriots, who had met death in this foreign land, were returned to their ancestral homes for proper burial. This time, he made sure there was a bunk for him on ship and that his trip home would be more pleasant than his trip over, for now he could afford better accommodations.

To while away the time on board, Fatt Hing and his fellow travelers fell into the habit of playing *pai-gow*. Before the journey's end, each man's hoard of gold had exchanged owners several times. When the ship docked at Canton, Fatt Hing was lucky enough to have retained half of what he started out with.

This was enough to enable Fatt Hing to take a bride, build a house, and buy four *mous* of land. His parents and relatives could not believe their eyes when he unwrapped his packets of gold, and Fatt Hing had moments of regrets about his gambling losses on board the ship. He could have stayed home, farmed his land, and lived unpretentiously, but within a year Fatt Hing became restless. He missed the excitement of California, and he was eager to get back to the mines. But his parents would not allow him to depart until he had presented them with a grandson. Nevertheless, as soon as Fatt Hing knew that his wife was pregnant, he bought passage back to California. This time

[6] *Ibid.*, p. 80.

there was no need to slip aboard surreptitiously. California gold had enriched the county, and the magistrate was happy to see the men come and go.

A lot of changes took place in San Francisco during Fatt Hing's year or so of absence. It was certainly not like the same San Francisco that Fatt Hing saw when he landed the first time. Houses were strung out like beads on a string. Ships of every nation were anchored in the bay. Goods were piled high on the piers. There were so many Chinese faces in the crowd, he almost felt as if he were standing on a wharf in Canton.

Gold mining was another story. The furious pace of activity had died down. The surface gold was pretty much worked over. That below the ground was more difficult to get at, and a day's labor yielded less. More and more, the Chinese were moving into the city. Fatt Hing was uncertain. He knew the hills and he had been unusually lucky before. He wanted to try again. He finally decided to prospect for his own gold and work his own claim if he found one. One of his brothers was persuaded to join him.

Month after weary month, the two trudged up and down the river banks and mountain ravines. First they followed the Sacramento north and then they swung south to follow the San Joaquin. Throughout the vast expanse, they found that other miners held prior claim to the choice areas while abandoned claims yielded little. To keep themselves in food and supplies, Fatt Hing and his brothers gathered firewood, worked in the sawmills, watered other men's horses, or cooked for other miners.

"We are opening a restaurant on Jackson Street," said his cousin. "Tong-Ling charges a dollar a meal and his place is overflowing with foreigners throughout the day. What did he know about cooking before he came to *Gum Shan*? If the foreign devils will eat his food, they will eat ours. Why don't you two brothers join us?" By then, the two needed little persuasion. Fatt Hing, who had picked up a smattering of English, worked in the dining room. When business was slow, he stood outside the door banging on his gong entreating customers to come in. No matter what the request, Fatt Hing always answered his customers with repeated nods of the head, a broad smile, and several yeses.

For Fatt Hing, this life was more comfortable than mining or prospecting. Business picked up steadily, and the money came in regularly. "Let others go after the gold in the hills," he said. "I'll wait for the gold to come to the city."

In 1864 the chairman of the Six Companies received a call for workers from an entirely new line of work—railroad construction. After thirty years of bickering and wrangling, mistrust and contention, the Federal government finally decided to build a transcontinental railroad linking the West with the East. The Act of 1862 called for the construction of a railroad and telegraph line from the Missouri River to the Pacific coast.

The Union Pacific and Central Pacific were commissioned to build the railroad. The Union Pacific was to start at the Missouri River and build westward while the Central Pacific was to begin from the west coast building eastward, both rails to link up and form one continuous line after completion. The railroad companies were paid by the miles of rails laid. Thus the stage was set for a furious race between the Union Pacific and Central Pacific to see which could lay more miles of track.

An immediate cry went up for men, for boys, for any pair of hands that could do the work. Labor was made more scarce by men diverted to battle in the Civil War. Charles Crocker, one of the Big Four partners of the Central Pacific in charge of construction, was faced immediately with the acute shortage of labor. Of the thousands sent into the hills during 1863 to 1864, only two in five reported for work, and of these all but a few quit as soon as they had earned enough to pay stage fare to Virginia City, where new discoveries in mineral wealth excited the adventurers' hopes for a windfall fortune. For a while, there was talk about importing peons from Mexico; at another time, Crocker thought of hiring prisoners or asking the government to send out rebels captured during the Civil War.

The situation was desperate; there was little likelihood that the railroad could be completed within the fourteen years called for, or be completed at all, as long as labor continued to be such a thorny problem. Charles Crocker, an ingenious and resourceful man, thought of the Chinese. His superintendent, J. H. Strobridge, was skeptical. "They are physically incapable of the heavy manual labor," he argued. But at no one time could Crocker recruit more than 800 whites. He issued circulars, posted ads in the post office, and gave work to any person who applied. After pay day, the force would dwindle to 600 and gradually increase to 800 but no more.

> When no other recourse appeared in sight, Strobridge dubiously decided to try the experiment and fifty Chinese were hired. They were hauled to the end of the track. They disembarked, glanced without curiosity at the surrounding forest, then tranquilly established camp, cooked a meal of rice and dried cuttlefish and went to sleep. By sunrise, they were at work with picks, shovels and wheelbarrows. At the end of their first twelve hours of plodding industry, Crocker and his engineers viewed the results with gratified astonishment. Those who through the day had been momentarily expecting the weaklings to fall in their tracks from exhaustion permanently revised their opinion of the Chinaman's endurance.[7]

Crocker came to rely on and place his trust completely in the Chinese laborer, so much so that they were labeled "Crocker's pets." At first the Chinese worked as graders, leveling the ground with their picks and shovels for the railbed. A shortage of masons temporarily halted the work. Strobridge reported to Crocker who boomed, "Put your Chinamen to work."

With all his faith in the Chinaman as a grader, Strobridge protested, "Make masons out of Chinamen?"

"Sure," replied Crocker, "didn't they build the Chinese wall, the biggest piece of masonry in the world?"[8]

At one time, over 10,000 Chinese were employed on the Central Pacific. Their heroism in making the Central Pacific a reality is described vividly in a book by Oscar Lewis entitled *The Big Four*.[9]

Almost immediately after work began on the western terminal of the Central Pacific, the builders were up against the sheer granite

[7] Oscar Lewis, *The Big Four* (New York, Alfred Knopf, 1938), p. 71.

[8] Edwin L. Sabin, *Building the Pacific Railway* (Philadelphia, J.B. Lippincott Co., 1919).

[9] The Big Four were Leland Stanford, Collis P. Huntington, Mark Hopkins, and Charles Crocker, the four partners who organized and directed the work of the Central Pacific.

walls of the Sierra Nevadas. Work had to be continued, for the Union Pacific was racing across the western plains, and every mile of rail laid by the Union Pacific meant more money in their pockets and less for the Central Pacific coffers. Yet the blinding snowstorms, the extreme cold, and the rearing avalanches defied man to pitch himself against the elements. This is Mr. Lewis' description of the heroism of Crocker's men:

> The winter of 1865–1866 was severe as any on record. Snow fell in quantity as early as October, and the next five months saw an almost continuous succession of storms. As ground froze and the tracks and construction lines were blanketed under an icy mass fifteen feet thick, the work slowed down to a walk.[10]

Nearly half of the work force of 9,000 men had to be put to work clearing the snow. Five locomotives strained futilely to drive a snow-plow through thirty-foot drifts. Before half the winter was up, they had to admit defeat except in tunnels or in the deep cuts. Mr. Lewis continues:

> Tunnels were dug beneath forty-foot drifts, and for months, three thousand workmen lived curious mole-like lives, passing from work to living quarters in dim passages far beneath the snow's surface. This eerie existence was complicated by constant danger, for as snows accumulated on the upper ridges, avalanches grew frequent, their approach heralded only by a brief thunderous roar. A second later, a work crew, a bunkhouse, sometimes an entire camp, would go hurtling at a dizzy speed down miles of frozen canyons. Not until months later were the bodies recovered; sometimes groups were found with shovels or picks still clutched in their frozen hands.[11]

Oswald Garrison Villard, in his testimony to a House Committee on Chinese exclusion, paid tribute to the heroism of the Chinese who worked for him under the same conditions on the Northwest Pacific line. He said:

[10] Lewis, *op. cit.*, pp. 72–73.
[11] *Ibid.*

> I want to remind you of the things that Chinese labor did for us in opening up the western portion of this country. I am a son of the man who drove the first transcontinental railroad across the American Northwest, the first rail link from Minnesota to Oregon and the waters of the Puget Sound. I was near him when he drove the last spike and paid an eloquent tribute to the men who had built that railroad by their manual labor for there were no road-making machines in those days.
>
> He never forgot and never failed to praise the Chinese among them, of whom nearly 10,000 stormed the forest fastnesses, endured cold and heat and the risk of death at the hands of the hostile Indians to aid in the opening up of our great northwestern empire.
>
> I have a dispatch from the chief engineer of the Northwestern Pacific, telling how the Chinese laborers went out into eight feet of snow with the temperature far below zero to carry on the work when no American dared face the conditions.[12]

Winter had its hazards, but summer had its share too. Again, to quote from Oscar Lewis:

> Throughout the summer of 1866, "Crocker's pets," six thousand strong, swarmed over the upper canyon, pecking methodically at the broken rock of the cuts, trooping in long lines beneath their basket hats to pour wheelbarrow-loads of debris down the canyon-side, threading precarious paths with seventy pound kegs of black powder suspended from both ends of bamboo poles, refreshing themselves at intervals with sips of tea kept near at hand in whisky kegs emptied and abandoned by their white confreres. The Chinese were presently found to be adept at the backbreaking work of drilling and placing blasts, by then a major part of the work, for the upper ridges were scraped clear of soil by the winter deposits of ice.
>
> Track-layers followed close behind the graders, and locomotives pushed strings of flatcars loaded with construction iron,

[12] Villard, O.G. "Justice for the Chinese," *Christian Century* Vol. 60 (May 26, 1943), pp. 633–634.

lumber, explosives, food, drink and more men to the rail head. Cape Horn, a sheer granite buttress, proved the most formidable obstacle of the year; its lower sides dropped away in a thousand-foot vertical cliff that offered no vestige of a foothold. The indomitable Chinese were lowered from above on ropes, and there suspended between sky and earth, chipped away with hammer and chisel to form the first precarious ledge which was then laboriously deepened to a shelf wide enough to permit the passage of cars. Three years later, when overland trains crept cautiously along this ledge, passengers gazed straight down from their windows into thin air.[13]

John Galloway, famous transportation engineer, in his book, *The First Transcontinental Railroad, Central Pacific and Union Pacific,* called the construction of the transcontinental railroad—1,800 miles across grassy plains and sagebrush desert, through the passes of the Rockies and High Sierras—without doubt the greatest engineering feat of the nineteenth century.

The majority of the workmen on the Central Pacific were Chinese, while on the Union Pacific the Irish predominated. So, in addition to the fierce race to add trackage to their own lines, there was an undercurrent spirit of competition between the Irish and the Chinese.

Some of this competition resulted in outright animosity, but it was a spur in their flanks, each side driving the other to outperform themselves.

One day, the Union Pacific men laid down six miles of track and boasted to the Central Pacific of their accomplishment. The Central Pacific answered with seven.

"No Chinaman is going to beat us," replied the Irish. Thus goaded, they laid down seven and a half miles of track and said they would lay eight if Crocker didn't call it quits.

Crocker pulled up his haughty frame and promised the Union Pacific ten miles. Durant, president of the Union Pacific, immediately put up $10,000 in wager that Crocker couldn't do it.

"Wait and see," smiled Crocker.

[13] Lewis, *op. cit.*, pp. 74–75.

Crocker was a sly devil. He waited until the day before the last sixteen miles were to be laid. Then he assembled his men and his supplies and laid down the ten miles of track with 1,800 feet added for good measure. It was an achievement that has never been equaled nor approached even by modern methods in the United States.

Of the two portions of the railroad, there was no doubt that the Central Pacific portion was the more difficult. The Central was obliged to overcome 7,000 feet of mountain rise in 100 miles whereas the Union Pacific had 500 miles in which to overcome a gradual rise of 5,000 feet and fifty miles more of a leeway in which to attain the summit of the Black Hills, 2,000 feet higher. This appeared slight compared with the rise of 2,000 feet in twenty miles accomplished by the Central Pacific. Editor Bowles of the *Springfield Republican* proclaimed that the building of the Union Pacific from Omaha to the Rocky Mountains was mere baby work in comparison.

Chinese labor also built the Northwest Pacific Railroad, extending the benefits of the transcontinental to the Northwest Territory. They were also the main labor force of the Southern Pacific, which began pushing its tributaries southward and westward.

When work on the railroads slackened, some Chinese turned to manufacturing, as goods imported from the East were expensive. One day, a farmer sent into town for some temporary farm hands to pick his tomato crop. Much of the crop was already overripe, but in farming as with the railroads, labor was scarce and temperamental. When workers could be found, they were roughnecks who bruised the fruit and caused heavy losses.

When told that he should try the Chinese, the farmer asked for a group of workers who were told to report in the morning. Even before the sun came up, the Chinese were at the farm ready for work. Diligently and quietly, they plucked the ripe tomatoes from the stalks, laying them gently in the baskets. At sundown, the baskets were arranged and piled neatly in rows and the workers faded away. Before dawn the next day, the workers were back in the fields.

By word of mouth the news spread, and the Chinese were in great demand as agricultural workers. According to Carey McWilliams, Chinese made up one-tenth of the farm labor supply in 1870. In

1880, they constituted one-third. By 1884, half of the farm workers in California were Chinese.[14]

Much of the city of San Francisco today stands on man-made land. When the first white settlers saw her, she was a half-submerged peninsula of marshland, swamps, lagoons, and rocky hills covered with sagebrush. Five million acres of lush garden and farm land at the mouths of the Sacramento and San Joaquin rivers were reclaimed by hardy Chinese laborers who performed their tasks without benefit of drainage machinery, cranes, bulldozers, or trucks when malaria took a heavy toll of white laborers.[15]

Early historians of California are unanimous in their opinions about the contributions rendered by the pioneer Chinese. Theirs were the muscles that opened up the bowels of the earth and wrested from her the riches of gold to add to the wealth of the nation. They tilled the land and harvested the fruit so that the vast hordes pouring into the West to populate and tame the wilderness would not hunger. They added dignity and stability, order and tranquility to a frontier land where laws were yet to be made. They were a colorful part of the scenery; their dress and their ways so different from what the Occident was accustomed to seeing. Their patronage and their lion's share of the taxes kept many a county from bankruptcy. Their feats and heroism in the construction of the transcontinental railroads and tributaries are recorded in history. Their industry and physical stamina salvaged for the West millions of acres of the richest farm lands and urban real estate.

They could not have given more!

[14] Carey McWilliams, *California, the Great Exception* (New York, Current Books, Inc., 1949), p. 152.

[15] Testimony of George D. Roberts, President of the Tideland Reclamation Co., 1877 Report, p. 436.

4

The Chinese Must Go

For their contribution to the early development of the West, the Chinese deserved recognition and gratitude. But as their ranks increased, alarm developed. Popular sentiment shifted from welcome to hatred and from praise to blame. Hounded and persecuted, the Chinese were driven from the West and excluded from the country.

How come? Why the abrupt about-face in attitude? Did the Chinese change for the worse? Were they at fault to cause the people to turn against them? No, the reasons were not logical; they grew out of the social, economic, and political climate of the West at that time.

In 1848, the population of California hovered around 15,000. The gold fever quickly increased this figure tenfold within two years. The 1860 census reported 380,000 residents in California. Ten years later, this figure had more than doubled.

Only one man in twenty was a native of the state in 1860. In Gold Rush slang, the other nineteen were Argonauts (as the gold-seekers were called) "come to see the elephant." The elephant was California and all that it embodied of that period. The Argonauts, in the main, were young, energetic men in the prime of health and life; otherwise they would not have survived the rigors of the journey around the churning waters of Cape Horn, through the steaming tropical jungles of the Isthmus of Panama, over the deserts and mountains of the North American continent, or in the holes of freighters hastily converted to carry human cargo. They came from all walks of life—farmer, sailor, hunter, merchant, criminal, minister, doctor, poet. They came from every country—Ireland, Spain, Mexico, China, Germany, Russia, and the hardly settled eastern states of America. They came with a dream—not to settle a new frontier land, but to strike it rich in gold.

Historian H. H. Bancroft estimated that during the years 1849 and 1850, the gold taken out averaged $600 per miner. "Averages are usually misleading; this one, on examination, can mean only that for every miner who struck it rich, there must have been a platoon who hardly got to see what gold looked like."[1]

There is unanimous agreement among observers and historians about the social climate of California at that time. It was a wild, uninhibited, lawless frontier given to frequent outbursts of temper and belligerency helped along by drink and gambling losses.

If the miners were not sifting for gold, they were at the saloons or the gambling tables. "Bancroft claimed 537 places sold liquor in San Francisco in 1853. . . . If San Francisco allotted one saloon to every street corner (four per intersection), there would still be some left over. . . . California consumed an annual five million gallons of liquor."[2]

Norton, in his *The Story of California*, wrote: "Drinking and gambling were the natural outcome of sudden riches where there were no more worthy objects for their expenditure. . . . Few indeed were the men who were not to a greater or lesser extent the prey of these professionals. Everybody in the town joined in the game. Easy gain made losses easier to bear."[3]

Elizabeth Margo wrote: "Gambling like drinking was at the heart of the gold-rush mood serving alike those who would celebrate success and those who would obliterate the nagging memory of failure. . . . The kind of excitement and thrill that was the essence of gambling beat in precisely the same tempo as did the rapid pulse of the gold fever."[4]

Fights, murders, and cruelty were commonplace. In her detailed and descriptive letters to her sister back East, Dame Shirley wrote: "In the short space of twenty-four days, we have had murders, fearful

[1] Ralph K. Andrist, "Gold Fever Took Thousands of Victims," *Long Island Press*, April 28, 1963, p. 8.

[2] Elizabeth Margo, *Taming the Forty-Niner* (New York, Rinehart & Co., 1955), p. 56.

[3] Henry K. Norton, *The Story of California* (Chicago, A. C. McClurg & Co., 1913), p. 229.

[4] Margo, *op. cit.,* p. 42.

accidents, bloody deaths, a mob, whippings, a hanging, an attempt at suicide, and a duel."[5]

By 1873, yield from the gold mines was petering out. Surface gold was exhausted, necessitating the use of more elaborate mining methods involving the use of machinery and equipment which meant capital resources. For the average miner with his pick and axe, sifting pan or rocker, the days of get-rich-quick opportunities were over. However, the inevitability of nature was no consolation to those whom fortune had deluded, so discontent was widespread.

California gold and the Civil War had resulted in intense agitation for a transcontinental railroad. On May 10, 1869, 2:47 P.M. (eastern time), a magnetic ball fell from the dome of the Capitol in Washington and a roar rose from the crowds waiting on the Capitol steps. At the same moment in San Francisco the city went wild. Fire bells pealed from the City Hall tower. The boom of 220 guns from Fort Point split the air. In Philadelphia, the Liberty Bell chimed. Throughout the nation, people were celebrating a historic moment taking place on Promontory Point, Utah. The last tie was ceremoniously laid in place. The last spike forged of gold was hammered in to mark the joining of the tracks of the Central Pacific with those of the Union Pacific. The transcontinental railroad was completed. The nation was welded. One of the greatest engineering feats of the nineteenth century was finished. While the country celebrated the welding of the nation, 25,000 workmen from the railroads lost their jobs, their labor dumped en masse on the western labor market.

The East was experiencing a depression in the aftermath of the Civil War and Reconstruction. There had been hopes that the completion of the transcontinental railroad would open up boundless horizons and unlimited prosperity in the West. But the drainoff of excess labor in the East only aggravated the conditions in the western labor market. "In 1869, the Central Pacific handled almost 30,000 through passengers. In 1870, the Union Pacific passengers numbered 142,623. These were but the feeble advance tricklings of a mighty flood. In 1869 the population of the five States and Territories tra-

[5] Louise Clappe, *The Shirley Letters from the California Mines* (New York, Alfred A. Knopf, 1961), p. 161.

versed by the Pacific Railway was 820,000; within a year it was over a million."[6]

Discovery of the Comstock Lode in 1857 with its bowels of silver, copper, and quartz relieved the economic problems of the West for a time. But unlike the placer mining methods of California, where every man was for himself, the mining companies of the Comstock Lode were huge corporate holding companies which sold stock. Everybody gambled in mining stocks, from railroad kings down to maidservants. When the bottom fell out of the market in 1876, everybody was hard hit. "The railroad kings could stand their losses, but the clerks and shop assistants and workmen suffered, for their savings were gone and many were left heavily in debt, with their houses mortgaged and no hope of redemption."[7]

Farmers fared no better. The Southern Pacific held extensive land grants from the government along the right-of-way of the tracks. Other large tracts were held by the early arrivals who had the foresight to buy themselves large parcels. Of those who swarmed into California, some were farmers who came with the intention of buying and tilling small tracts such as they had known at home. But small tracts were hardly ever sold; the few that were offered for sale were outrageously overpriced, their owners holding out for large profits. Meanwhile, they could hire farm hands to work the fields. The farm hands were recruited in the spring and laid off after the harvest.

The political climate of California led James Bryce to conclude in his *The American Commonwealth*:

> Both in the country and in the city there was disgust with politics and the politicians. The legislature was composed almost wholly either of office-seekers from the city or of petty country lawyers, needy and narrow-minded men. Those who had virtue, enough not to be "got at" by the great corporations, had not intelligence enough to know how to resist their devices. It was a common saying in the State that each successive legislature was

[6] Edwin L. Sabin, *Building the Pacific Railway* (Philadelphia, J.B. Lippincott Co., 1919), p. 308.

[7] James Bryce, *The American Commonwealth* (New York, The Macmillan Co., 1927), p. 430.

> worse than its predecessor. . . . County government was little better; city government was even worse. The judges were not corrupt, but most of them, as was natural, considering the scanty salaries assigned to them, were inferior men, not fit to cope with the counsel who practiced before them. Partly owing to the weakness of juries, partly to the intricacies of the law and the effects of the recently adopted code, criminal justice was halting and uncertain, and malefactors often went unpunished.[8]

California was ripe for a demagogue, who emerged in the person of Dennis Kearney. Kearney, an Irish sailor, had ridden the tides of modest success, but on the advice of a friend, had committed himself heavily in mining stocks. Caught in the landslide, he was reduced to practically nothing. Embittered, he took to haranguing in the empty sand lots where construction was going up. At first, only a few hoodlums and vagabonds paid any heed to his thundering vituperations. These would have been passed off as the blubberings of another malcontent if the *Chronicle*, one of the two leading newspapers in San Francisco, had not championed him.

In keen rivalry with the *Morning Call*, the *Chronicle* was looking for a popular issue that would boost its circulation. A reporter was dispatched to the sand lots and instantaneously recognized the makings of a circulation booster. The reporter polished up Kearney's harangues, making them spit fire and venom. Each day, his "utterings" were reported faithfully by the *Chronicle* until he was built into a hero—champion of the "downtrodden workingman." His followers were organized into the California Workingmen's Party.

The *Morning Call*, having missed the boat in bidding for the support of the workingmen, made up for lost time. Each tried to outdo the other in reporting Kearney's demagoguery, most of which they helped write.

Kearney's targets were the land and rail monopolies and the Chinese. The Central Pacific, with the only transportation line to the Mississippi Valley and the Atlantic coast, held a strangle hold on the economy of the West. With its enormous power, influence, and wealth, it proceeded to dictate the policies of government. Leland

[8] *Ibid.*, p. 431.

Stanford, president of Central Pacific (which later became the Southern Pacific), was also governor of the state and subsequently senator from California.

In this explosive social, economic, and political climate, the heavy concentration of Chinese in California made them a convenient scapegoat for the relief of pent-up frustrations and emotions. In 1870, there were 63,000 Chinese in the United States, 99 percent of whom were on the west coast. Every tenth person in California in 1860 was Chinese. Their large numbers, their physical differences, the retention of their national dress, the custom of wearing their hair in pigtails, their habits and traditions, so incomprehensible to the Occidental mind, made them a target easy to spot.

When employment with the railroad ceased, the Chinese sought work in the mines, on the farms, in land reclamation, in domestic service, and in the cigar and woolen factories. These were jobs which the white man scorned, for the white man was looking for a quick bonanza. Nevertheless, they were jobs that gave the Chinese employment while the white man was out of work.

So whereas the Chinese had been praised for their industry, their honesty, their thrift, and their peaceful ways, they were now charged with being debased and servile coolies, clannish, dangerous, deceitful, and vicious. They were accused of being contract laborers, although there was no shred of evidence to show that the Chinese were anything but Argonauts of a different skin coloring. Degenerate traits were ascribed to them, in direct contradiction to the praises heaped upon them a few years earlier. The workingmen accused them of undermining the white man's standard of living. It was alleged they could work for less because they subsisted on next to nothing. The word was spread that the land and rail monopolies hired Chinese instead of white men because the Chinese accepted employment at any price. Yet the books kept by Charles Crocker of the Central Pacific showed that white men were paid at the rate of $35 per month plus keep, and the Chinese were paid $35 per month without keep, mainly because the Chinese preferred cooking their own food.

The charge of accepting slave wages was shortly disproved after the exclusion laws took effect. The drastic curtailment in immigration brought about a shortage in Chinese laborers. Quick to take advantage of the situation, Chinese laborers demanded and got higher wages for their services—this in spite of a surplus in white labor.

However, reason and fact could not prevail. Elmer Clarence Sandmeyer wrote: ". . . there would have been a depression in the 1870's if the entire population had been made up of lineal descendants of George Washington. . . . If the Chinese in California were white people, being in all other respects what they are, I do not believe that the complaints and warfare against them would have existed to any considerable extent."[9] But once the charges were made, they spread like a prairie fire, fanned red-hot by Dennis Kearney.

Kearney invariably began his speeches with an attack upon the monopolies—the rich, huge corporate enterprises. He pointed out their owners' ornate mansions on Nob Hill and blamed these moguls for the plight of the workingmen. He accused the Chinese of working hand-in-hand with monopolies, of accepting slave wages, and of robbing the white man of his job. His wrath was directed against both the Chinese and the land and rail monopolies, but the latter were powerful, impregnable, organized, while the Chinese were docile, eager to avoid conflict, and ineffectual in court because their testimony could not be accepted as evidence. Kearney's speeches always ended with the slogan, "The Chinese must go!" So the blame fell upon the Chinese, and thus supplied with a hate object, the frenzied, incited mob would dash off to another orgy of attacks upon the defenseless Chinese.

During this period, the Chinese were stoned and robbed, assaulted and murdered. Hoodlums would organize attacks against the Chinese camps as sport, for they knew the Chinese could not obtain redress.

In the spring of 1876, the Chinese were driven from small towns and camps, their quarters burned. Some Chinese were killed or injured. In June of 1876, a violent attack was made upon them at Truckee.

In 1877, employers of Chinese labor in Chico received threatening letters. In March of that year, six tenant farmers were attacked and five killed. The murderer who was caught confessed to being under orders from the Workingmen's Party.

[9] Elmer Clarence Sandmeyer, *The Anti-Chinese Movement in California* (Urbana, Ill., University of Illinois Press, 1939), p. 88.

In July 1877, a great riot broke loose. Twenty-five wash houses were burned, and there followed an outbreak of riots. For months afterwards, no Chinese was safe on the streets. Arson and personal abuse spread to adjacent counties. Chinese laundries were burned, and when occupants tried to escape, they were shot or left to die in flaming buildings.

In 1878, the entire Chinese population of Truckee was rounded up and driven from town.

In 1885, the infamous massacre of 28 Chinese in Rock Springs, Wyoming, occurred. Many others were wounded and hundreds were driven from their homes.

In 1886, Log Cabin, Oregon, was the scene of another brutal massacre.

Professor Mary Coolidge wrote: "During the years of Kearneyism, it is a wonder that any Chinese remained alive in the U.S."

Murdering Chinese became such a commonplace occurrence that the newspapers seldom bothered to print the stories. Police officials winked at the attacks, and politicians all but incited more of the same. There were thousands of cases of murder, robbery, and assault, but in only two or three instances were the guilty brought to justice.

If murders were commonplace, the indignities, abuse, brutalities, and injustices practiced against the Chinese were outrageous. An old-timer told of the indignities he suffered at the hands of drunken white men:

> Every Saturday night, we never knew whether we would live to see the light of day. We operated a laundry near a mining camp. Saturday was the night for the miners to get drunk. They would force their way into our shop, wrest the clean white bundles from the shelves and trample the shirts which we so laboriously finished. If the shirts were torn, we were forced to pay for the damages. One night, one of the miners hit his face against the flat side of an iron. He went away, but we knew that our lives were now in danger so we fled, leaving all of our possessions and money behind. The miner came back with a mob who ransacked our shop, robbed us of the $360 that was our combined

savings and set fire to the laundry. We were lucky to escape with our lives, so we came east.

Whereas most Chinese had gone straight to San Francisco upon their arrival in the United States, they now began to disperse. Some had already gone north to work on the Northern Pacific and Canadian Pacific Railroads. Others sought work in the silver and coal mines of Nevada, Oregon, Wyoming, and Colorado. But prejudice and hatred confronted them everywhere. The anti-Chinese sentiments had spread like a cancerous growth to other parts of the West.

On February 11, 1870, a joint resolution passed the legislature of the Territory of Colorado, affirming the desirability of Chinese immigration. "The preamble stated that the immigration of Chinese labor to Colorado was calculated to hasten the development and early prosperity of the Territory by supplying the demand for cheap labor. It was, therefore, resolved that such immigration should be encouraged by legislation that would guarantee the immigrants security of their persons and property."[10] Ten years later, the seeds of hatred sprouted in Colorado. Anti-Chinese feelings reached their pitch in Denver for the November elections, and these feelings soon gave way to open violence.

There were two versions to the story of how one riot started. The *Rocky Mountain News* version was that a Chinese laundryman charged ten cents more than a white customer was willing to pay. An argument ensued, whereupon the Chinese slapped the white man in the face with a knife. The injured man ran into the streets and a crowd gathered, so the Chinese fired a gun into the crowd.

The other version was revealed in a government publication as a result of an investigation to determine if indemnity was due the Chinese. The riots, said the government publication, began when a game of chance between two Chinese was broken up by a couple of drunken white men. Both versions then agreed about the crowd that gathered.

Because only fifteen policemen were on the Denver force, the Mayor called out the fire department, promising the crowd a drenching if they did not disperse. The crowd became so angry that they

[10] "The Chinese in Colorado," *Colorado Magazine* (October, 1952), p. 273.

began a destructive rampage lasting throughout the night. Every Chinese laundry, business, and home was destroyed. The Mayor, with his pitiful law-enforcement staff, was helpless. An appeal was made to the Governor for help. A light artillery battery and the Governor's guards were dispatched to Denver. The Chinese were rounded up and locked in jail for their own safety. One Chinese was killed and several white men wounded, but the homes and property of the Chinese were completely destroyed.

The Chinese had no recourse. Neither the state, the federal, nor the Chinese government provided them any protection. China had not wanted her citizens to roam abroad. Nor did she relish the thought of permitting the white man to step foot on her territory. China was proud of her culture, her civilization, and her ways. She had no use for the barbaric white men who had hair on their arms, chests, and legs and whose bodies gave off offensive odors. The white men she knew were mostly sailors, arriving on the ships that insisted upon coming into her harbors. China could well do without such contamination.

But the white man persisted. He wanted to trade. He wanted the silks, the tea, the porcelains, the lacquers that China had. In return, he sought a market for the goods that he carried. His persistence went to the extent of shooting his way in.

The United States was anxious to have her share of the China trade too. The development of the west coast, the inauguration of the Pacific Mail Steamship Line and the transcontinental railroad opened up limitless opportunities for facilitating that trade. Missionaries, determined to bring their god and their brand of salvation to this heathen nation, were knocking on the doors, panting to be let in. Contractors, engineers, and investors were jumping the gun in the race to get started in this vast undeveloped area. But China said no. The white man was not welcome.

Whereas the European nations sent gunboats, the American government sent a diplomat in the person of Anson Burlingame to pry open the doors of China. He was dispatched to the Imperial Court in 1860. During the six years of his mission in China, he had become a trusted adviser to the Chinese government. When he was about to resign in

1866, the Chinese government made a most unusual request. He was asked to represent China as the Chinese Envoy to the United States and principal European nations.

With the consent of the American government, Anson Burlingame accepted the honor conferred upon him by the Chinese. As Chinese Minister, he negotiated the Burlingame Treaty of 1868, which contained the provisions long sought by the United States. The Preamble of the Burlingame Treaty reads:

> The United States of America and the Emperor of China cordially recognize the inherent and inalienable right of man to change his home and allegiance and also the mutual advantage of the free migration and emigration of their citizens and subjects respectively, from one country to the other, for the purpose of curiosity, of trade or as permanent residents.

The United States was anxious to get into China for the pursuit of trade and commerce. The Treaty would secure this privilege for American citizens. Although the United States had promised the same privilege to the subjects of the Emperor, she had not banked on the traffic running both ways.

The Treaty secured reciprocally for citizens of both nations, freedom from religious persecution, privileges to maintain their own schools, and the right of residence and travel in the other's country according to concessions granted to the most favored nation. The United States pledged herself to respect the territorial integrity of China and to refrain from interfering in her internal administration or trade.

The Treaty granted the same privileges, immunities, and exemptions with respect to travel and residence that it granted to citizens of the most favored nation, "but nothing contained herein shall be held to confer naturalization upon citizens of the United States in China, nor upon the subjects of China in the United States." To suit her purpose, the United States later interpreted this clause as specifically prohibiting the naturalization of Chinese in the United States.

Ratification was speedy in the U.S. Senate, but when some delay developed in Peking, uneasiness arose in Washington and the American minister was instructed to exert his influence toward an early ratification.

The Burlingame Treaty was hailed as a triumph for American diplomacy. The United States congratulated herself for bringing China out of her seclusion, and the President spoke of it as a liberal and auspicious treaty. In his message to Congress, he said:

> Unquestionably the adhesion of the Government of China to these liberal principles of freedom of emigration with which we are so familiar and with which we are so well satisfied, was a great advance towards opening that Empire to *our* civilization and religion and gave promise in the future of greater and practical results in the diffusion throughout that population of *our* arts and industries, *our* manufactures, *our* material improvements and the sentiments of government and religion which seem to us so important to the welfare of mankind. [Italics mine]

It was obvious that the nation's mind was on a single track, concentrating only on the benefits derived and not on the obligations assumed, for the United States was not only unprepared to assume the obligations, she was also unwilling. The ignominious treatment of the Chinese, related previously, bear witness to that.

Few perpetrators of crime against the Chinese were ever brought to justice. In evidently flagrant cases, indictments were returned and light sentences passed in the form of token punishment. For example, in 1871 a group of toughs attacked Chinatown. Twenty-one Chinese were killed, fifteen were lynched on the streets of Chinatown, and the stores and homes were looted and mobbed before the riot was quelled. A grand jury scored the city officials for failing to give protection to the Chinese and handed down 37 indictments against the hoodlums. Yet, only eight rioters received sentences of two to eight years—a mockery of justice for twenty-one murders.

According to the provisions of the Burlingame Treaty, under the most-favored-nation clause, the United States government was obligated to exert all its powers to secure protection to the persons and property of all Chinese subjects in the United States. Yet, when the Chinese minister protested about the lawless ill treatment of the Chinese, the federal government feebly replied that it could not interfere with the enforcement of laws by the states. However, in a riot at Seattle, when the federal government did threaten to send in federal troops, peace and order were quickly restored.

The southern states—staunch supporters of the principle of white supremacy—joined forces with the West. Only the eastern states opposed the tactics and motives of the West.

Whereas mainly the Democratic Party had capitalized on the Chinese issue, the Republicans were fearful of losing control if they did not jump on the band wagon.

> In 1880, six of seven California electors cast their votes for the Democratic presidential nominee although the state legislature had an overwhelming Republican majority. The reason for this switch was that the Californians were dissatisfied with the position which the Republican Party had taken on the issue of Oriental immigration. In 1884, California was back in the Republican column because the Democrats had not taken a sufficiently extreme position on the same issue. The vote in 1880 and 1884 demonstrated conclusively that the Chinese issue determined the electoral vote of California. And, since the strength of the two major parties was so nearly equal during these years, the Pacific Coast States held the balance of power and largely determined national elections on the basis of a single issue.[11]

In running for office as Senator, Leland Stanford, who had repeatedly extolled the virtues of the Chinese and who had given credit to their part in building the Central Pacific, expediently added his voice in condemnation of the Chinese. Henry K. Norton wrote in his book, *The Story of California*: "Every man in public life was under so binding a necessity to accept the popular belief in regard to the Chinese and to truckle to it at every turn, that for one to seek the real truth of the matter was to end forthwith his political career."[12]

With complete disregard to the provisions of the Burlingame Treaty, Congress passed an exclusion law in 1879 prohibiting further

[11] Carey McWilliams, *California, the Great Exception* (New York, Current Books, Inc.), p. 183.

[12] Norton, *op. cit.*, p. 291.

immigration of Chinese laborers. Because this was in direct contravention of the Treaty, President Hayes was forced to veto it. But an election was coming up and the West had to be placated.

A commission of three distinguished men were dispatched to Peking in 1880 to seek a revision of the Burlingame Treaty. That they were successful was evident in the Treaty of 1880, in which China conceded permission to the United States to regulate, limit, or suspend immigration, but not absolutely prohibit it. The limitation or suspension was to be reasonable and enacted in good faith. The limitation or suspension applied to the laboring classes only, other classes not being affected. Those who were already in the country were entitled to stay or come and go of their own free will. The Treaty reaffirmed the responsibility of the United States to protect all Chinese subjects from abuse and mistreatment, according them the same privileges and exemptions as may be enjoyed by citizens or subjects of the most favored nation.

The Treaty was ratified, and toward the end of 1881, Congress immediately passed a bill suspending Chinese immigration for twenty years. President Arthur vetoed the bill, calling it unreasonable and unjustified. Suspension of twenty years is tantamount to prohibition, he declared. But instead of reducing the years of suspension, a few hot-headed members of Congress introduced a flurry of bills calling for suspension periods of twenty-five, forty, and even fifty years.

In the end, it was evident that a suspension period beyond ten years would meet with a Presidential veto, so a bill suspending the immigration of Chinese labor for ten years was passed and became law. That was the infamous original Chinese Exclusion Act of 1882. It was to father many similar acts, each more severe than its predecessor.

It was the intention of the Chinese government and American commission when they drafted the Treaty that the term "laborers" should denote only unskilled labor, but it was soon broadened and interpreted by the United States to include skilled as well as unskilled labor. On the other hand, the following stipulation in the Treaty was narrowed to suit the purposes of the United States with the same intent—to keep out as many Chinese as possible:

"Chinese subjects, whether proceeding to the United States as teachers, students, merchants, or from curiosity, together with their body and household servants . . . shall be allowed to go and come of their free will and accord." The specific classes mentioned were interpreted by the U.S. Attorney General not as illustrative examples but as meaning those classes *only*, in spite of the fact that the preceding article stated: "The limitation or suspension shall be reasonable and shall apply only to Chinese who may go to the United States as laborers, other classes not being included in the limitations." So a Chinese physician was classified a laborer and, not being in the five named categories, was refused permission to land. The same applied to an editor and a priest.

Their appetites whetted by the first taste of exclusion, the West was soon clamoring for more stringent measures. Hardly two years had gone by before an amendment was passed to the Exclusion Act. Masters of vessels were made responsible for illegal entry of Chinese laborers. Laborers already in the U.S. were permitted to remain, depart, and re-enter at will, but the amendment required that all departing Chinese obtain a certificate from the Chinese Consul General and another certificate from the immigration inspector at San Francisco. The latter was the holder's sole right of re-entry.

Those Chinese coming to the United States for the first time had to obtain a certificate from the Chinese government which was to be visaed by a diplomatic officer at the port of departure. Here already was a double check to insure that the traveler was not a laborer, but upon arrival, a Chinese was still subject to detention.

A trip across the Pacific Ocean was not a minor expense, and for a merchant to be turned back without the accomplishment of his mission caused many business firms to think twice before sending a man to the United States. In one case, and many others similar to it, a group of merchants arrived in San Francisco with a large potential order for machinery. They had obtained a certificate from the Chinese government and their papers were properly filled out in Chinese. But the U.S. diplomatic officer at the port of departure had inadvertently omitted some of the information on the English forms. The merchants were denied permission to land and were detained in the filthy detention house at San Francisco. A hurried dispatch to Chang Yen Hung himself, the Foreign Minister of China, did not alleviate the suspicions of the immigration inspector. The merchants were given the choice of returning to China or moving on. The merchants moved on. They went right to England and placed their order there.

By this time, Chinese immigration had been reduced to a trickle. The following table is taken from the *Historical Statistics of the United States, 1879–1945*, put out by the Census Bureau. Listed are only those figures from 1880 to 1924, when the law to exclude all aliens ineligible for citizenship took effect with the express intent to prevent any further immigration of the Mongolian races.

TABLE 4–1
Immigration from China, 1880–1924

Year	*No. Entering U.S.*	*Year*	*No. Entering U.S.*
1880	5,802	1903	2,209
1881	11,890	1904	4,309
1882	39,579	1905	2,166
1883	8,031	1906	1,544
1884	279	1907	961
1885	22	1908	1,397
1886	40	1909	1,943
1887	10	1910	1,968
1888	26	1911	1,460
1889	118	1912	1,765
1890	1,716	1913	2,105
1891	2,836	1914	2,502
1892	—	1915	2,660
1893	472	1916	2,460
1894	1,170	1917	2,237
1895	539	1918	1,795
1896	1,441	1919	1,964
1897	3,363	1920	2,330
1898	2,071	1921	4,009
1899	1,660	1922	4,406
1900	1,247	1923	4,986
1901	2,459	1924	6,992
1902	1,649		

SOURCE: U.S. Census Bureau, *Historical Statistics of the United States, 1879–1945*.

During this period, fourteen separate pieces of legislation relating to Chinese exclusion were passed. The table shows that only a few thousand Chinese came to the United States each year compared with the millions of other nationalities that flocked to this country. For instance, in 1882, when the first of the exclusion laws was enacted against the Chinese, 102,991 immigrants from Great Britain and 250,630 from Germany were admitted against 39,579 Chinese. In 1924, when the last of the exclusion acts was enacted against the Chinese, 89,336 Mexicans, 59,490 Britishers, and 20,918 Russians or Baltic states subjects were admitted against 6,992 Chinese. And in almost every year during this period, the number of Chinese leaving the United States was greater than the number coming in.

While the number of Chinese entering the country was drastically reduced, their concentration in the Far West was also diluted. The Chinese began to disperse and move eastward. Some went to Boston, New York, Chicago, and Denver. They took up unobtrusive occupations—mainly opening and operating laundries. It could hardly be said that the Chinese offered white labor any sort of competition, but whenever a national election came up, the Chinese question was again tossed into the political arena.

So far, the Democratic Party had carried the ball of opposing Chinese immigration, but in the election of 1887, the Republicans were not to be outdone. They went one step further.

A glance at Table 4–1 shows that for the year 1887, only ten persons emigrated to the United States from China. Yet zealous politicians were rolling up their sleeves for an all-out campaign against Chinese immigration. The politicians were tilting with windmills, although windmills would probably have posed a more formidable challenge.

Suspension of immigration was now too mild a weapon. Although it was expressly denied in the Sino-American Treaty of 1880, legislators clamored for outright prohibition. Accordingly, the United States pressed for a revision of the Treaty.

But before the Treaty could be revised and ratified, Congress prematurely passed the Scott Act in 1888, which expressly *prohibited* the coming of Chinese laborers to the United States, permitting only the five specific classes: officials, teachers, students, merchants, and travelers. But even these were harassed and burdened to the point of exclusion.

The Scott Act redefined *Chinese* as any member of the Chinese race, whether subjects of China or any other nation. It callously prohibited the return of any Chinese who had been employed as a laborer or miner, whether he held a validated return certificate or not. This prohibition was another direct contravention of the Treaty of 1880 still in force, as well as an ex post facto law and hence unconstitutional. This meant that 20,000 Chinese laborers who had gone back to China for a visit with re-entry permits and with every intention of returning to their jobs or their businesses here were locked out of the country. Many owned property and some had set up families, but they were denied re-entry.

The Scott Act furthermore required that returning Chinese, but not laborers, re-enter at the same port of departure. In other words, if they left the United States from San Francisco, they were to re-enter at San Francisco. They were not permitted to vary their itinerary and come in through Seattle.

After the passage of the Scott Act, the Chinese Minister in Washington registered his government's protest with the State Department. He was not even given the courtesy of an answer or acknowledgment. Six months later, he called upon the Secretary of State to repeat his protests against the violation of the Treaty. The Secretary was ill-disposed even to discuss the matter. He dismissed the Chinese Minister with these words: "Congress makes and repeals laws; the President can only veto. As Secretary of State, I can do neither." This from the Secretary of State, whose responsibility is the conduct of foreign affairs!

Protests were also made to the American Minister, Denby, in Peking, but in a note to the State Department, Mr. Denby wrote that he did not deem it prudent to discuss the Scott Act with the Tsung Li Yamen or "the mode of reconciling China to its results."

American violation of the Treaty by passage of the Scott Act strained Chinese-American relations to the breaking point. The Chinese Minister in Washington bitterly remarked: "I was not prepared to learn that there was a way recognized in the law and practice of this country whereby your country could release itself from treaty obligations without consultation or the consent of the other party. . . ." Throughout President Harrison's term of office, diplomatic exchanges between China and the United States were severed until 1894, when a new treaty between China and the United States was negotiated.

At the same time that the U.S. government showed such scant regard for her treaty obligations, she was demanding special treaty concessions and benefits for her merchants, missionaries, and sailors in China.

The legislators in Washington were unconcerned about the flagrancy of their act. The Republicans wanted to be on record as having outdone the Democrats on the Chinese question and they had demonstrated their ferocity. No thought was given for a moment to the fact that they were making a mountain out of a molehill and the tiniest of molehills at that.

The election of 1888 passed, and the country settled down to another four years. With the coming of 1892, the whole story was repeated. Harsher measures were demanded and harsher measures were passed. This time, the bill was called the Geary Act of 1892. It practically stripped the Chinese of any protection in courts, singled out the Chinese to be denied the rights upon which western justice is based, and subjected to suspicion all Chinese in the United States.

The Geary Act extended all bills in force against the Chinese for another ten years. No bail was to be permitted the Chinese in habeas corpus cases. All Chinese were required to obtain a certificate of eligibility to remain in the United States. And if a Chinese was arrested without such certificate, the burden of proof fell upon him.

When the Geary Act was passed, the Chinese Consul advised his fellow countrymen not to register. It was unconstitutional, he reasoned, and would soon be declared so. But reason was not to prevail. To the surprise of the world and the legal profession, the Geary Act was declared "constitutional" by the Supreme Court. Chief Justice Field shamefacedly acknowledged that the law was in violation of the Treaty of 1868 and 1880, as well as contrary to the Constitution, but he tried to justify it on the grounds of public interest and necessity.

Always, the Chinese had found eventual relief in the judicial system of the United States from the discriminatory and irrational laws passed against them by politically motivated legislators. And though the executive and legislative branches of the government were wont to submit to the emotional expediencies of the times, the judicial branch had always served to check and restore the dignity of the U.S. Constitution. But with the Geary Act, the judicial, too, flung reason and right to the winds. The phrase "not a Chinaman's chance" was born of this period and accurately reflected the position of the Chinese at the time.

Chinese exclusion legislation rode the waves of political elections. And though Chinese immigration was a dying cinder, the heat of the elections generally managed to fan a little more life into it. The Chinese were yet to see many other acts of Congress directed specifically at them. In 1898, when Hawaii was annexed as a U.S. territory, the exclusion laws were made applicable to the Territory even though Chinese immigration had never been an issue in Hawaii, the Chinese population in Hawaii was a large one, and the Chinese were well assimilated.

The same thing happened in the Philippine Islands when it became a U.S. territory. For centuries, the Chinese in the Philippines had come and gone freely. Sino-Philippine relations were warm and cordial. It was U.S. possession of the Islands that set up immigration barriers for the Chinese, whose centuries-long intercourse with the Philippines had rendered them an integral part of the Philippine population.

In 1902, Chinese exclusion was extended for another ten years. If President Arthur, who first vetoed an exclusion bill for twenty years because it was tantamount to prohibition, could foresee that Chinese exclusion would last for sixty-one years he would have been aghast.

Further acts to strengthen and enforce the exclusion acts were passed in 1904, 1911, 1912, and 1913. The Chinese also suffered further restrictions under the general immigration acts of 1917 and 1924. The former set up specific zones including China and other Asiatic countries, whose nationals were to be barred from U.S. shores. The latter act excluded from immigration into the United States all aliens ineligible to citizenship.

The Immigration Act of 1924 was not thought to be applicable to the Chinese, for it seemed that forty years of Chinese exclusion legislation had encompassed the whole field and plugged up every loophole, but it was to have a dynamic, disruptive influence on the lives of the Chinese in America and on their families. The Act of 1924 virtually condemned the Chinese in the United States to a life of forced celibacy, bachelorhood, or trans-Pacific marriages.

Never in the history of the United States had the nationals of another friendly, sovereign state been so humiliated, so disgraced. Later, the Japanese were also excluded, but it was the Japanese government under a Gentlemen's Agreement with the United States that undertook to screen the emigrants. The Chinese were the only people specifically named in legislation to be excluded from the United States. It was an affront that still rankles in the hearts of many Chinese.

5

Taking the Consequences

THE wound was deep. Somehow, it hurt more because it had been dealt by the United States, in all other respects a traditional friend of China. Was it not under similar circumstances that Caesar cried out, "Et tu, Brute"?

During the nineteenth and early part of the twentieth century, imperialism was the keynote of international relations. Nations with gunboats and big guns sliced off chunks of territory belonging to other nations. Africa and the Americas were portioned out in this manner. So was Asia.

China was a proud and haughty nation. Her empire once spread from the northernmost tip of Manchuria to the South China Sea, encompassing Burma and Indo-China. And from east to west, from Formosa to Asia Minor, the mileage was equally vast. But one by one her tributary states were wrested from her. Burma went to Great Britain; Korea and Formosa to Japan; Indo-China to France. Hong Kong was ceded to Britain after the Opium War. Manchuria fell to Japan in 1931, and the rest of the China coast was carved out into spheres of influence in which foreign powers staked their claims, insisted that Chinese law did not apply to the white man, and undertook to collect China's customs duties for her—a clear infringement of her sovereignty.

While everyone had been greedy and grabbing, the United States consistently upheld the political integrity of China. On the slightest pretext, the British and French gunboats would steam up the Yangtze River or storm the Chinese forts. Germany never hesitated to make her military might known, nor did Russia, and Japan was the worst offender of them all. But imperialism was repugnant to the American mind. It was unexpected circumstances that the United States found herself in the position of a colonial power as in the case of the Philippines and Puerto Rico.

Somehow the Americans had gained a fondness for the Chinese people inconsistent with their treatment of the Chinese in America. Because of the China trade—the silks, the carvings, the lacquers, the chinaware, and the arts which the merchants brought back with them—the American people gained a high respect for this ancient civilization. Chinese goods, along with the fact that most missionaries sent to China were from small towns and supported by small parishes, gave the average man a hazy interest in China. And then, too, China had managed to put up an imposing, if false, front of her invulnerability.

Repeatedly, foreign powers had tried to gain an audience with the Emperor or even with the governor of Kwangtung Province (where Canton is situated), but they were rebuffed. The Emperor refused to acknowledge the existence of such barbaric states unless they came as tribute-bearing nations.

There is a long and interesting tale about the various attempts of the western nations to gain an audience with the Emperor and the devious ways by which they were put off. The western envoys refused to kowtow before the Emperor. The Chinese would not grant an audience unless the diplomats made the proper obeisance. The Chinese cared little whether the foreign envoys were received or not, but it seemed of paramount importance to the western nations.

When the Chinese could deter no longer, the diplomats were finally received en masse. To the West, this was a signal success. Three formal bows were substituted for the kowtow (a subject of wrangling for several months). The Russian minister, dean of the diplomatic corps in Peking, made a speech. Then each diplomat in turn laid his letter of credence before the Emperor. Prince Kung, brother to the Emperor, acting as foreign minister, expressed the friendly sentiments of the throne and the ceremony was over. But the Chinese felt they had had the last word. In their sight, the diplomats had lost face. The ceremony had been held in the Pavilion of Purple Light, the place traditionally set aside for the reception of envoys from tributary states. The Emperor had neither risen from his throne nor uttered one word.

Merchants who came to trade with China were allowed only to

dock at Canton and make whatever purchases or sales with specified *hong* merchants. They were allowed no other contacts. A strip of land was allocated along the docks for residence and business purposes. Beyond this strip, they were forbidden to trespass. For more than half a century, foreigners abided by the rules set down by the Chinese imperial government for fear that their trading privileges would be rescinded. This held the foreigners in check, for the China trade was much too valuable.

China's brittle veneer was shattered by the Opium War in 1839. Great Britain, with her monopoly of opium from India, sought to force a market for this deadly opiate upon the Chinese people. Importation of opium was banned by a decree from the Emperor, but when the British defied the decree, the governor of Kwangtung strode down to the docks, ordered the confiscation of all opium stocks, and had them burned before his eyes. This brought war with Britain and, in its wake, a host of national disgraces that were to plague China for the next century.

The United States refused to cooperate with Great Britain, and when the ban on opium was decreed, the United States complied readily, agreeing to have nothing more to do with the trade. Besides, American interest in opium was very minor because Britain held a virtual monopoly.

Time and again, the United States refused to participate in the mad scramble for territorial concessions or spheres of influence that characterized the China policy of the European nations. She was eventually to share in the spoils through the most-favored-nation clause in treaties concluded after each grab, but on the whole, American behavior was proper and correct.

Much can be said for this restraint of the United States government, for domestically, commercial interests did their best to influence the government toward grabbing its share. And during the nineteenth century, imperialism was the fashion, the sport of "strong nations." The goal was to collect as many colonies as possible before the other fellow got wind of it, for once the scramble was on, jealous rivalry generally thwarted plans of outright annexation. In many instances in the history of colonialism, countries were unmolested or allowed to remain independent because jealous rivals would not allow another to have her.

The United States consistently upheld and defended the independence, territorial integrity, and sovereignty of China. On other occasions, the United States was instrumental in seeing that other nations did likewise. Yet in spite of American intercession, the plum of China was ripe for plucking. If China was not divided up, it was because of the Open-Door Policy formulated by John Hay, United States Secretary of State in 1899. He proposed to England, France, Germany, Russia, Italy, and Japan that China be regarded as an open market for international commerce, that these powers refrain from their intense competition against each other, and that they help China to regain her political independence and to reform her government.

The motivation behind the Open-Door Policy was twofold. As mentioned previously, the American people had always had a warm spot in their hearts for the Chinese people. On the other hand, clear, cold business logic prevailed too. If China was dismembered, the United States, who had not participated in the grab, would be left with nothing. The Open-Door Policy was in the best interests of the United States and also happened to be in the best interests of China.

For this reprieve, China was grateful. Again and again, the United States demonstrated her good will for China by aiding her in problems created by the demands of other nations: by President Grant's visit to China in 1879 to mediate the dispute with Japan over the Liuchiu Islands; by returning to China the American indemnities exacted during the Boxer Rebellion, which went toward the establishment of a university and scholarships for study in the United States; by aid and donations for flood and drought relief; and by many other expressions of good will. The bonds of friendship were firmly cemented during World War II, when they were both allied against Japan—China's archenemy.

Up until the Communist take-over in mainland China, the only scar on Chinese-American relations was the issue of Chinese exclusion! The previous chapter mentioned that relations became so strained after passage of the Scott Act, that diplomatic ties were broken off during the entire period of President Harrison's term in office. With a new treaty concluded in 1894, diplomatic relations were resumed, but with the expiration of the treaty ten years later, Congress, callous to the "face" and pride of the Chinese, re-enacted the entire body of Chinese exclusion laws.

This precipitated a violent reaction in the coastal ports of China. It was not so much the exclusion of laborers that the Chinese objected to, although on this score alone, the Chinese realized that they were the only nationals specifically singled out by name to be barred. The Chinese were sensible enough to know that by the emigration of the laboring class, a distorted impression had been given of the Chinese people as a whole. They, too, were eager to put their best foot forward, and the laboring class did not represent the best of China.

When China first gave its consent for the suspension of Chinese labor into the United States, China was given to understand by express provision in the treaties negotiated that classes other than laborers would be freely admitted. Specific examples raised were merchants, students, teachers, travelers, and government officials. The United States seized upon these five categories named in the treaties, ruling that only these five groups of Chinese would be admitted. To make matters worse, the Treasury Department and later the Bureau of Immigration interpreted the exclusion laws as if their sole object was to keep out every possible Chinese.

Merchants, students, and teachers were treated like common criminals—subjected first to suspicion, then detained in a place worse than a jail, and forbidden communication with anyone until they had undergone intensive questioning. If there was the slightest discrepancy in a person's papers, he was given 48 hours to make a written appeal. The burden of proof in all cases rested upon the person claiming admittance, and in all doubtful cases the benefit of the doubt was resolved against the Chinese. Students and merchants, after expending a small fortune for passage across the Pacific, never knew whether they were to be admitted until they had undergone this degrading experience at the port of entry, although they held valid visas or certificates signed by American consuls in China.

That there was circumvention of the law by some Chinese is not denied, but the real gripe of the Chinese people against the United States was the abuse and vilification they received at the hands of the immigration inspectors. Let me relate the experience of Wang Kai-kah, China's vice-commissioner to the St. Louis World's Fair.

In 1903 an American emissary, John Barret, was dispatched to China with the mission of inviting Chinese merchants to participate in the forthcoming World's Fair at St. Louis. This was the first time that China had ever participated in an affair of this sort, so she graciously accepted the kind invitation of the United States. A liberal appropriation was set aside, and merchants were instructed to ready their best wares for the exposition. A prince of royal blood was named to preside at the opening of the fair.

Adjunct to the invitation came rulings from the Treasury Department for admittance of the Chinese delegates to the U.S. exposition. These were discriminatory conditions not required of the other nationals attending:

(1) All Chinese delegates were to be photographed.

(2) They were to submit to personal examination by the Bertillon system of identification used only on criminals.

(3) A bond of $500 was required of each delegate to insure that he would leave the country immediately after the closing of the fair.

(4) Delegates had to present satisfactory evidence that they had no intention of remaining in the country.

(5) On being admitted, the delegates were to proceed by direct and continuous travel to the site of the fair. Within thirty days after the closing, the delegates were to return by direct and continuous travel to the port where they were admitted and depart on the first vessel sailing.

(6) On no condition must the delegates leave the exposition grounds unless a pass was obtained from the proper authorities. Such pass would entitle the holder to leave the exposition grounds for 48 hours. If the delegate did not return within 48 hours, his bond of $500 would be forfeited and the delegate subject to deportation.

This is like being formally invited by special courier to a friend's house for dinner. You graciously accept only to find a list of conditions for acceptance of the invitation in your morning mail:

(1) Submit to personal examination at the door.

(2) Bring some form of identification with you.

(3) Swear that you will not become a permanent guest.

(4) Post a bond so that the host can be sure you will leave after the repast.

(5) Go direct to the dining area. Immediately after dinner, hail the first taxi and go home.

(6) You are allowed twenty minutes to go to the washroom. If you are not back within twenty minutes, we will come after you and eject you from the house for violation of the rules.

Surely no friend would invite a guest to dinner under such preposterous conditions. Yet, these were precisely the conditions under which China was invited to participate in the fair.

It took two students sixteen months to get from San Francisco to Oberlin College, where they intended to take up the study of medicine. The students had come with returning missionaries who had sold them on the idea of coming to the United States for a medical degree. The students held passports signed by Li Hung Chang, who held the position equivalent to foreign minister of China. They also held certificates from the American consul in Tientsin, but he had made an unfortunate mistake in filling out the certificates. For this, the students were held in the notorious detention shed in San Francisco for a week, in spite of the assurances given by their American missionary friends. The Chinese consul was obliged to bail them out for $2,000, pending communication with Peking.

Their stay in San Francisco lasted six months, for meantime Li Hung Chang had died. Finally the matter was cleared up and the students left for Oberlin, but not being fully acquainted with the routes of travel, they chose the least expensive one, which happened to be the Canadian Pacific. The train crossed into Canada, and as soon as the train returned to American soil, the students were taken off, even though they held valid entry papers. They were told that they could not re-enter the United States once they had left its soil, although they had never left the train.

Stranded in Canada, they again wired the Chinese consul in San Francisco, who demanded that they return to San Francisco as soon as possible, as the American authorities were ready to forfeit their bonds of $2,000. Yet, the railroad could not sell them a return ticket because another law forbade selling a ticket to any Chinese unless he had the proper papers.

The two students waited in Canada for another three months while friends wrote letters on their behalf. Sixteen months after they arrived in San Francisco from China, they were finally permitted to proceed to Oberlin. By that time, the funds they brought with them for their education were almost depleted. In spirit, they were totally disgusted and depressed.

There are enough instances of this sort to fill a whole volume in itself, but the two examples above should suffice to give the reader a general idea of what a Chinese went through after he set sail for these shores.

Of course tales of these incidents were taken back to China, and a proud people like the Chinese were naturally incensed. Their indignation must have been deep, for other things considered, Chinese friendship for the United States was profound.

It therefore came as a shock and surprise to American officials when one of the first demonstrations against a foreign nation, after the birth of nationalism in China, was directed against the United States. It came in the form of an economic boycott.

The boycott sparked off in Shanghai and spread south. Its effects were felt even in Malaya, where large numbers of Chinese were resident. Merchants banded together and refused to buy or sell American goods. They agreed not to ship goods in American ships. Chinese children were not to be sent to schools operated by Americans. No Chinese was to work for an American firm as interpreter or comprador, and Chinese servants in American homes were asked to resign. Merchants violating the boycott were publicly denounced and ostracized, or were reported to the banker's guild where they soon found their credit cut off.

In 1904, the United States was doing between thirty and forty million dollars' worth of trade with China. This figure was drastically reduced by the boycott.

In China, work was forbidden on buildings that were being erected by Americans. American ships could not discharge their cargo. Contracts with American firms were annulled or not renewed. Chinese newspapers refused advertisements from American firms and canceled existing contracts. Flour, oil, tobacco, and shipping were hard hit by this boycott, which proved effective in substantially reducing American trade with China.

President Theodore Roosevelt, in a speech to southern textile manufacturers who had been hit by the boycott, said:

> We cannot expect China to do us justice unless we do China justice. The chief cause in bringing about the boycott of our goods in China was undoubtedly our attitude toward the Chinese who came to this country. . . . Our laws and treaties should be so framed as to guarantee to all Chinamen, save of the excepted coolie class, the same right of entry to this country, and the same treatment while here, as is guaranteed to any other nation. By executive action, I am as rapidly as possible putting a stop to the abuses which have grown up during many years in the administration of this law. I can do a great deal and will do a great deal even without the action of Congress, but I cannot do all that should be done unless some action is taken. . . .
>
> The action I ask is demanded by considerations that are higher than mere interest for I ask it in the name of what is just and right. Americans should take the lead in establishing international relations on the basis of honest and upright dealings which we regard as essential between man and man.

The action that President Roosevelt took was to send out an executive order instructing all immigration officials to desist from arbitrary mistreatment and abuse of the Chinese on pain of dismissal.

Congress, too, took note of the boycott to the extent of conducting hearings into the whys and wherefores of this expression of protest against the United States. The main witness was Charles Denby, a man who had served his country in China for twenty years. He pinpointed the cause of the boycott directly to the Chinese exclusion laws, for which he blamed the immigration inspectors at the ports of entry. Merchants are not excluded from this country, he declared, yet they have been subjected to humiliating experiences, suspected as coolies posing as merchants.

The boycott lasted a year. When the Chinese merchants lost heart after sustaining heavy losses, the students and press carried it on. By this time, both the American and Chinese governments were thoroughly alarmed at the dangerous proportions the movement had assumed. Secretly, the Manchu government was delighted at this defiance and resistance put up by her people, but on the other hand, she feared the movement might explode into another uprising which might rock the very throne upon which the Emperor sat. An imperial edict was issued to suppress the boycott.

Upon cessation of the boycott, business picked up and American businessmen soon forgot about the cause that led to the protest. With the pressure off from businessmen, Congress dropped the matter. In spite of specific orders from President Roosevelt, immigration officials soon continued their old habits.

But if there was no further eruption of their feelings against the exclusion laws, Chinese resentment remained to smolder in the latent recesses of the national subconscious. In light of present-day relations between the United States and Mainland China, historians, statesmen, and experts scratch their heads in bewilderment at the turn of events that have deposited these two traditional friends in opposite camps. The exclusion laws may not have been the sole culprit, but as A. Whitney Griswold prophesied as far back as 1938 in his book, *The Far Eastern Policy of the United States*, ". . . the germs of race prejudice had polluted American relations with both China and Japan and had profoundly influenced the development of the Far Eastern policy of the United States."

Assessing the situation from another angle Professor Coolidge, in her book *Chinese Immigration*, felt that the development of the West was retarded by the loss of Chinese labor and that laborers from other countries brought in to replace the Chinese were not as useful, just as unassimilative, and far more menacing both to labor and to citizenship.

Agriculture is one of California's basic industries. But unlike farming communities elsewhere, California had a peculiar agricultural system all her own. Because of the large land holdings held by a small group of men, actual work on the farm was not performed solely by the owner and his family. Farming was more like a vast industrial enterprise. It was not uncommon to find farms 4,000 acres in size. Labor was hired for the planting, the cultivating, and the harvesting. Labor was hired when needed and discharged after completion of the task at hand. Conditions like these generally led to mechanization of equipment and methods, but in California, mechanization was not the answer because tractors, plows, and combines do not lend themselves to orchard crops. Potatoes can be dug, separated from the vines, sorted, and sacked as the farmer rides over his fields, exerting no more energy than stepping on the gas pedal. Harvesters can cut the wheat, thresh it, sack the wheat, tie the straw up neatly in bundles, and gently deposit the straw back on the field. But machines have not been devised to pick soft, ripe fruit from trees without bruising a goodly portion.

So after the Chinese left the railroads, most of them went into farming. They were well experienced in this sort of work, as they knew the feel of soil and the satisfaction of coaxing the most from it. In 1870 about one-tenth of the farm labor was Chinese. By 1880, this proportion was increased to one-third, and four years later more than half the labor force in farming was Chinese.[1]

Farm employers valued the Chinese workers highly. They were industrious, reliable, honest, and unobtrusive. When an employer hired a Chinese farm hand, he knew without overseeing that without fail, the Chinese would be on hand when needed. This was important because ripe fruit must be picked promptly. A delay of a day or two could ruin the crop.

"If a Chinese labor leader in California agrees to pick the fruit of an orchard, he will do it to the last 'cot' or prune. Not so the white laborer. You may contract with him at so much for the job, and a day or two, he is apt to ask for a small advance to buy necessary shoes or whatnot; and when the morrow's sun has ripened the fruit to the point of rottenness he is not to be found."[2]

Farmers lament that there has been no substitute for the efficiency

[1] Carey McWilliams, *California, the Great Exception* (New York, Current Books, Inc., 1949), p. 152.

[2] Statement by Chauncey R. Burr, Senate Document 449, Vol. 4915, 59th Congress, 1st Session.

of Chinese farm labor. Nevertheless, in 1882, the gates clanged shut in the face of the Chinese laborer. His only crime was that he worked hard and he looked different.

However, the peaches still had to be picked. The prunes, the apricots, the oranges were rotting on the branches. The tomatoes burst their fiery red jackets and spilt themselves on the ground. Other produce grew to seed and replanted themselves helter and skelter. But hands to gather the fruits of nature's bounty were not to be had.

Imbalance in the economic scheme of things generally corrects itself. The demand for farm labor was acute, and the supply had been arbitrarily cut off. It wasn't long before some sort of substitute was found. It came in the form of Japanese immigrants.

Japan did not allow her citizens to leave the Fatherland until 1880, so there was no problem of Japanese immigrants prior to this time. But with passage of the Chinese Exclusion Act in 1882 and the acute demand for farm labor, Japanese laborers stepped in to fill this vacuum. By 1900, there were 24,326 Japanese in the United States and by 1910, there were 72,157, a threefold increase in ten years. The Japanese did not rely solely upon immigration to increase their ranks. They brought their women with them, thereby adding to their numbers from within as well as from without.

The Japanese differed little from the Chinese in physical characteristics. They supplanted the Chinese in the farms and homes, and for the same reasons that the Californians objected to the Chinese, they objected to the Japanese—only more so.

The Japanese were not as docile as the Chinese. They took exception to the discrimination against them, and they made themselves heard through a strong, militaristic government in Japan. On several occasions, President Theodore Roosevelt thought the United States would be drawn into war over the treatment of the Japanese in California. In 1906, when California segregated Japanese children from white schools, Japanese protest was so vehement that President Roosevelt asked for a ship-by-ship comparison of the U.S. Navy with the Japanese Navy. In a letter to his son, he wrote:

"I am horribly bothered about the Japanese business. The infernal fools in California and especially San Francisco insult the Japanese recklessly and in the event of war, it will be the nation as a whole which will bear the consequences."[3]

In 1908, anti-Japanese feeling ran so high in California that the federal government was compelled to accede to her demands for some form of restriction. But Japan was not to be treated with disparagement like China. Japan had a strong navy. Her military potential was impressive. Her minister in Washington was not to be kept waiting nor to be dismissed contemptuously or casually. Japan realized that the problem of Japanese emigration to California would be a constant thorn in the side of U.S.-Japanese relations, but she would not suffer the United States to expressly exclude her citizens.

Accordingly, Japan agreed to regulate emigration of her own citizens to the United States in what is known as the Gentlemen's Agreement of 1908. In the Agreement, Japan promised to stop issuing passports to laborers, skilled or unskilled, except those previously domiciled in the United States, or to the wives or children of such persons. Thus Japan retained control over the emigration of her citizens and in good faith tried to regulate the emigration flow to the United States.

In 1907, Japanese immigration reached 30,226, and in 1908 the figure dropped to 15,803, but after 1908 as after 1882, Japanese immigration became insignificant.

Again a vacuum developed in the California labor market; again the artificial barriers of exclusion could not hold back the influx. When the Japanese stopped coming, the Hindus came. This period also saw the beginning of large-scale immigration from Mexico. Between 1920 and 1930 the number of Mexicans increased fourfold, and by the end of the decade, some 75,000 Mexicans joined the migratory labor ranks in California. When there was talk of restrictive legislation against the Mexicans, farm employers turned to the wooing of Filipino workers. By 1930, some 30,000 Filipinos tried to fill the yawning gap in farm labor.[4] Also migrating to California were Russians and the most recent arrival, Puerto Ricans.

[3] A. Whitney Griswold, *Far Eastern Policy of the United States* (New York, Harcourt, Brace & Co., 1938), p. 251.

[4] McWilliams, *op. cit.*, p. 154.

When exclusion was set in motion in 1882, California perpetuated for herself a chronic headache of an army of intransigent, migratory population. This rootless, hapless horde moves with the crops. Working from south to north, they are here one day and gone the next. They eat when they have work and go on relief the rest of the time. Their instability lends instability to the state. Children growing up among this migratory group have no benefit of education. Living conditions among them are appalling. When they are contracted to harvest a crop, they take their own sweet time in their own sweet way and who can blame them when the completion promises them nothing better than the beginning? What matters if the employers tear their hair and wring their hands at the "inefficient, happy-go-lucky, worthless lot"? The land does not belong to the worker or the worker to the land. He feels no attachment to it. As McWilliams points out, "If ever a system was calculated to make for bad labor relations, it is this system of farm labor employment in California."

During the ruckus over Chinese exclusion, it was contended that if this "undesirable element" pervaded the state, more "desirable" immigrants might be discouraged from coming in. This has certainly not been the case, and California found herself in the predicament of the little girl who hated her red hair. Having been taunted by her playmates all day, she asked in her prayers that night for a different shade of hair. "Please God," she prayed, "I'd rather be bald than have this horrid red hair." Shortly afterwards, she became ill and her red hair began to fall out. When she surveyed herself in the mirror, she screamed, "But God, I was only joking."

We have considered the international, the Sino-American, and the local consequences of Chinese exclusion, but what about the Chinese to whom these laws were directed? In former years, economic necessity was dominant in determining Chinese emigration to the United States. When famine, pestilence, poverty, and hopelessness threatened to engulf them, a pioneer group of southern Chinese looked toward the United States, the land of opportunity. To them, the United States symbolized hope, the contentment of a full stomach, a better station in life, perhaps education for their children. They did not ask for much. They were neither greedy nor avaricious. They were not out for sudden wealth or fabulous fortunes. The migrant Chinese only asked for the opportunity to earn a livelihood. He would have given his best and more for this opportunity, which was soon denied him.

Coming as the first wave of migration to a pioneer country, the Chinese did not bring their wives or children with them. This was generally true of most newcomers to the West, but as the frontier country became more settled, families joined the menfolk. When men have a normal family life, they put down roots and society becomes stabilized.

With the enactment of the exclusion laws, the Chinese knew that they were not welcome in this new land. It was a horrible experience for the Chinese to realize that they were unwanted and unwelcome; it was a feeling similar to that of a child who realizes his parents think him a burden, but who knows that there is no place else for him to go. The Chinese who were in the United States clung to their opportunity to stay here for the sake of their livelihood. To have returned to China meant a bleak economic future and most likely the severance of the family source of income. And with the Chinese, the sense of family obligation was greater than personal considerations.

To send for the family required financial resources greater than most of the early Chinese commanded, and after paying for passage across the Pacific, there was absolutely no guarantee that the wife or children would be admitted. And with laws enacted against him regularly every four years, the Chinese was never sure when he, too, would be ejected from these shores.

Most of the Chinese who came to the United States were already married. Chinese boys generally marry at sixteen or seventeen and are fathers shortly thereafter. When these men arrived in the United States, they were family men with mouths to feed and heads to look after. They could not take their duty lightly. The dilemma was to stay in hopes of a better future for their children but be separated for the major part of their lives from the warmth and love of the family circle, or to go back and pit themselves against a seemingly losing battle for survival against the rocky hills and terrain of southern China.

That a great many did go back is verified by the figures: the number of Chinese departing exceeded the arrivals. But for those who stayed, the choice meant condemnation to a life of celibacy or bachelorhood, although in actuality they may have been married. They were denied the joys and cares of seeing their children grow up. They no longer knew the feast days, the holidays when faces dear and close swarmed about to lend gaiety and festivity to the air. They were deprived of performing the thousand-and-one small gestures of gratitude and love to their parents, who had brought them into the world and sacrificed for them what they were now sacrificing for their children. Yes, these men were condemned, sentenced to a life of loneliness, boredom—a life shorn of love and warmth, of home and family in a land where prejudice surrounded them and fate was benign if one did not suffer bodily attack.

The ones who stayed sometimes managed to make an occasional trip to China, but this was another hazardous gamble. It was easy enough to leave, but it was not so easy getting back in. It was necessary to get a certificate from the Chinese consul and another certificate from the immigration officials at the port of departure, the sole evidence of the holder's right to return, but if this was the end of it, the lot of the Chinese might have been much easier. There was no guarantee that with the issuance of the return certificate that such certificate would be honored upon re-entry. With the passage of the Scott Act, those Chinese out of the country temporarily, even though they held valid return certificates, were forbidden to re-enter. Professor Coolidge estimated that 20,000 Chinese were trapped outside of the country in this high-handed manner.

But even when treaty stipulations and the law gave the Chinese right of re-entry, immigration officials took it upon themselves to suspect every Chinese of forging his papers. No matter how many times a Chinese had come back into the country, he was not permitted to step from ship to shore after the examination of his papers, but was automatically detained for a grueling period of questioning designed to trap or trick the Chinese into giving an incongruous answer and expose himself to deportation.

Hurdles and indignities like these made most Chinese in the United States think twice about making a trip to China to visit their families. The exclusion laws were not only unjust; they were inhuman!

By 1924, it seemed as if no more exclusion laws could possibly be enacted against the Chinese, but not so. Although the Immigration Act of 1924 did not specifically mention the Chinese, it definitely affected them, for the law excluded all aliens ineligible to citizenship. This circuitous phraseology meant that *all non-whites*, except those of African descent who were granted right of citizenship under the 15th Amendment, were to be forbidden entry into the United States as immigrants.

This Act was to work extreme hardship upon the remaining Chinese still in this country and especially upon American-born Chinese men. By all rights, they were U.S. citizens entitled to the guarantees of the U.S. Constitution to life, liberty, and the pursuit of happiness, but what happiness lay in store for them when the very basis of human society, the family, was denied them?

Prior to 1924 and in spite of the exclusion acts, American citizens, Chinese included, were allowed to bring in their wives and children, provided they could raise the passage, take a calculated risk that the wives and children would be admitted, and buck the traditions by taking the family away from the ancestral home. The Immigration Act of 1924 took away this right granted to white and Negro citizens. As Chinese women were aliens ineligible to citizenship, they were no longer admitted even though they may have been the wives of American-born Chinese men.

The framers of this law probably never realized the heartaches that this Act would bring to American citizens of Chinese ancestry. Chinese women were extremely scarce in this country. The discrepancy in numbers between men and women was fantastic. In order to marry a girl of his own race, an American-born Chinese invariably had to go and find a wife in China. Most American-borns brought their wives back with them and established their homes here. But after 1924, American-born Chinese with every right as native-born citizens found that their wives could no longer join them. If these men went back to China and married Chinese girls, they had to maintain split families, living the major part of their lives like bachelors. If they craved a wholesome family life, they were forced into intermarriage with its disadvantages and social ostracism. The last choice was for them to forsake marriage. Neither of these alternatives could be considered appealing or satisfactory.

The Chinese exclusion laws were more than exclusion laws. They were punitive laws inflicted upon innocent victims by incident of birth!

In the last analysis, the upper-class Chinese, the educated, the wealthy, the big merchants kept away from the United States. They would not subject themselves to the degrading humiliation that they knew would be meted out by American immigration authorities. If they were on a pleasure tour, surely "pleasure" would be a misnomer if one were to be locked up perhaps for weeks and months on Angel's Island, Ellis Island, or some similar detention house to be grilled, cross-examined, and suspected of criminal behavior. Would the reader plan a trip to Europe if he knew that similar treatment awaited him at the border of the European countries?

In the end, it was left to the poorer classes—the ones who had little to lose, the ones who had no choice but to swallow their pride—to risk the chance of getting in and to suffer whatever indignities the immigration authorities willed. This is not to insinuate that the Chinese who did come to the United States were the scum of the earth. True, they were of the lower economic class, but these were men of courage, of endurance, of intelligence, and yes, of cunning, to pitch themselves against a seemingly impenetrable wall. However, these men did not have the benefit of education or knowledge, the skills or the polish of a civilization that was centuries old. They knew only how to struggle for survival, rice and salt being their main concern. They reflected these basic concerns in their behavior and manners because they had been so conditioned.

But China had the finer things of life to offer. She had a glorious and ancient civilization dating back thousands of years. Her philosophies and literature reflected the wisdom and maturity of the ages. Her porcelains, her silks, her paintings, and her multiform art were unsurpassed for their beauty and handiwork. But the American people did not get to know this facet of China. They did not get to know the scholar, the poet, the painter, nor did they get to know the wares and products made in China, for merchants, too, had pride.

And so the American people knew the Chinese only as a miner, domestic servant, laundryman, farm laborer, or restaurateur. Surely these Chinese did not disgrace their race, but neither were they in a position to truly represent the Chinese people or its civilization.

In sum, the exclusion laws set into motion forces that were to pollute Sino-American relations, perpetuate an unnatural migratory labor situation in California, inflict inhuman punishment against some of her own citizens by depriving them of the right to a home and family, and insulate the American people against a true understanding of the Chinese and their civilization.

6

A Crack in the Door

THERE was general agreement among responsible leaders of the United States that the Chinese exclusion laws were a mistake. They were rammed through Congress at the insistence of an adolescent frontier state and concurred in because of political expediency. The laws were unjust; in some instances, downright unconstitutional. They flagrantly violated treaty stipulations between traditionally friendly nations. They were exceedingly difficult to enforce or administer. They were outmoded, archaic, useless; for Chinese immigration was but a mere trickle, and even this trickle was dammed by the Immigration Act of 1924. Besides, complete trust and amity between allies in World War II were impossible when such discriminatory statutes directed against the Chinese were still part of American law. As President Franklin D. Roosevelt said in his message to Congress requesting repeal, "Nations like individuals make mistakes. We must be big enough to acknowledge our mistakes of the past and to correct them."

In 1943, the time was propitious for repeal. American public sentiment was certainly strongly in favor of it. And surprisingly enough, strongest support for belated justice came from the West Coast, the very region which originally meted out exclusion. It was Warren Magnuson, Democrat from the state of Washington, who sponsored the bill for repeal, which eventually passed the House and in the same form was sent to the Senate. In the Upper House, it was Senator Charles Andrews of Florida, a Southerner, who pushed the bill through. Even the *San Francisco Chronicle*, formerly a staunch supporter of exclusion, reversed itself.

It was the California department of the American Legion that bucked the parent organization and resolved to urge the enactment of repeal. It was the same with the Veterans of Foreign Wars. Although the national organization went on record opposing repeal, the California department disagreed with the national organization and vigorously called for abolition of the exclusion acts.

The grounds were further softened by the nationwide tour of Mme. Chiang Kai-shek in the spring of 1943. She was invited to address a joint session of Congress—the first such honor ever accorded a woman. Conscious of the remaining scar upon Sino-American relations, Mme. Chiang took the opportunity to invite a number of key Congressmen to dinner, among them influential members of the House Immigration Committee. Pointedly, she brought up the subject of the possibility of repealing the exclusion laws, and she emphasized the great boost that such a measure would provide for Chinese morale.

After Mme. Chiang's triumphant tour, strenuous opposition against repeal virtually melted away. It remained for public sentiment to be translated into actual legislation.

The Democratic Party as a whole was definitely pro-repeal. President Roosevelt twice sent messages to Congress asking for passage of the bill. Only the Southern Democrats, with a keen fear of racial issues, were hesitant, but the Senate version of the bill sponsored by Senator Andrews of Florida mitigated Southern opposition.

The Republican Party was not inclined to support legislation of a Democratic Administration, but Wendell Willkie, defeated Republican candidate and titular head of the Republican Party, lent his support and used his influence to persuade Republican members of Congress that the measure was non-partisan. The day before the repeal bill came up for debate in the House, Wendell Willkie held a three-hour conference with more than a hundred Republican Congressmen. As a result, there was no partisan opposition against repeal.

There were three main provisions to the repeal bill. The first abolished all existing legislation pertaining to exclusion of persons of the Chinese race. The second provided for an annual quota of 105 for all persons of the Chinese race, 75 percent of the quota being reserved for those emigrating from China. The third gave the right of naturalization to those Chinese who had lawfully entered the United States.

All three provisions of the bill were equally important, for there were a few legislators who were willing to repeal the entire body of exclusion laws specifically naming the Chinese but without providing for a quota or for naturalization of the Chinese. Such a bill, however, would have been an empty gesture. The Chinese would still have been forbidden right of entry into the country by the Immigration Act of 1924. So technically, while discrimination against the Chinese might have been erased, discrimination against Asians still persisted, and a Chinese was an Asian. There would have been little comfort in being re-classified for discrimination.

The quota of 105 was arrived at by computing one-sixth of one percent of the number of Chinese resident in the United States in 1920 as determined by the census of that year. The same formula was used to determine the quotas for all countries whose nationals were eligible for U.S. citizenship, but as applied to the Chinese there were two inequities. First, as the Chinese had been excluded from the country for more than sixty years, the number of Chinese resident in the United States in 1920 was insignificant—only 61,639. It was hardly a realistic base to compute a quota for a national group numbering more than 600 million.

Second, for all other nationalities, a person was judged the citizen of a particular country on the basis of country of birth, not on the basis of national extraction. For example, a person of Italian extraction born in France would be considered a Frenchman for immigration purposes and admitted under the French quota. Not so with the Chinese! A person of Chinese extraction applying for entry to the United States, whether he be a citizen of Ireland, Thailand, Venezuela, or any other country, could only be admitted under the Chinese quota. This meant that only 75 percent or specifically 79 places were reserved for those emigrating exclusively from China proper, the other 26 out of the 105 quota were reserved for nationals of Chinese extraction from other parts of the world.

A separate quota of 100 was set up for non-Chinese persons emigrating from China. Thus, in effect, China had two quotas: one for Chinese and one for non-Chinese. Again, it was unique in that China was the only country so treated.

The third provision of the bill was the most significant. It gave the Chinese already in the United States the right of naturalization. It enabled them to transfer their allegiance to their adopted country. It gave them a chance to share in the benefits that this country so generously offers, and it gave them the privilege of shouldering the responsibilities of an American citizen. One of the most frequent criticisms directed against the Chinese in the United States was that they were unassimilable. Yet it is difficult to see how they could adapt themselves completely to American life when laws specifically forbade them to become an integral part of the country and its people.

Another provision, suggested but not included in the final repeal act, was the right of wives and minor children of Chinese-American citizens to be admitted as non-quota immigrants, a right accorded other nationalities. It was feared that this right, if extended to the Chinese, might jeopardize the whole repeal bill. Treading cautiously, the Citizens Committee, guiding force in the repeal campaign, yielded. On this issue the Citizens Committee underestimated the extent of pro-Chinese sentiment, for an amendment embodying that right was passed without a murmur three years later.

In the House as well as the Senate, debate on the bill was limited. The majority who went on record spoke in favor of the bill. In perusing through the *Congressional Record*, I found that only Compton I. White of Idaho reverted to the hashed-over arguments against the Chinese as he knew them fifty years ago. Forced to admit that a lot of changes had taken place since 1882, White retreated.

Neither House nor Senate felt the need for a count of votes. The die-hards against repeal knew that they were in the minority, and a count of votes would only reveal their pitiful ranks. The bill for repeal of the Chinese exclusion laws passed by voice vote in the House on October 22, 1943. A month later, the Senate followed suit. On December 17th, the last vestige of the humiliation of the exclusion laws passed into history as President Roosevelt put his signature to the repeal act.

With the lowering of the gates what happened? Did a floodtide result? What types of immigrants came or rather what types were allowed to come? Were they male or female, young or old, professionals or laborers? What bearing does the pattern of immigration have on the Chinese communities in the United States?

In answer to those who envisioned a deluge of Chinese immigrants after repeal, the annual quota of 105 was an effective cork. Up until 1946, the only Chinese admitted for permanent residence were those admitted under the quota. And these were few indeed. In the three years dating from repeal, this number added up to 213 Chinese admitted. For a ten-year period following repeal of the exclusion acts, only 558 Chinese persons were admitted to the United States under the quota.[1] This averaged out to 56 persons a year. If the Chinese were not entirely barred, they were certainly effectively barred. Table 6–1 below gives the number of Chinese immigrants admitted under the quota for the years 1944 to 1965.

TABLE 6–1

Chinese Admitted to the U.S. as Quota Immigrants
Years Ending June 30, 1944 to June 30, 1965

Year	*Numbers Admitted*	*Year*	*Numbers Admitted*
1944	19	1955	1,066*
1945	105	1956	470*
1946	89	1957	267*
1947	65	1958	304*
1948	80	1959	371*
1949	36	1960	454*
1950	60	1961	117*
1951	97	1962	84
1952	64	1963	82
1953	107*	1964	47
1954	1,363*	1965	708*

* Includes those who had adjusted their status in the United States by suspension of deportation, by private law, or as displaced persons by mortgage on future quotas.

SOURCE: U.S. Immigration and Naturalization Service

Actually the quota was never fully utilized between the years 1944 to 1952. The main reason was that quota entry called for further qualifications and acted as another barrier.

Persons who applied for quota entry were not granted visas according to numerical order. A preference system was set up as a selective

[1] Figures for Chinese persons and China differ because of the two-quota system.

process to screen the immigrants. There were four such preference categories. The first 50 percent of a country's quota was reserved for skilled aliens whose services were determined by the Attorney General as needed urgently in the United States because of high education, technical training, specialized experience, or exceptional ability. Such immigrants would substantially benefit the national economy, the cultural interests, or the welfare of the United States. Accompanying spouses and children of such skilled aliens were also given first preference status.

Second preference, or 30 percent of the total quota, was set aside for parents of Chinese-American citizens over 21 years of age.

Third preference, or the remaining 20 percent, was first made available to spouses and children of permanent resident aliens lawfully admitted and residing in the United States.

Fourth preference permitted up to 25 percent of any portion of a quota not required for visa issuance to first, second, or third preference quota immigrants to be made available to brothers and sisters of American citizens and to sons and daughters of American citizens, if such sons and daughters did not qualify for non-quota status because they were married or over 21 years of age.

All in all, over a period of 22 years that the quota restrictions were in force, 5,891 Chinese entered the country. If it were not for the non-quota provisions and some of the relief measures later enacted, the quota would have been almost as restrictive as exclusion.

In 1946, under the impetus of the War Brides Act, Congress passed a measure permitting the wives and children of Chinese-American citizens to apply for admission as non-quota immigrants. However, the husbands and children of female citizens were not accorded this same privilege until 1952. Table 6–2 below gives the number of non-quota immigrants admitted from 1946 to 1965. The peak year of admissions was 1959, when 5,660 entered the country. Most of the women and children who came to join their menfolk were admitted under the non-quota provision.

The few thousand Chinese that entered the country as quota and non-quota immigrants were few when compared with the numbers from other countries. In the 22 years after repeal, 52,959 Chinese persons were admitted as immigrants. In comparison, for the year

TABLE 6–2

Chinese Admitted to the U.S. as Non-Quota Immigrants
Years Ending June 30, 1946 to June 30, 1965

Year	*Numbers Admitted*	*Year*	*Numbers Admitted*
1946	144	1956	3,980
1947	1,063	1957	4,856
1948	3,494	1958	2,891
1949	2,454	1959	5,660
1950	1,229	1960	3,218
1951	986	1961	3,400
1952	1,088	1962	1,496*
1953	986	1963	2,124*
1954	1,384	1964	2,931*
1955	1,562	1965	1,353*

* NOTE: After 1961 separate figures were not kept for Chinese persons, non-quota. These figures also include non-Chinese born in China.

SOURCE: U.S. Immigration and Naturalization Service

1965 alone, 29,923 immigrants were admitted from Great Britain and Northern Ireland while 21,621 came from Germany.

Table 6–3 compares the total immigration to the United States by country over a period of 146 years, from 1820 to 1965. Ostensibly 417,000 persons came from China. This figure is not an accurate reflection of Chinese immigration because immigrants from China and Chinese immigrants are not synonymous. Besides, nearly half of this figure entered during the peak years during the 1870's and 1880's, an influx which led to the first exclusion act. For comparative purposes, true Chinese immigration is less than the number given. A report released by the Immigration and Naturalization Service in February 1964 shows that between the years 1899 and 1961 merely 110,480 Chinese persons were admitted to the United States.

Not only have the Chinese come to this country, they have also left it. For practically every year since the beginning of the century, departures have exceeded arrivals. Even after repeal of the exclusion laws, this pattern held true until 1948 when male citizens of Chinese ancestry began to bring in their families as non-quota immigrants. This caused a reversal of the trend, but even then when immigration

TABLE 6–3

Total Immigration to the United States, by Country for 146 Years, 1820–1965 (000 Omitted)

All countries	43,291		
Europe	35,106	Asia	1,202
Albania	2	China	417
Austria-Hungary	4,285	Japan	345
Belgium	194	India	16
Bulgaria	67	Turkey in Asia	208
Czechoslovakia	130	Other Asia	216
Denmark	356		
Estonia	1	America	6,548
Finland	29	Canada & Newfoundland	3,799
France	709	Mexico	1,367
Germany	6,845	West Indies	739
Great Britain	4,692	Central America	168
Greece	506	South America	373
Ireland	4,704	Other America	102
Italy	5,041		
Latvia	2	Africa	57
Lithuania	3	Australia & New Zealand	88
Luxembourg	2	Pacific Islands	22
Netherlands	343	Not Specified	268
Norway	848		
Poland	465		
Portugal	297		
Rumania	160		
Spain	197		
Sweden	1,260		
Switzerland	334		
Turkey in Europe	162		
U.S.S.R.	3,345		
Yugoslavia	72		
Other Europe	50		

SOURCE: *Annual Report,* U.S. Immigration and Naturalization Service 1965, Table 13

overtook emigration in 1948, 3,574 came in, but 2,238 departed. This left a net increase of 1,336. If the restrictionists had looked at the immigration statistics put out by U.S. governmental agencies, their fears of a flood of Chinese immigration would long ago have been allayed.

TABLE 6–4

Comparison of Chinese Immigration and Emigration
Years ending June 30, 1944 to 1958*

Year	*Immigrants*	*Emigrants*
1944	34	49
1945	109	257
1946	233	770
1947	1,128	2,168
1948	3,574	2,238
1949	2,490	547
1950	1,289	674
1951	1,083	560
1952	1,152	397
1953	1,093	293
1954	2,747	733
1955	2,628	921
1956	4,450	224
1957	5,123	283
1958	3,195	2

SOURCE: U.S. Immigration and Naturalization Service

* Emigration figures for Chinese persons not available after 1958.

From 1948 to 1953, almost every Chinese immigrant who disembarked at an American port or airport of entry was a young woman with or without young children in tow. For these six years, the preponderance of females averaged close to 90 percent. This is apparent from Figure 6–A on page 87.

The overwhelming number of females reflected four conditions. First, the unbalanced sex ratio among the Chinese in this country was correcting itself after the artificial barriers were removed. Second, the Communist take-over in China caused an exodus among those who had connections with relatives overseas. It used to be that the men emigrated while the women stayed behind in the ancestral home. Third, enactment of the War Brides Act on December 28, 1945 enabled men who had served in the Armed Forces to bring in their wives and minor children. Fourth, whereas Chinese-American men were permitted to send for their spouses, Chinese-American women were not allowed the same privilege under the non-quota conditions. Not until 1952, with the passage of the omnibus Immigration and Nationality Act, was this inequity against Chinese-American women removed. By 1954, a more balanced ratio between male and female immigrants was achieved.

The normal age pyramid is shaped like an isosceles triangle, but the age pyramid when plotted for Chinese immigrants is broadest at the middle instead of the base. This is readily seen in Figure 6–B on page 88. Several significant aspects can be deduced from the graph:

(1) Chinese immigration is predominantly female and no doubt will continue to be so until the sex ratio among the Chinese population in the United States becomes more equalized.

(2) The largest age group among females is between 20 and 29 years. Among males it is between 30 and 39. In other words, Chinese immigrants are predominantly adults in the prime of their lives. This means that the United States receives the full productive energies of these people without having to assume responsibility for rearing and educating these human resources.

(3) Men and women in their twenties and thirties are fairly well set in their ways and habits. They will tend to perpetuate the customs of the old country. Their schooling is behind them, so that opportunities for their learning English are limited. Immigrants tossed into the melting pot would melt much quicker if they were predominantly in the younger age brackets.

(4) An unusual phenomenon seen in the upper age brackets reverses a trend of former years. For instance, 100 men in the 60-to-64 age group, 93 in the 65-to-69 age group, and even 8 in the 80-and-over age group were admitted in 1961. (See Appendix Table A–2.) In years gone by, older Chinese always went back to China to retire or to die. Even after death, their bones were sent to China for interment. The Chinese communities in the United States had no old-age problems to contend with.

Immigration of the aged must be taken as a clue to the degree of acculturation. This means that even the old folks have given up

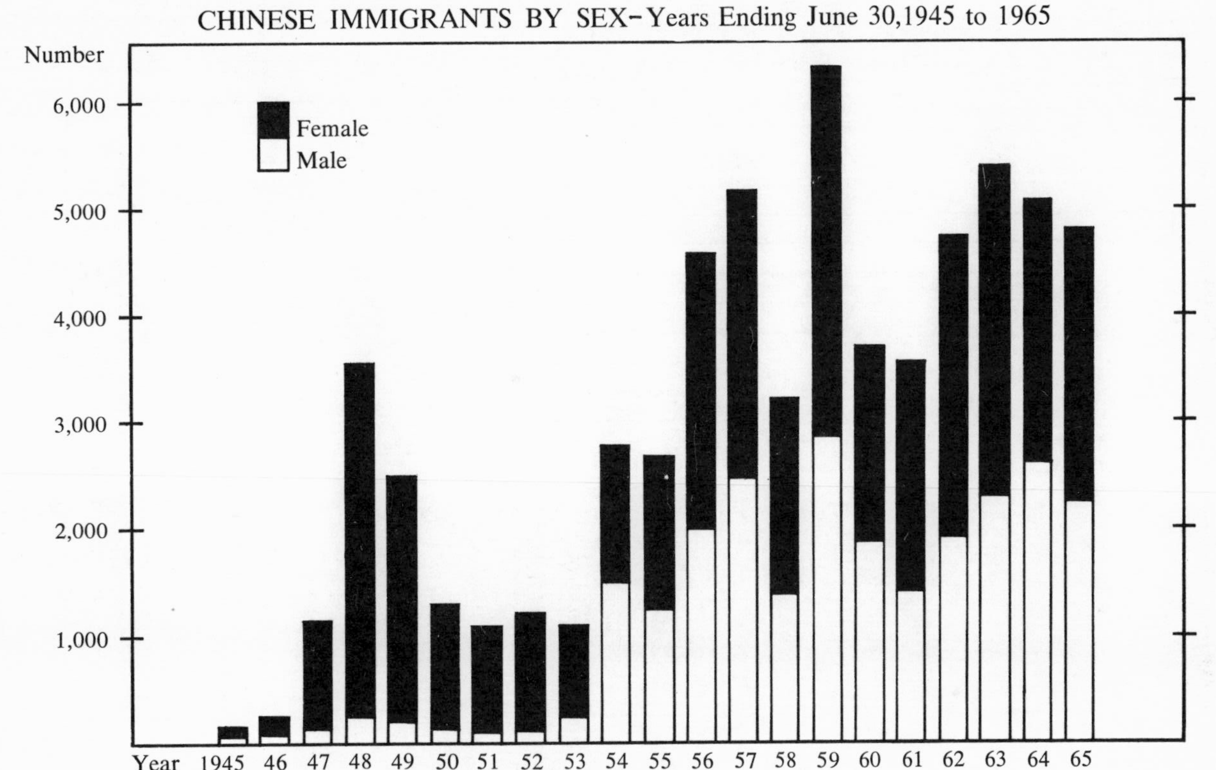

SOURCE: See Appendix, Table A-1

Figure 6-A

CHINESE IMMIGRANTS ADMITTED, BY SEX AND AGE GROUPS

Years Ending June 30, 1956 to 1961

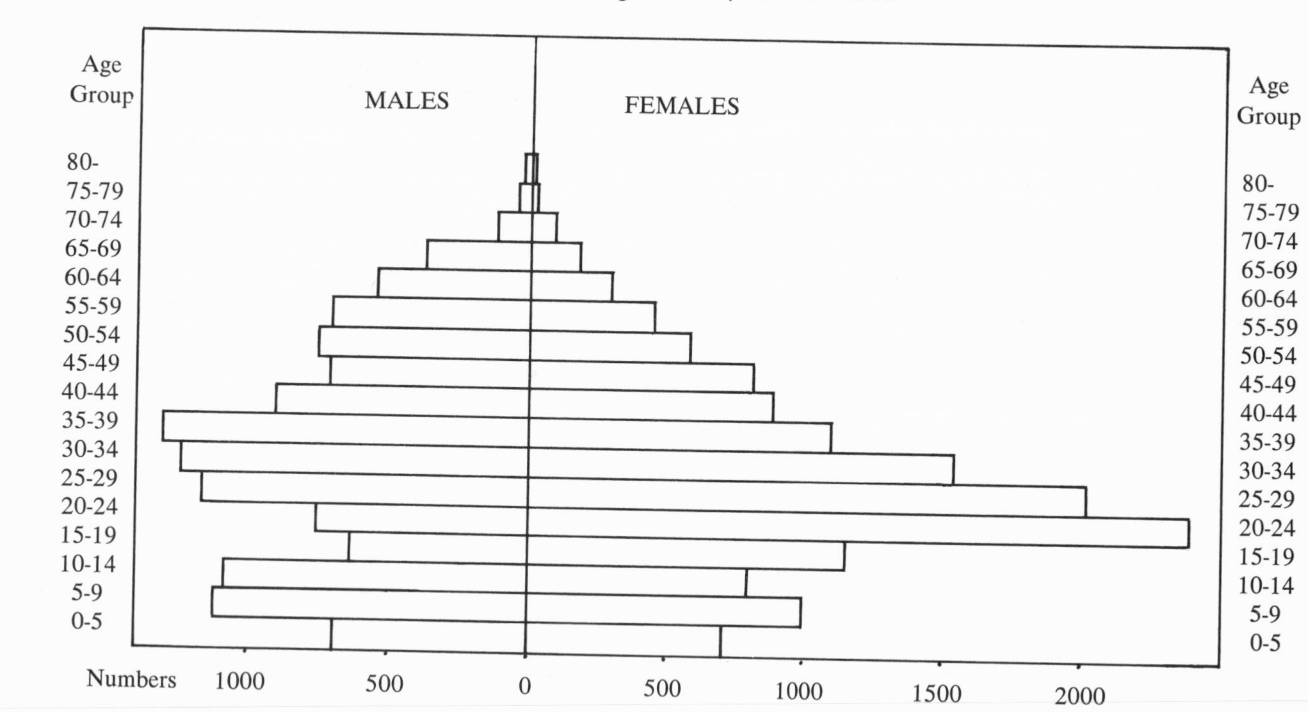

SOURCE: See Appendix, Table A–2

Figure 6 -B

maintaining and continuing the ancestral home. They have pulled up roots and come to join their children here.

The greatest antagonism against Chinese immigration in former years was directed against the threat of cheap labor. Not that the Chinese were different from other immigrant nationalities in this respect, for most immigrants invariably take up the lower rung, manual jobs when they first arrive in this country. But it was felt that because of the greater endurance and efficiency of the Chinese laborer, he was a threat to the job tenure of the white laborer.

Since the repeal of the exclusion acts, Chinese immigration has included few laborers, in fact hardly any at all. In Table 6–5 we have a ten-year total of the immigrants from China and Hong Kong by major occupation groups. A total of 46,000 were admitted. Over half of these were women and children who came to make a home for their menfolk. This group has had little immediate impact on the labor market.

The largest true occupational group are professional and technical people, screened and selected for their special training or skills. There are valid reasons for this influx of the elite:

(1) It is the intelligentsia that writhes under a totalitarian form of government and seeks, if possible, to escape from it.

(2) Since it is difficult, to say the least, to get a United States visa, those in China or even Hong Kong and Taiwan who can effect their entry into this country must have more than the usual financial and mental resources.

(3) The preference system under the quota gave first priority to those who possess skills and knowledge of benefit to the United States. As the Chinese quota was so tiny and the demand so great, American consuls had their pick of the very cream of the crop.

The service workers and managers and proprietors listed in Table 6–5 no doubt have jobs in the traditional occupations of laundries and restaurants usually operated by friends or relatives. The few in the other occupational groups are insignificant.

There is little unemployment among the Chinese. In fact, restaurants and laundries are clamoring for help that they cannot get. Some men work at more than one job to pay off any debts incurred for

TABLE 6–5

Major Occupation Groups of Immigrants from China and Hong Kong 1956–1965

Major Occupation Group	*Ten-Year Total*
Number Admitted	46,060
Housewives & Children or No Occupation	26,200
Professional & Technical	5,966
Service Workers	3,251
Managers, Officials & Proprietors	2,272
Clerical	1,983
Operatives	1,558
Craftsmen	521
Sales Workers	415
Private Household Workers	360
Laborers	181
Farmers	114
Farm laborers	112

SOURCE: *Annual Report,* U.S. Immigration and Naturalization Service, 1956–1965, Table 8.

their trip and passage. They are astonished at the relative ease of finding work and earning money. In this respect, the United States fulfills their dreams as the Mountain of Gold.

An aspect of Chinese immigration that bears watching is the pattern of distribution, or rather concentration. California is the most populous state for persons of Chinese ancestry, followed by Hawaii and New York. States like Illinois, Massachusetts, and Washington trail far behind with a few thousand each, while an isolated few are scattered among the other 44 states.

According to the Immigration and Naturalization Service, approximately one-third of the new immigrants intend to make California their future home. One-fourth elect the state of New York. Hawaii has not been getting many immigrants.

Since U.S. immigration laws favor the reunion of family and relatives, it is inevitable that the states that already have Chinese residents would get more immigrants. It would be well to recall, however, that the heavy concentration in California causing the group to be especially noticeable once led to antagonism and exclusion. The Chinese should give thought to dispersion to other areas of the country.

Only persons intending to reside here permanently are considered immigrants. Others come into the country as government officials, students, visitors, and businessmen. Their stay is only for a definite and limited period of time. Non-immigrants generally depart after expiration of their visas.

Again, the Communist take-over in China altered the situation. I know of many ex-ministers, ex-ambassadors, ex-generals, and ex-governors not directly attached to the Chinese embassy or consulates, living a quiet life of semi-retirement in this country. These are officials who had served in the Nationalist government, and because of their former positions are afraid or unwilling to return to China. Some of these have adjusted their immigration status under the Refugee Relief Acts, and have become permanent residents or naturalized American citizens.

The student group is another non-immigrant class that has settled down for a long and perhaps permanent sojourn in the United States. Of course their original intent was to come here for one, two, or three years of advance study and return to China. But caught in the web of international politics, they were stranded. Some were unwilling to return to China under a Communist form of government. Some liked it here and wanted to remain. Some found the choice of returning or remaining a difficult and uncertain one to make, meanwhile postponing their decision and staying on. And some were forbidden to return to China because they had acquired skills and knowledge in this country which could be employed against the United States in event of war. This restriction was removed in the latter part of 1955, but there was no wild scramble among the former student group to leave the United States. For the most part, many were already comfortably settled in jobs and homes and had become a fixed element of the Chinese population in the United States.

The Immigration Act of 1924 and the Walter-McCarran Act of 1952 both adhered to the national-origins quota. Both unabashedly discriminated against those who were not white Protestants and most severely against persons of the Asia-Pacific triangle. For the many decades that these laws were in force, the Chinese in this country suffered extreme hardships. The stringency of the quotas rendered the laws inhumane and often unworkable.

Fortunately a number of measures provided some modicum of relief. The first of these was the Displaced Persons Act of 1948, which was amended and extended to June 30, 1954. The Displaced Persons Act provided for mortgaging up to 50 percent of future quotas, so that many Chinese already in the country were permitted to adjust their status and remain as permanent residents during the crucial period of the Communist take-over in China. Relief was limited, however, by the tiny quota allotted Chinese persons, and within a short period of time the quota was mortgaged far into the twenty-first century.

The Refugee Relief Act of 1953 provided for the issuance over a three-year period of 205,000 non-quota visas to certain refugees, escapees, and expellees; to relatives of U.S. citizens; and to alien residents; plus 4,000 non-quota visas for alien orphans; and 5,000 changes of status for refugees already in this country without charge to the quota. Of this allotment, the largest number, 90,000, went to German escapees and expellees. Two thousand were reserved for Chinese Nationalists. The act expired on December 31, 1956.

Further liberalization of immigration came with the Refugee Escapee Act of September 11, 1957. Unused allotments at the expiration of the 1953 Act were extended. Some of the mortgages against the national quotas were removed. Adjustment of status for highly skilled specialists and diplomats already in the United States was made possible. Over two thousand persons from China took advantage of the provisions of this act to gain immigration status.

By the Act of September 22, 1959, non-quota status was granted to aliens who were on quota waiting lists prior to December 31, 1953, and whose petitions had been approved prior to January 1, 1959. In other words, the 115 persons from China who benefited from this act had already waited at least six years for a visa.

In May 1962, in one of the most puzzling anomalies of Chinese Communist behavior, 60,000 refugees were permitted to swarm across the Kwangtung borders into Hong Kong. This tiny British-held colony, already swollen with more than three and a half million population quickly strung up barbed wire, rounded up as many refugees as they could find, and sent them back behind the Bamboo Curtain.

An uproar rose from an incensed American public. President John F. Kennedy immediately invoked the provisions of existing legislation to permit the entry of "several thousand" refugees from Hong Kong as parolees. From June 4, 1962, to the end of 1965, when the program terminated, over 15,000 Chinese refugees were paroled into the United States. Most of the beneficiaries of this relief measure had long been on the waiting list for visas. Two-thirds were housewives, children, or students with no occupation. Again, this executive order helped more to reunify families than to aid the refugees who actually swarmed across the Red China border, but it did relieve Hong Kong or Taiwan of the population pressure of 15,000 people.

On October 3, 1965, one of the most sweeping changes in U.S. immigration law was enacted. The national-origins quotas were abolished, the change-over to extend over a period of three years. By 1968, immigrants were to be processed in order of their application. A total annual quota for all countries was set at 170,000. No one country's immigrants could exceed 20,000 in any one fiscal year.

It was emphasized that the new law would be on a first-come-first-served basis. This is not exactly the case, as there are seven preference classes that have priority over chronological order. These are (1) unmarried sons and daughters of U.S. citizens; (2) spouses and unmarried children of permanent resident aliens; (3) professionals and cultural persons; (4) married children of U.S. citizens; (5) brothers or sisters of U.S. citizens; (6) skilled labor whose services are in great demand; (7) refugees.

Within each preference class, the visa applicants are processed according to chronological order, but the first-preference classes always have priority over the subsequent preferences. In other words, the unmarried son of a U.S. citizen, though he may file later than a skilled laborer, would have priority obtaining a visa. After all preference applicants are exhausted, the remaining quotas are made available to non-preference applicants on a first-come-first-served basis.

Theoretically then, the Chinese, instead of being restricted to a quota of 105, may use up to 20,000 of the annual quota. Country of origin will be based on place of birth—not on nationality or race except in cases where families would be separated by strict interpretation of this provision. Persons born in Hong Kong may apply for immigrant visas available to Great Britain, but this number shall not exceed 1 percent of that country's maximum number of visas. A Chinese born in Brazil would come under the regulations for immigrants from the Western Hemisphere.

The law and its operation are often at variance. As of this writing, the law has not fully gone into effect. Official statistics after the change-over were not yet released. How will the new law affect the pattern of Chinese immigration?

Preliminary figures from the Immigration and Naturalization Service showed that 13,736 persons from China (including Taiwan) and 3,872 from Hong Kong were admitted for the fiscal year 1966. This compares with a total of 4,769 from both places for the preceding year. Obviously this is a substantial increase, and it reflects the tremendous backlog of waiting applicants.

The impact of this enlarged immigration will be felt in many quarters. I have already seen letters in the press reviving racist fears that such a large influx of Chinese will prove indigestible, especially if they continue to concentrate in a few places. Will this focus of attention work to the detriment of the good will and social status that the Chinese now enjoy?

How will this affect the Chinatowns and their community facilities? How will the old-timers receive the newcomers? Will this rate of immigration keep up or will it taper off? These are intriguing questions. We need the answers.

7

Honorable Deception

UNITED States immigration laws and procedures have dominated the entire spectrum of Chinese-American life—not just in the legal sense, but as an all-pervading influence. We perceived in Chapters 5 and 6 that they determined the size and composition of the Chinese-American community in this country. They perpetuated a predominantly male society leading to lack of families and family life. They have jumbled up family relations and mixed up family names. But most disturbing of all, they still create a constant uneasiness and pose a potential threat to any Chinese-American who cannot produce a birth certificate to prove himself a native-born citizen.

One would assume that after sixty-one years of exclusion, the Chinese population in the United States would have been extinct. But at the time of repeal, there were approximately 78,000 persons of Chinese ancestry in this country, of which 80 percent were foreign-born. These people were not vestiges of immigrants who had been admitted prior to 1882. They had entered in spite of the exclusion laws. How they were able to accomplish this feat is the subject of this chapter.

For centuries, Confucian ethics was the foundation of Chinese culture, and the average Chinese possesses a very strong sense of moral values. He is inclined to do what is right because he lives in such intimate proximity with his family and neighbors. If he is lazy, it is not just his parents or his wife who is displeased and who will censure him; he faces the disapproval of a large family or multitudinous clan. If he has done wrong, it is not just the individual who is shamed. He has brought dishonor upon the family name. His duties, his behavior, and his conduct are rigidly defined, but what is right must be morally right. It must stand the test of common sense, logic, and justice.

This is evidenced by the extremely low crime rate of the Chinese in America. It explains why a Chinese farm hand will work diligently whether there is an overseer or not. A Chinese will try not to contract a debt, but if he does, he will honor it as soon as he is able. Businessmen throughout the world have always praised this trait of the Chinese. Their word is as good as a bond, it is said.

Whenever the Chinese have circumvented the law in the United States, the law usually broken dealt with illegal entry. To the Chinese way of thinking, however, no moral issue was involved here. The exclusion laws were discriminatory and unjust. The West was virgin land with wide-open spaces that crowded no one. This was new country to be developed and the Chinese wanted to participate. Here was work to be done and the Chinese were willing to do it. The gates of the United States were open freely to everyone, and she proclaimed herself a haven for the poor and oppressed. Then why were the Chinese the only people to be denied entry? It did not make sense to a logical mind, but instead of belligerent opposition, the Chinese resorted to nonviolent disobedience in the form of cunning ruses to outwit the immigration authorities.

Nonviolent civil disobedience has been advocated by some of the foremost thinkers and leaders in the world. Alluding to statutes passed by some Communist governments, Pope Pius XII spoke of the "right, even the duty, of non-obedience on the part of citizens whenever in a state some laws should be unjust because they were contrary to the common good, the natural law, and positive divine or ecclesiastical law."[1]

Henry David Thoreau, a strong advocate of civil disobedience, wrote: "Unjust laws exist: shall we be content to obey them until we endeavour to amend them, and obey them until we have succeeded, or shall we transgress them?" Transgress them at once, he answered, through direct, personal action.

Mahatma Gandhi was one of the most dramatic and effective practitioners of the art of nonviolent civil disobedience. By deliberately defying British laws, he succeeded in rallying his people around

[1] *The New York Times,* Nov. 21, 1955.

him and freeing India from British rule. Gandhi's modern-day disciple is Martin Luther King, who employs nonviolent but direct action as a protest against laws that are unjust.

Since the Chinese had no recourse against the exclusion laws in the courts (their testimony was not accepted in courts), and since the Chinese government offered them no backing, they had to resort to their own wits and ingenuity to outsmart the immigration authorities.

Smuggling across the border was not a satisfactory method, nor physically speaking, the safest. The danger of detection was great, for the Chinese were required to carry registration cards. At any time, a Chinese could be accosted and commanded to show his registration card. Periodic raids were made against Chinese establishments, and anyone unable to produce a registration certificate was bundled off to a place of detention for deportation.

Fear of detection was a hovering concern, but the problem of getting out of the country if one wanted to go to China for a visit compounded the difficulties. After 1923, Canada and Mexico passed their own exclusion laws, which meant a double barrier for smugglers to overcome, so that smuggling was not a commonly used method of illegal entry.

The tactics employed by the Chinese remind me of a story I once read about the atomic-powered submarine *Nautilus*. The *Nautilus* was to make a test run for the New England coast through one of the thickest nets of sea and air power combined. The purpose, of course, was to find out if an enemy submarine could penetrate the United States coastal defense barriers.

Coastal defense authorities knew that the *Nautilus* was coming and were alert to employ every means at their command to prevent any breakthrough. Far out in the Atlantic, her position unknown, the *Nautilus* devised her strategy. Through her eyes and ears, radar and radio, she would steer clear of all vessels. If a submarine or ship approached, she would use her superior speed to break away; for once her position was known, it would be broadcast, and a swarm of airplanes, battleships, and submarines would converge and close in upon her. It was a game of hide-and-seek, of patience and waiting; for if a ship picked up the ping of her engine, the game would be over.

Dodging and turning, breaking away and waiting for the other vessel to make the first move, the *Nautilus* bided her time. She knew that once she was able to maneuver herself into a commercial sea lane, she could ride in behind a liner or freighter. She had to be careful to select a ship whose motor vibrations were similar to that of her own, so that she could synchronize the sound of her motor to the one ahead.

The strategy proved effective. As soon as the proper ship came along, the *Nautilus* fell in line and rode in under the camouflage without the slightest fear of detection. Within three miles of the New England coastline, she surfaced in triumph. The United States was still vulnerable to sneak attack.

The Chinese employed the same strategy. They selected situations in which it was difficult to tell the real from the false. They took advantage of American ignorance of Chinese customs. They capitalized on situations in which it was difficult to check the records.

The only crack in the door, practically, for a person of Chinese ancestry was American citizenship. According to U.S. laws, a person born in the United States is a citizen, and a child of a U.S. citizen inherits his parent's citizenship. This child, as a citizen, would be entitled to enter the country to take up residence here. The number of Chinese actually born in the United States prior to 1943 was few, and acquiring citizenship by naturalization was expressly denied the Chinese. Fate, however, played into their hands.

In 1906, an earthquake shook San Francisco and started a fire which practically razed the entire city. The old Chinatown was wiped out, and so were the municipal buildings that housed the public records. At that time, a large majority of the Chinese in the United States were concentrated in and around San Francisco. Dating from the Great Fire, many, many Chinese became "born in the United States," and there was no means to disprove the claims because the records were completely destroyed. This is not to say that all such claims were false, but to separate the wheat from the chaff was difficult, and a native-born citizen was not to be denied his constitutional rights.

The immigration authorities were aware of this ruse, and they sought to cull the real from the false by means of rigorous and intensive examination. The Chinese anticipated this and were ready with fabricated biographical sketches to fit their new status. They studied their stories and memorized them so well they knew their cover stories better than their true ones.

Now armed with his citizenship, the father could claim citizenship for his children born in China. In subsequent trips to China, the father would invariably report the birth of a son or two upon his return. What puzzled the immigration officials the most was that these men reported only sons, seldom a daughter. In fact, the ratio was something like four hundred sons to one daughter.

Again, there is a plausible explanation for this, for it is the usual custom in China to register only the names of male offspring in the village temple. Girls were not considered part of the genealogical line. This abnormal ratio of sons to daughters reported may not have been intentional, but again, it was the device of the *Nautilus* riding in behind the motor of a similar ship. Anyhow, it created another loophole.

If a man had sons, he would send for them when they came of age. Under such circumstances, there would be a true father-son relationship. In some instances, the sons died or else the father had reported extra "sons." Such slots were available for sale to boys who had no family connections in the United States, and these sons were known as "paper sons."

These paper sons memorized the family histories of their paper fathers so that they could pass the rigorous examinations of the immigration authorities. All incoming or returning Chinese were detained and questioned unmercifully from every angle in an attempt to trip them up and break their stories. Questions and answers were compared and cross-checked with the answers given previously or subsequently by every single member of the family. It got so that a bona fide citizen would find himself denied entry unless he, too, made an extensive study of his family tree and family history. And woe to him if his answers did not jibe with those of his paper relatives.

Sometimes true and false family relationships became hopelessly entangled after two or three generations. A true Chen could have a Wong paper brother and a Lee paper brother. Eventually, he could have a Moy paper nephew and an Eng paper nephew. All of these would use their paper name Chen for American purposes and retain their true names in Chinese circles. However, offspring of these Wongs, Lees, Moys, and Engs born in the United States would also have to use the paper name Chen. Some American-born Chinese children could never understand the jumbled relationships or the mix-up in names.

Five classes of Chinese were exempt from the exclusion laws—officials, teachers, students, merchants, and travelers. Officials were diplomatic personnel; and teachers, students, and travelers were limited to very short stays. Only merchants with a business establishment in the United States could remain in this country for any length of time. Therefore, a Chinese desiring to come to the United States could buy a partnership in a business firm. This would rightfully make him a businessman, but some of the businesses had an unusually large number of partners. Only a few of the partners were needed to run the business; the others merely put in an occasional appearance. Again, however, it was difficult for immigration authorities to differentiate between the real merchant and the quasi-merchant.

To counter any possible circumvention, the immigration authorities resorted to many questionable practices to discourage the Chinese. Often, those with legitimate business purposes were prevented from entering the country. In other instances, paper sons and quasi-merchants slipped through the net.

All Chinese seeking entry to the country, whether teacher or student, immigrant or merchant, used to be detained at the port of disembarkation. They were taken to Ellis Island, Angel's Island, or some similar detention house. There they were put under lock and guard until they could be questioned at length. The period of detention lasted from two weeks to four months. At Ellis Island in New York, at least, the conditions were sanitary and the detainees were not abused. They were generally questioned within two to six weeks, after which they were released and admitted, or they were held for deportation or released on bond. At any rate, two to six weeks was considered a speedy rate of processing.

On the West Coast it was different, for prejudice against the Chinese was deeply ingrained there. For many years, the United States had no immigration building in San Francisco. A shed, rented from the Pacific Mail Steamship Company, served as the detention house. It was a cheap wooden two-story building extending out over the water, where the odors of sewage and bilge gave off a constant stench. The shed was situated at one end of a wharf reached by a long, narrow stairway. The interior was about 100 feet square, into which were herded as many as 200 people at one time. The occupants were separated only by sex—the men on the first floor and the women on the second. There were no tables and no chairs. Food was served on the floor, and the guards had no qualms about kicking and swearing at the hapless detainees.

During their period of detention, the Chinese were called up, one by one, for questioning and cross-examination. Only one friend was allowed to be present during the questioning, but the friend could not act as legal counsel because none was allowed. The questions were devised to trap or trick a person into giving contradictory information so that he would expose himself. Then his answers were checked and cross-checked against those of persons claiming relationship to him. If any discrepancy was found, the authorities could accuse the person of fraud and subject him to deportation.

The questions asked were often ludicrous and ridiculous, having nothing whatever to do with the right or identity of a person to enter the United States. A typical questioning session went like this:

Q: How far is your home village from town?

A: Five *li*.

Q: You are wrong. We happen to have ascertained that it is seven *li*. Do you deny that this is not your true home village?

A: I have lived in this village all my life, and I believe it is five *li*. Besides, it depends upon which end of the village you figure the distance from.

Q: Where is the village pond?

A: In front of the village.

Q: I mean in what direction in relation to the village? Northwest? Southwest?

A: I believe it is to the north.

Q: Surely if you have lived there all your life, you would know in what direction the village pond lies.

A: I am confused about what is north and south. All I know is that when I leave the front door and turn left, that is the direction of the village pond.
Q: How many pigs does your family keep?
A: Two.
Q: How many chickens?
A: It depends. When we kill one, there are fewer chickens until the hen hatches more eggs.
Q: Where is your water urn situated?
A: At the kitchen door.
Q: Is your house one story or two stories?
A: There is an attic.
Q: Are there steps to the attic?
A: Yes.
Q: How many?
A: Twelve.
Q: How do you know?
A: I counted them because I was told you would ask me questions like these.
Q: Then you were coached in the answers to be given. You rehearsed and memorized all this information to make us think you are the son of Wong Hing?
A: (slightly flustered) No, no, no. I was not coached. I am the true son of Wong Hing, my father, who is now in San Francisco. He told me that you would ask me questions like these and that I was to be prepared to answer in the most minute detail.

The questions and answers were all taken down verbatim and easily ran to 150 pages. Most of the examination was concerned with farfetched questions, repeated attempts to trip the applicant by scaring him, confusing him, or threatening him. Supposedly if he was led through a rambling, circuitous route, he would shed some of his assumed veneer and reveal his true colors. It is the principle of the third degree.

All these questions and answers became part of the permanent files; and if the person ever left the country and sought to enter again, he would have to undergo this same process and give the same answers; for any glaring discrepancy would subject him to intense suspicion, a longer period of detention, and possible deportation. These answers were also checked with the files of any relatives in the United States for discrepancies.

In the end, all those who wished to enter the United States had to undergo interrogation and detention whether they were perfectly entitled to enter or not. Only the naïve, the true merchants, the students, and the teachers, who believed in the letter of the law and were unfamiliar with its administration, came unprepared and in many cases were turned down, although they were entitled as citizens or protected by treaty in their right of free transit. These tactics were employed against the Chinese because the immigration authorities felt quite helpless at times in administering a basically unjust law.

Today, Ellis Island, Angel's Island, and other detention houses are no more. The investigation and questioning now take place in the consulates overseas. In Hong Kong, where most of the applications for Chinese immigrants are filed, the processing of a visa takes on the average of four years and eight months by the State Department's own admission.[2] The bulk of these applications are for non-immigrant status as wives or children of Chinese-American citizens. The task of validating these claims is doubly difficult because there are no birth, death, or marriage certificates issued in China. And even if there were registration of births and marriages in the village temples, it is now impossible to check these.

In the absence of legal papers, the American consuls fall back on intensive investigation and interrogation. The applicant is questioned for hours on trivialities. He is called back repeatedly to answer the same questions to see if he deviates from his previous testimony. His answers are checked with those of other members of the family, and if they do not jibe, the visa is denied.

The applicant and his parents must submit to blood tests. The blood type of the children must match that of either parent, in spite

[2] J. Campbell Bruce, *The Golden Door* (New York, Random House, 1954), p. 188.

of the fact that blood tests are not conclusive, and they are not accepted as evidence of paternity in American courts. Furthermore, the Chinese are the only people subjected to this requirement.

American consuls complained that the Chinese lie about their age and that it is hard to tell the true age of a Chinese by just looking at him. So, in addition to the blood tests, the applicant must also undergo radiological and clinical examinations. X-ray plates are taken of specific bones and joints to determine the degree of maturation and thus establish the age of the applicant.

Few, if any other national groups, are subject to such indignities to qualify for a visa. The process is so involved, so time-consuming, and so frustrating that some applicants fear that by the time their investigations are completed, they will be too old to qualify for rightful entry as children of Chinese-American citizens. The conditions are highly conducive to bribery and extortion.[3]

In my own experience several years ago, I sought the advice of one of Hong Kong's sharpest lawyers in connection with the slow pace of issuance of a perfectly routine visa. I was shocked when he advised me to "pass $200 under the table." I told him I would never be a party to a bribery attempt. "This is not bribery," he replied; "this is extortion. If you won't play the game, be prepared to wait indefinitely."[4]

The long shadow of the immigration inspector still stalks even those Chinese already in the United States. One would think that with repeal of the exclusion laws in 1943, offenses committed under those laws would be forgiven after twelve years. But in 1955, the State and Justice Departments suddenly decided to expose the "mystery of the paper sons," even though the ruses used by the Chinese had long been known to the immigration authorities.

The Chinese in the United States were called upon to confess and reveal their true identity. Those who complied within a specified period of time were granted immunity from prosecution and deportation. However, their citizenships were revoked, and if they wanted to be citizens, they had to reapply for naturalization.

To force confessions from the Chinese, investigators were sent

[3] *Ibid.*, p. 203.

[4] The consul in question was later tried and convicted.

into Chinatowns during the height of festivities during the Chinese New Year's season in February 1956. People were accosted and questioned on the streets. Officers of the family and district associations were subpoenaed to produce the association books and records. A federal grand jury was impaneled to weigh testimony on passport frauds.

Chinese communities throughout the country reacted with fear and apprehension. The suddenness and national scope of the investigation led them to believe that this was a backlash of emotions from the Korean War and a portent of greater persecution against the Chinese. They stayed away from Chinatowns. Many New Year's banquets were canceled. Chinatown business in New York City slumped to the loss of $100,000 a week.

When the number of confessions proved disappointingly low, the government decided to attack the "slot brokers" or men who acted as middlemen between paper fathers and paper sons. Singled out for prosecution were a handful of prominent leaders in the Chinese communities. Among them were Sing Kee, a war hero decorated by Congress with the Distinguished Service Cross for extraordinary bravery in World War I and Arthur Lem, a highly respected and popular civic leader among the Chinese and Americans on Long Island, New York.

In a two-page spread on August 27, 1961, the *Daily News* of New York City chronicled the trial of Arthur Lem. What began as an attempt to convict Lem of being a slot broker wound up as a trial to prove that Arthur Lem's name was not Arthur Lem but Chin Dong Art.

Arthur Lem, then age 46, was brought to the United States when he was 12, allegedly by his paper father. He attended high school in Hempstead and worked in laundries after school. His was the record of a poor boy who made good. He operated a highly successful restaurant where patrons from all over Long Island and New York City went for real Chinese cuisine. As a local boy who had lived in Hempstead almost all of his life, Arthur was well known, respected, and loved by the townspeople. He did volunteer work for the FBI and the Immigration and Naturalization Service and was a special court interpreter. In 1958 he was chairman of a drive which netted $25,000 for the local YMCA. That same year he was voted "Man of the Year" by his fellow businessmen.

A year later, a disgruntled employee, spurred by the confession program, went to the immigration authorities and informed them that Arthur Lem's real name was Chin Dong Art and that he was a paper son. The informant also confessed that he himself was a paper son whose entry had been facilitated by Arthur Lem acting as broker.

The authorities seized upon this opportunity to clinch what they thought was an air-tight case with a prime witness. But the trial dragged out to be one of the longest in the history of federal cases tried in the Brooklyn Federal Court. The trial ended in a hung jury.

An impressive array of character witnesses testified on Arthur's behalf. These included Joseph Carlino, Speaker of the New York State Legislative Assembly, judges, a college president, a special deputy sent by Thomas E. Dewey, and other distinguished men in public life. These men believed in the American sense of fair play, and they had urged Arthur to fight the case. But it was the entire resources of the federal government against one man. Arthur had sold his profitable restaurant and mortgaged his home to pay for the legal battle. The lengthy trial had sapped his spirit and his financial resources. A re-trial, which the government planned, would reduce him to penury. He decided to plead *nolo contendere* (I will not contend), but the prosecuting attorney would not accept his plea. Lem was forced to plead guilty to a single count of conspiracy and was given a token sentence.

In toting up the results of the government's campaign to uncover the names of the Chinese who had gained entry to the United States under false pretenses, what do we find? Humane considerations forbade their deportation to mainland China, where they would find worse than a hostile reception. Neither Hong Kong nor Taiwan could accept these people on their already overcrowded islands. What more could the government do except change their names and make them re-apply for naturalization? On the Lem trial alone, the federal government spent hundreds of thousands of taxpayers' dollars. What did it accomplish? Perhaps the consensus was best summed up by the author of the *Daily News* story in her closing paragraph:

> . . . he [Lem] has been ruinously punished for lying about the way he and others came to this country. His fortune is gone, his business long since sold to pay the expenses of his case. . . . He could be subject to deportation from the land he loves. Just what is justice in the case of Arthur Lem?

That many Chinese did come to the United States under false pretenses is evident, but 61 percent of the Chinese population in the United States today are American-born citizens, though they may still go by the names of their paper ancestors. If the exclusion laws were repealed in 1943, then the violations of those laws prior to that date should also be forgiven. The ghost of the past should not be allowed to haunt the Chinese in the present or in the future.

8

Counting Heads

If you were a resident of Maine, the chances of your coming across a person of Chinese descent would be one in ten thousand. In Ohio the odds are three in ten thousand, whereas in New York they are two in a thousand. But even in California, where Oriental faces are more common, the numbers reveal that the likelihood is still only six in a thousand.

One tends to lose perspective when one becomes personally identified or emotionally involved with a group or situation, and herein lies the value of statistics. It frees one from the human involvement of personal prejudices and opinions by reducing the facts to impersonal numbers. For example, I was under the mistaken impression that the Chinese population in the United States was a sizable one. And why shouldn't I be? My life revolved around my family and friends, most of whom were my own ethnic group. I gave little thought to the fact that the vast majority of Americans have little or no contact—nor will they ever have—with a Chinese person.

This revelation was brought sharply into focus for me when I was invited to speak to a sociology class taking a course in minority relations at Adelphi University in Garden City, New York. Hoping to learn from them as well as to impart information to them, I began my talk by asking the class how many of them had ever known a Chinese personally. Only one boy raised his hand. He had had a Chinese schoolmate.

Incredulous, I repeated my question. The rest of the class all shook their heads. Their contact did not even extend to a nodding acquaintance or conversation with one.

Regaining my perspective, I began to delve into the total demographic picture of the Chinese population in the United States, and I found an excellent source in the U.S. census dating from 1860. That year, when mass hysteria intensified the fear that the country was threatened by a "yellow peril," Congress voted to incorporate special questions pertaining to the Chinese in the census questionnaire. Specific and detailed data on the Chinese for the past one hundred years is therefore available.

Considering that the census is an all-inclusive sample, it is undoubtedly the best source of demographic data obtainable. However, the census information should not be taken at face value without a few qualifications.

First, the Chinese are very suspicious of anyone asking them personal questions. This attitude is partly a carry-over from China, where the average citizen tries to live his life as far apart as possible from any government outside of his village council. To him government means only increased taxes, conscription of forced labor, or impressment into military service. Any snooper asking questions on behalf of the government can be up to no good, and the appearance of a head-counting representative of the government can cause a mysterious disappearance of most of the able-bodied men into the hills. Suspicion of census takers is, therefore, a holdover from China. Families will often underreport members and their income to the census taker for these reasons.

To take a case in point, I happened to be visiting in the home of a relative one day when the census taker showed up. Instead of answering the census taker's questions, my relative feigned ignorance of the English language. Frustrated by her seeming inability to make herself understood, the census taker soon left without getting any information.

In my naïveté, I attempted at first to interpret for my relative, but visual daggers soon convinced me that my services were not welcomed. Immediately after the census taker's departure I was told, "When you have eaten a few more bags of salt you will discover that it is wiser to give out as little information to the government as possible. Who knows but that this information will be used against you?"

Second, the hesitancy to give out information stems also from the many ruses and extralegal tactics employed by the Chinese to get into this country during the period of exclusion. The many fictitious family relationships made it difficult to explain one's family to a census taker. Even if a person could answer truthfully for himself, his answers could set off a chain reaction that might affect others. The simplest thing to do, therefore, was to elude the census taker.

Third, in the attempt to get an accurate count of the Chinese in the United States or of any other non-white minority group, the census taker works under a handicap. He is instructed not to ask point-blank whether a person is Negro, Chinese, or Japanese but to determine this fact by observation. Obviously the discernment of whether a person is Chinese, Japanese, or Filipino by observation is not a reliable method. Physical differences, if any, are slight, and it is all too easy to mistake Chinese for other Asians and vice versa.

Census data pertaining to the Chinese must be weighed with these qualifications in mind. Nevertheless, the decennial censuses are still the most inclusive, the most comprehensive, and the best source of demographic data about the Chinese in this country.

Over the span of a century, the Chinese population in conterminous United States has never exceeded 200,000 owing to the exclusion laws. (See Table 8–1.) Immigration legislation over the last two decades has done away with past discrimination so that the Chinese population in 1960 is nearly six times what it was in 1860. Yet the ratio to total U.S. population is roughly the same today as it was a century ago—approximately 0.1 percent.

In fact, the Chinese population decreased steadily between the years 1890 to 1920, and only a slight increase was registered between 1920 to 1940. Since 1940, however, there has been a better than 50 percent increase each decade. Although a 50 percent increase sounds large the numerical increase is slight. The incorporation of Hawaii and Alaska into the Union between the census years of 1950 and 1960 brought the total Chinese population for the country up to 237,292. By 1970, this figure should well exceed 300,000. The bulk of the increase will come from immigration as a result of the elimination of the national origins quotas.

TABLE 8–1

Chinese Population in Conterminous United States
By Decades, 1860–1960

Year	*Number*
1960	198,958*
1950	117,629
1940	77,504
1930	74,954
1920	61,639
1910	71,531
1900	89,863
1890	107,488
1880	105,465
1870	63,199
1860	34,933

* Excluding Hawaii and Alaska

SOURCE: *The World Almanac*, 1962

The Chinese are also one of the smallest non-white minority groups. Negroes constitute more than 10 percent of the U.S. population. There are twice as many Japanese and Indians as Chinese.

Negroes	18,848,619
Indians	523,591
Japanese	464,332
Chinese	237,292

Though few in numbers, the Chinese should not be dismissed as inconsequential, insignificant, and unworthy of note. The Chinese, too, spice the potpourri that makes up the American people. They are an exotic group that has lent color to the American scene. The experiences of this group, once hated and persecuted, may serve as a guide to dealing with present-day minority problems and peoples.

Table 8–2 shows the distribution of Chinese by states. Chinese are found in every state in the Union, including 137 Chinese in Alaska. At one time the British boasted that the sun never set on the Union Jack; the Chinese can still boast that the sun never sets on the Chinese people. Some Chinese will always be found in the remotest recesses of the globe.

TABLE 8-2

Distribution of Persons of the Chinese Race by States
1950 and 1960

	1950	*1960*		*1950*	*1960*
United States	150,005*	237,292	Missouri	519	954
Alabama	187	288	Montana	209	240
Alaska	n.a.	137	Nebraska	202	290
Arizona	1,951	2,936	Nevada	281	572
Arkansas	592	676	New Hampshire	93	152
California	58,324	95,600	New Jersey	1,818	3,813
Colorado	458	724	New Mexico	166	362
Connecticut	450	865	New York	20,171	37,573
Delaware	85	191	North Carolina	345	404
District of Columbia	1,825	2,632	North Dakota	82	100
Florida	429	1,023	Ohio	1,542	2,507
Georgia	511	686	Oklahoma	397	398
Hawaii	32,376	38,197	Oregon	2,102	2,995
Idaho	244	311	Pennsylvania	2,258	3,741
Illinois	4,207	7,047	Rhode Island	403	574
Indiana	496	952	South Carolina	101	158
Iowa	310	423	South Dakota	44	89
Kansas	315	537	Tennessee	230	487
Kentucky	335	288	Texas	2,435	4,172
Louisiana	526	731	Utah	335	629
Maine	77	123	Vermont	34	68
Maryland	795	2,188	Virginia	565	1,135
Massachusetts	3,627	6,745	Washington	3,408	5,491
Michigan	1,619	3,234	West Virginia	99	138
Minnesota	720	1,270	Wisconsin	590	1,010
Mississippi	1,011	1,244	Wyoming	106	192

* Includes Hawaii

SOURCE: U.S. Decennial Censuses, 1950 and 1960

In the United States, concentration overshadows distribution. Roughly three-fourths of the total are concentrated in the three states of California, Hawaii, and New York. (See Figure 8–A.) Another 8 percent is divided among the states of Illinois, Massachusetts, and Washington. To further intensify the concentration, 96 percent live in urban areas. They cluster mainly in and around the metropolitan

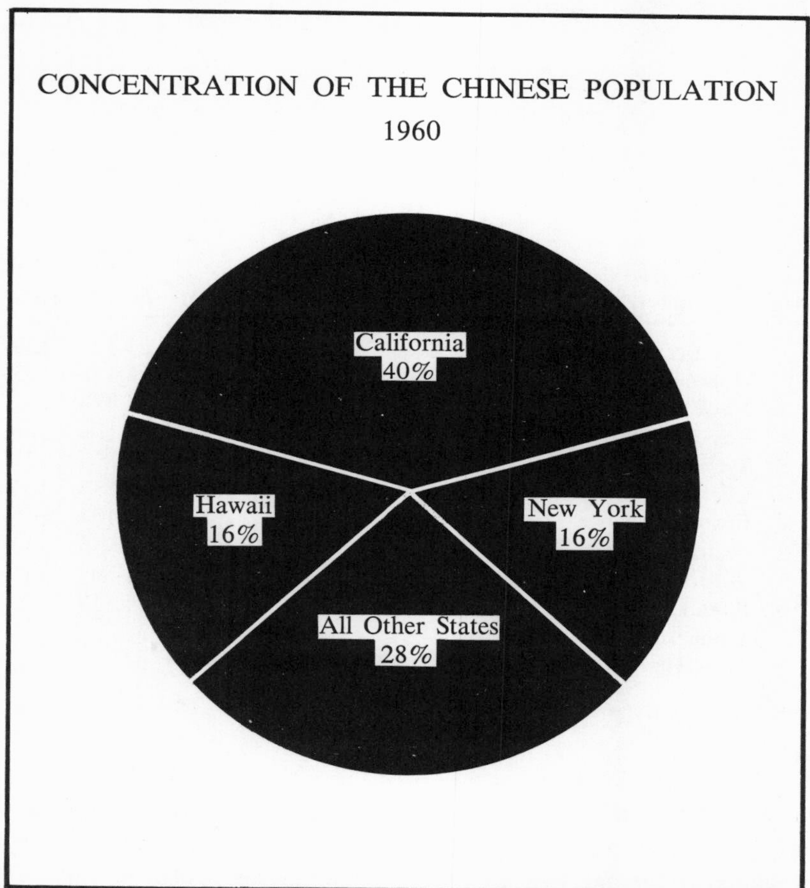

Figure 8-A

SOURCE: See Appendix, Table 8-3

areas of San Francisco, Honolulu, New York, Los Angeles, Sacramento, and other cities.

TABLE 8-3

Chinese Population in Selected Metropolitan Areas
Total, by Sex, Sex Ratio, and Percentage of
Total Chinese Population in U.S., 1960

Metropolitan Area	*Total*	*Percent to Total Chinese Pop.*	*Male*	*Female*	*Sex Ratio*
1. San Francisco-Oakland	53,250	22.4%	29,928	23,322	128
2. Honolulu	36,875	15.5%	18,723	18,152	103
3. New York	36,503	15.4%	22,509	13,994	161
4. Los Angeles-Long Beach	19,402	8.2%	10,902	8,500	128
5. Sacramento	6,457	2.7%	3,540	2,917	121
6. Chicago	5,866	2.5%	3,552	2,314	154
7. Boston	5,564	2.3%	3,463	2,101	165
8. Seattle	4,611	1.9%	2,686	1,925	140
9. Wash.D.C.-Md.-Va.	3,925	1.7%	2,361	1,564	151
10. Philadelphia-N.J.	2,544	1.1%	1,527	1,017	150
Total 10 Cities	174,997	73.8%			
Total Chinese Pop. U.S.	237,292	100.0%			

SOURCE: U.S. Census, 1960, *Nonwhite Population by Race*, p. 217

There are plausible reasons why the Chinese congregate in and near a few nuclei cities. First, immigration is generally a family affair. A man sends for his wife and children, and the family is reunited under one roof. If brothers, sisters, parents, or cousins are brought over, the newcomers want to stay close to their relatives, not only because of family connections, but also because the newcomers must often depend upon the oldtimers in the beginning for a job or for support.

Second, new arrivals do not want to be cast onto a virtual island surrounded by a sea of foreign faces and strange customs. They want the proximity of Chinatowns and the secure feeling that comes from familiar faces. This desire to be near one's fellow countrymen diminishes as acculturation progresses, but it never entirely disappears.

The heavy concentration, however, makes for a high visibility and is aggravated by the fact that the Japanese and Filipinos, who look like the Chinese, are also heavily concentrated in these same cities.

Sociologists contend that such visibility tends to retard acceptance and perhaps even provoke antagonism by the majority group toward the minority. At the same time acculturation is retarded. When the minority group is sizable, individual members are less likely to give up their speech and their ways.

A comparison of the distribution of the Chinese in 1950 with the pattern in 1960 reveals that the concentration has intensified. In a large number of states, the Chinese population doubled or nearly doubled from 1950 to 1960. For instance, in Delaware the increase was from 85 to 191; in Wisconsin from 590 to 1,010; in Florida from 429 to 1,023. In spite of the 100 percent increases, the numerical increases were small. In California and New York, however, though the percentage increases were smaller, the actual numbers rose from 58,324 to 95,600 and from 20,171 to 37,575, respectively.

In the decade from 1950 to 1960, all states except Kentucky gained in their Chinese population. In Oklahoma, North Dakota, and Montana, however, the gains were inconsequential. Maryland's jump from 795 in 1950 to 2,188 in 1960 is probably due not so much to an increase within the state per se as to a spill-over of suburbanites from Washington, D.C.

Succeeding generations of American-born Chinese may venture away from the vortex of Chinese centers as economic opportunities or jobs beckon, but the process will be a slow and gradual one. Even when the Chinese moved—and two out of every five did move during the five-year period from 1955 to 1960—only 7 percent went to a different state. (See Table 8–4.) Surprisingly, the Chinese rate of mobility is twice as high as that for the remainder of the United States. This indicates that the Chinese population has been in a volatile state of flux, having had to undergo either a trans-Pacific jump or readjustment to a new community or new home. Undoubtedly the stresses engendered have been great.

An extremely abnormal aspect of the Chinese population has been the scarcity of Chinese females. Take a look at Figure 8–B. The overwhelming predominance of males reminds one of an army in its

TABLE 8-4

Mobility Rate of the Chinese and Percentage Comparison with the United States
Persons 5 Years and Over
1960

Residence in 1955	*Number Chinese*	PERCENT *Chinese*	*U.S.*
Total	208,350	100.0	100.0
Same house as in 1960	99,113	47.6	80.1
Different house in U.S.	86,515	41.5	19.4
Same county	58,248	28.0	12.9
Different county	28,267	13.6	6.4
Same state	13,658	6.6	3.3
Different state	14,609	7.0	3.2
Abroad	18,099	8.7	0.5
Not reported	4,623	2.2	—

SOURCE: U.S. Census, 1960

wholly masculine character. That Chinese immigration has largely been male has already been stated. Explicit reasons for this are found in Chapters 4 and 10. Briefly, the combination of U.S. exclusion laws and Chinese customs that decree that womenfolk remain close to the ancestral hearth is responsible for the radically disproportionate sex ratio.

Only within recent years has the Chinese sex ratio even approached the equilibrium of 100. In 1960 it was 133.1, which means one and a third male to every female. In 1900 it was 1887.2 or 18.9 males per female. Even though the situation has improved nearly fifteenfold, the present ratio is still highly unbalanced. The disparity in some sections of the country is masked by the overall national average and especially by the inclusion of Hawaii in the 1960 census figures. Hawaii has traditionally had a more balanced sex ratio (103.9) than the mainland (139). The ratio of 129.8 in California is lower than the national average. New York's ratio of 163.4 is considerably higher.

The figures are further misleading in that a large number of the Chinese females are infants or children, so that age disparity between members of the opposite sex aggravates the situation when it comes

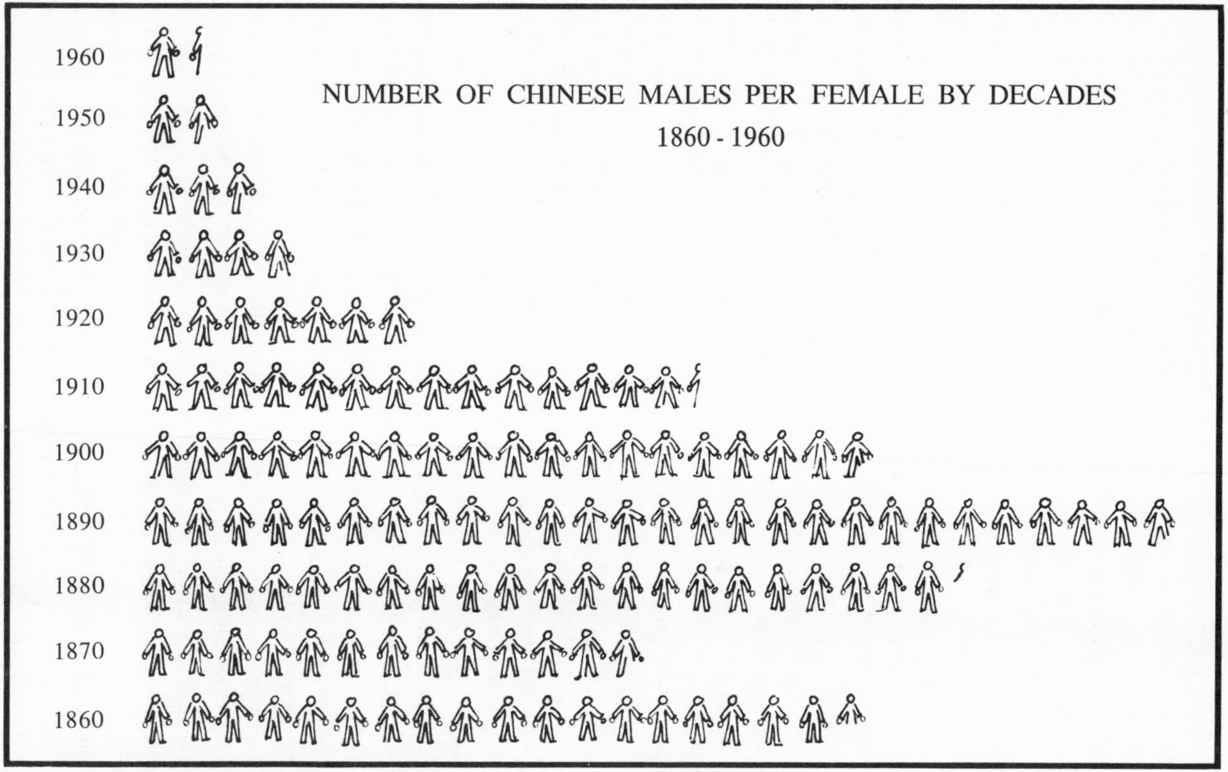

NUMBER OF CHINESE MALES PER FEMALE BY DECADES

1860 - 1960

1960

1950

1940

1930

1920

1910

1900

1890

1880

1870

1860

SOURCE: See Appendix, Table A–3

Figure 8-B

to pairing off. In a neighborhood Chinese restaurant that I patronize, I occasionally chat with the men who work there. Some confide their problems to me, and the most frustrating one is their inability to find female companionship with a member of their own ethnic group.

Of the six men who work there—the owner, the bartender, the headwaiter, and three waiters—only the owner is a married man. The others are young men in their twenties and thirties, eligible bachelors whose primary interest is girls. But poor fellows, the odds are great and the competition keen.

Fortunately, recent immigrants have been overwhelmingly female so that the sex ratio has been lowered significantly and within another decade should even out. A more balanced sex ratio will enable the men to get married and have a normal family life, thus stabilizing the Chinese communities. The offspring of these unions will be native-borns who will swing the makeup of the Chinese population from a predominantly foreign-born one to a native-born one. Because native-borns find it much easier to adapt themselves to the larger American society and to find acceptance within it, the rate of acculturation will be speeded up. The increased opportunities for Chinese men to find mates among Chinese women mean that intermarriages may decrease. When Chinese families are based in this country, the large sums formerly remitted to China will remain here.

Birth and death statistics for persons of Chinese ancestry are collected and tabulated by the U.S. Public Health Service. Prior to 1946, birth and deaths fluctuated between 1,000 and 1,500 annually. Most of the years, deaths exceeded births so that natural increase was a minus. It is almost asinine to point out that without women there could be no births.

The women came after 1946, and births took a big leap in 1949. In 1950 the crude birth rate for the Chinese rose to a fantastic 42.6. Each year thereafter the number of births remained in the 4,000's while the population continued to increase, thereby creating a decreasing birth rate. By 1960, the unadjusted crude birth rate for the Chinese sank to 24.6, which is comparable to the national average. This decreasing birth rate occurred in spite of the fact that the number of Chinese women was increasing.

Prior to 1950, the death rate for the Chinese in the United States

TABLE 8–5

Births and Deaths of Chinese Persons in the United States
1950–1964

	BIRTHS			DEATHS		
Year	*Total*	*Male*	*Female*	*Total*	*Male*	*Female*
1950	5,029	2,562	2,467	1,077	888	189
1951	4,870	2,560	2,310	1,188	1,046	142
1952	4,742	2,504	2,238	1,206	1,038	168
1953	4,592	2,408	2,184	1,195	1,031	164
1954	4,396	2,256	2,140	1,293	1,102	191
1955	4,429	2,252	2,177	1,165	989	176
1956	4,690	2,364	2,326	1,283	1,088	195
1957	4,666	2,364	2,302	1,356	1,150	206
1958	4,706	2,424	2,282	1,335	1,114	221
1959	5,024	2,614	2,410	1,343	1,134	209
1960	5,848	2,968	2,880	1,620	1,328	292
1961	6,172	3,160	3,012	1,677	1,376	301
1962	5,780	2,990	2,790	1,674	1,355	319
1963	6,048	3,198	2,850	1,729	1,427	302
1964	7,876	4,498	2,378	1,305	986	319

SOURCE: *Vital Statistics of the United States*, Dept. of Health, Education and Welfare, Public Health Service; annual reports

was meaningless. Many went back to China in their old age and died in their home villages. This practice is no longer feasible. The crude death rate for the Chinese in 1950 was 9.1, which was comparable to the national average of 9.5. By 1960, although the national average remained the same, the Chinese crude death rate sank to 6.8 in spite of the fact that there were more aged people among the Chinese.

In age composition, the Chinese population is shifting from a mature adult group to a more youthful one. Only one-fifth of the Chinese population in 1940 was under 14 years of age. By 1960, the percentage had increased to one-third. In actual numbers, the increase was almost fivefold—from 16,408 to 77,894.

Look at the age pyramids for 1940 and 1950 on page 120. On the male side, instead of being broadest at the base they bulge in the middle at the 35–39 age group. By 1950, correcting forces are in evidence in the enlarged base among Chinese males. The base of

AGE PYRAMIDS FOR THE CHINESE IN THE UNITED STATES 1940, 1950, 1960

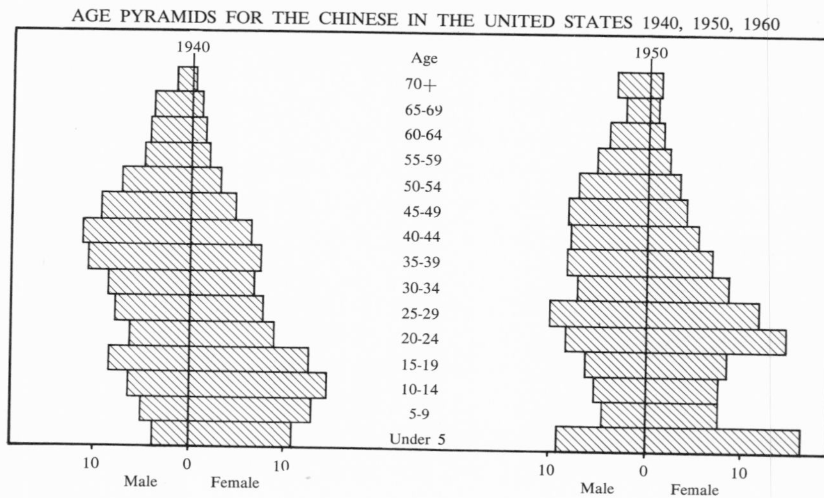

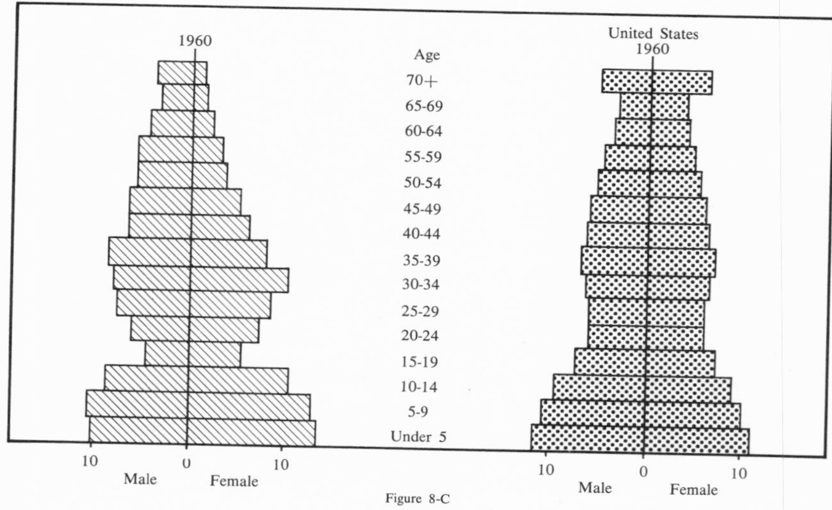

Figure 8-C

SOURCE: See Appendix, Table A–2

the pyramid is wider, and the bulge in the middle is less prominent. However, a bulge has developed on the female side of the graph, a reflection of the large influx of war brides and wives who were permitted to enter the country after 1946 as non-quota immigrants.

By 1960, the age pyramid has become more symmetrical. In other words, males and females in the same age groups are more balanced. The bases are widening although the pinch in the middle at the 15–19 age group for both males and females is rather unusual. The age pyramid for the entire United States was included for purposes of comparison.

This shift toward youthfulness has its implications. Youth is more adaptable, more pliable, and more receptive to change. Children under 14 years will attend school in this country and will be brought up in an American environment in their most formative years. Their outlook cannot help being different from the outlook of those who come to this country full-grown, already imbued with the ways of the old country.

Another aspect to note about the age composition of the Chinese population is the growing number of elderly men and women. In 1940 there were 6,000 persons 60 years or over. By 1960, there were about 20,000. Of these, men outnumber the women three to one.

These elderly men pose a problem—a new problem—for the Chinese communities. In former years, the aged returned to China to retire or to die. They left the country when they were in ill health or could work no longer. Back in their home villages, they were cared for by their families or relatives. According to Chinese custom, they were treated with dignity and respect.

The political change in China has cut off the traditional solution for the aged or infirm Chinese. He is forced to remain even when he can no longer work and when he needs someone to care for him. The three-to-one ratio of elderly men to women means that in all probability, these men are single or alone, without a family and without a home.

Eleven percent of the Chinese males are in the elderly age group, and this percentage has been increasing steadily. The problem is especially acute at present because it is a relatively new one, and there is no precedent or experience to go by. Most of the men in this upper-

TABLE 8-6

Age Groups and Percent Distribution of the Chinese by Sex 1940, 1950, and 1960

	MALES			FEMALES		
Age Groups	1940	1950	1960	1940	1950	1960
Children (14 and under)	8,756	14,703	40,676	7,652	12,597	37,218
Percent	15.2%	19.1%	30.0%	38.0%	31.1%	36.9%
Young Adults (15–29)	12,882	19,238	25,177	5,842	14,219	21,415
Percent	22.4%	24.9%	18.6%	39.0%	35.1%	21.3%
Mature Adults (30–44)	17,714	18,433	31,022	4,044	8,350	24,499
Percent	30.8%	23.9%	22.8%	21.1%	20.6%	24.4%
Middle-Aged (45–59)	12,396	16,613	23,498	1,977	3,863	12,270
Percent	21.6%	21.6%	17.4%	9.8%	9.5%	12.2%
Elderly (60 and over)	5,631	8,139	15,057	610	1,474	5,252
Percent	9.8%	10.5%	11.0%	4.0%	3.7%	4.2%

SOURCE: U.S. Census

age bracket were self-employed and do not have Social Security benefits or pensions. There are too many for the traditional Chinese organizations such as the family associations to take care of. Of course the old men can usually find a bed in the association headquarters, and they can grub a meal from relatives who own restaurants. Many must depend upon meager welfare checks for subsistence, and this is an enormous blow to their pride and dignity. Worse yet is the loneliness that comes from lack of family life and the absence of respect and care, which the aged in China are customarily accorded.

A very successful attempt to deal with the old-age problem is the Golden Age Club in New York. It was started by Mrs. Beatrice Dunham of the Community Service Society, a private service organization, in 1951. The club started out in one room, comfortably furnished and equipped with a television and games. The men came in to read the Chinese periodicals, or they just sat around dozing off or talking to one another, and Mrs. Dunham taught many of them handicrafts. For the lonely old men in Chinatown, the club was a place to go to.

The Golden Age Club was eventually taken over by the New York City Department of Welfare and moved to the Hamilton-Madison Houses on the fringe of Chinatown. As a publicly sponsored organization, membership now includes approximately 500 non-Chinese, among them Italians, Spanish, Negroes, and Jews. The large majority —about 2,000—are Chinese, of whom 12 are women. Among the non-Chinese, the men and women are equally divided.

During my visit to the Golden Age Club, I found the place hopping with activity. The noise was enough to put a teen-age club to shame. The members had just had lunch consisting of hash, soup, bread and butter, dessert, and coffee for 15¢ to 25¢. The meal was prepared by the members and subsidized by the Department of Welfare.

Activities offered by the club are the study of English, cooking, art, woodwork, drama, and discussion groups. There were recordings of Chinese operas and songs. A television was going full blast. A library served those who could read above the commotion. A public health nurse visits the club every Tuesday, and counseling service is offered by the staff members. Trips are organized to the parks and beaches.

To my eyes, these oldsters were vitally alive and happy. During my visit they were excited and eager to show me around. Somehow they did not fit my preconceived ideas of Chinese old folks.

Mr. Louis H. Chu, the director, said, "For the non-Chinese, the club is merely a place to get away from home. For the Chinese, the club *is* home."

The marital-status pattern reflects the abnormal sex ratio and age composition of the Chinese population of past years. All three are results of the stringent immigration regulations, and all three are trying hard to right themselves toward normality.

This is evident by looking at Table 8–7, which shows the marital status of the Chinese and total United States for 1940, 1950, and 1960. In 1940, almost half of the Chinese males were single and half were married, a really freakish situation. What the figures do not show is that a large percentage of the married men did not have their

TABLE 8–7

Marital Status of the Chinese and Total United States
14 Years and Over, by Percentage
1940, 1950, 1960

MALES	*Single*		*Married*		*Widowed or Divorced*	
	Chinese	*U.S.*	*Chinese*	*U.S.*	*Chinese*	*U.S.*
1940*	43.9	34.8	53.0	59.7	3.1	5.4
1950	36.9	26.2	58.1	68.0	5.0	5.9
1960	35.1	25.3	59.7	69.3	5.1	5.3
FEMALES						
1940*	33.4	27.6	57.4	59.5	9.2	12.9
1950	28.2	19.6	64.6	66.1	7.2	14.4
1960	22.0	19.0	69.4	65.9	8.6	15.1

SOURCE: Chinese figures from U.S. Censuses, *Nonwhite Population by Race*, U.S. figures from *Statistical Abstract of the U.S.*, 1962, p. 37.

* 15 years and over

wives with them (see Appendix Table A–4), so that, in effect, these men led bachelor lives. Being widowed or divorced also meant bachelorhood. In sum, this marital pattern meant almost a total body of single males.

A great improvement in the situation was evident by 1950, but the scarcity of eligible young girls can prove a frustrating problem and perhaps a heartbreaking experience to many a young man who wants to find a mate and establish a home.

For Chinese females 14 years and over, the percentages of those married are almost identical with the prevailing U.S. pattern. Chinese girls have no problem finding husbands unless they are particularly choosy. According to the 1960 census, 76.3 percent had found mates by age 20. Only 7 percent were unwed by the time they reached age 25.

Social scientists firmly believe there is no single item that is a better index of group achievement or of national human resources than education. Chinese respect for learning and for the scholar is a cultural heritage. Even when a college degree led to no more than a waiter's job, the Chinese continued to pursue the best education they could get, so that when opportunities developed, the Chinese were qualified and capable of handling their jobs.

Other minorities have not had the benefit of this reverence for learning. Their attitude toward centuries of closed economic doors was "What's the use?" As a result, many employers nowadays are willing to hire minority workers but become exasperated with their incompetence and inefficiency. For minority groups, it is always more convenient to shout discrimination.

Table 8–8 gives a comparison of school years completed for whites, Negroes, and Chinese 14 years and over for 1960. The large number of college graduates and post-graduates among the Chinese is immediately apparent. No doubt a good percentage of those in high

TABLE 8–8

Percentage Comparison of School Years Completed for Whites, Negroes, and Chinese by Sex, 14 Years and Over, 1960

Males:	*Whites*	*Negroes*	*Chinese*
None	15.2	5.0	14.6
Elem: 1–4 yrs	4.2	17.7	7.3
5 & 6 yrs	5.8	14.1	7.3
7 yrs	6.1	9.2	3.1
8 yrs	15.9	13.0	9.4
H.S.: 1–3 yrs	16.0	22.7	13.5
4 yrs	20.3	12.1	16.7
Coll: 1–3 yrs	8.5	4.0	11.5
4 or more	8.0	2.2	16.7
Med. Sch. Yrs. Completed	10.6	8.3	10.7
Females:	*Whites*	*Negroes*	*Chinese*
None	1.6	3.3	15.4
Elem: 1–4 yrs	3.5	12.5	6.2
5 & 6 yrs	5.5	13.0	6.2
7 yrs	5.5	9.3	3.1
8 yrs	16.7	13.5	7.7
H.S.: 1–3 yrs	23.6	25.7	13.8
4 yrs	29.0	15.5	23.1
Coll: 1–3 yrs	9.4	4.3	12.3
4 or more	5.3	2.8	12.3
Med. Sch. Yrs. Completed	11.1	8.9	11.7

SOURCE: U.S. Census, 1960

school who are yet in their teens will go on to complete college or post-graduate work. Especially significant is the fact that 16.7 percent of the Chinese males have finished four years or more of college in comparison with 8 percent of the whites and 2.2 percent of the Negroes.

The Chinese female is equally well educated. One-fourth of the Chinese females are in college or have completed four or more years of higher education. This is double the rate for that of her white sisters, and more than quadruple the rate for that of her Negro sisters. Surprisingly, the median number of school years completed for Chinese females (11.7) is higher than that for Chinese males (10.7).

On the other hand, the number of Chinese who have had no schooling at all is abnormally high. Approximately one out of every seven is an illiterate. A closer look at those who reported no schooling at all reveals that 11,490 of the 14,140 males and 5,905 of the 9,818 females in this category are 45 years or older. Most of them were born in China where only the well-to-do could afford to send their children to school.

Except when artificial barriers intervene, education is the best steppingstone to occupational advancement. This is dramatically evident from the change in the occupational profile of the Chinese in the United States for the last three censuses. Figure 8–D reflects this change by percentage distribution of the Chinese in the ten major occupational groups for 1940, 1950, and 1960.

In 1940, 2.9 percent of the Chinese were in the professional category. By 1960, this group claimed 17.9 percent, a sixfold increase! Household workers, farmers, and laborers are presently insignificant percentages. The clerical and sales group increase is due to the large number of Chinese females in these occupations. Operatives, which include laundry workers, and service workers, which include restaurant personnel, are still predominant occupations, but they are losing numbers rapidly.

More detailed information about the traditional occupations and economic opportunities open to the Chinese will be given in later chapters. Only broad categories are dealt with here to gain an overall perspective and to compare the group with the entire nation.

Table 8–9 shows how the Chinese stand occupationally in com-

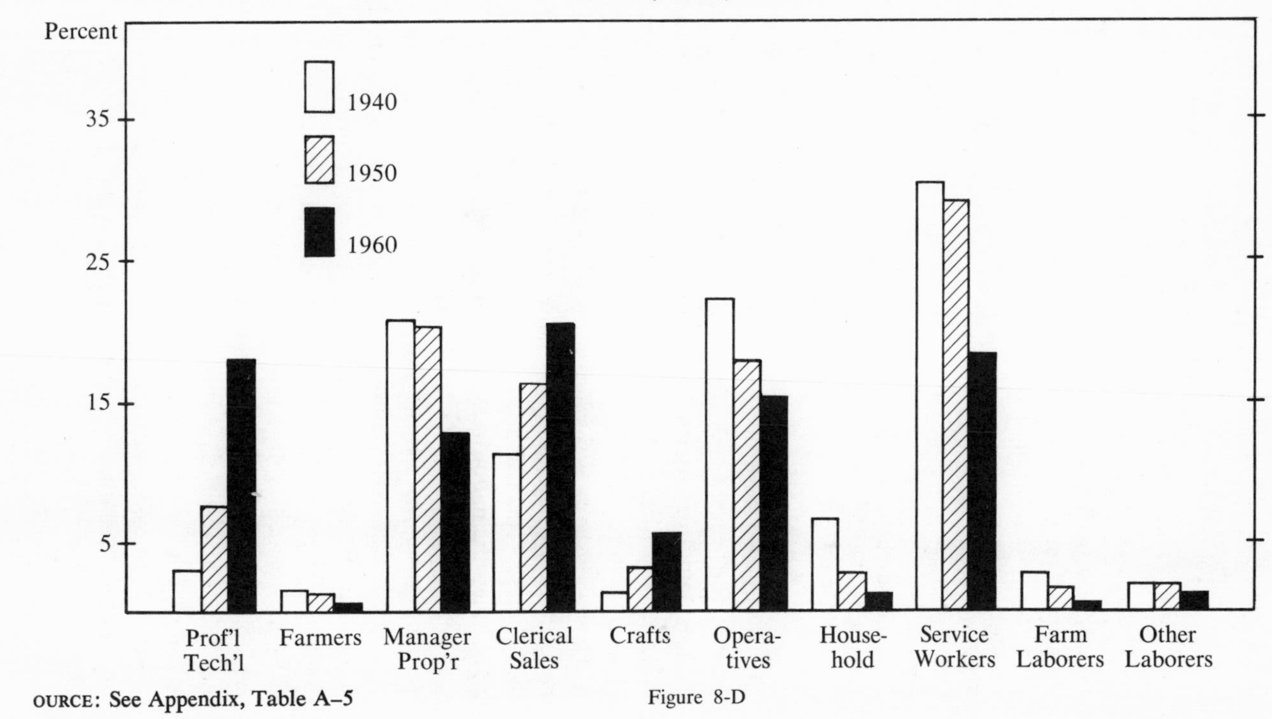

OURCE: See Appendix, Table A–5

Figure 8-D

TABLE 8–9

Percentage Comparison, Major Occupation Groups
Chinese and Whites, 1960

Major Occupation Groups	PERCENT *Whites*	*Chinese*
Professional, technical	12.0	17.9
Farmers, farm managers	4.3	0.6
Managers, officials, proprietors	11.6	12.7
Clerical workers	15.6	13.8
Sales workers	7.2	6.6
Craftsmen	13.7	5.2
Operatives	17.7	15.0
Private household workers	2.0	1.0
Service workers	8.2	18.0
Farm laborers	3.3	0.4
Laborers	4.5	1.3

SOURCE: U.S. Census, 1960

parison with whites according to the 1960 census. Fewer Chinese are in the manual or laboring jobs and more are in the professional and managerial positions, which may be interpreted as a favorable occupational picture indeed.

There is usually a significant correlation between education, occupation, and income, and this holds true for the Chinese. For 1959, the Chinese reported a median family income of $6,207, which is higher than the nationwide figure of $5,660. (See Figure 8–E).

No comparable figures on family income for 1939 and 1949 were available from the Census Bureau for comparison, but it would be safe to say that the Chinese family income has risen commensurably with their occupational advancement. As a group, they can be bracketed in the comfortable middle-income class.

We have caught only a fleeting glimpse of the statistical vignette of the Chinese in the United States as it stood at the time of the census in 1960. The information based on this enumeration has long been outdated, but we did see that the Chinese community has experienced a dynamic transformation in its size, its composition, and its social and economic status. The years spanning the decade from 1960 to 1970 will witness even greater changes, but that must await the results of the 1970 census.

PERCENTAGE COMPARISON OF CHINESE AND U.S. INCOMES, 1960

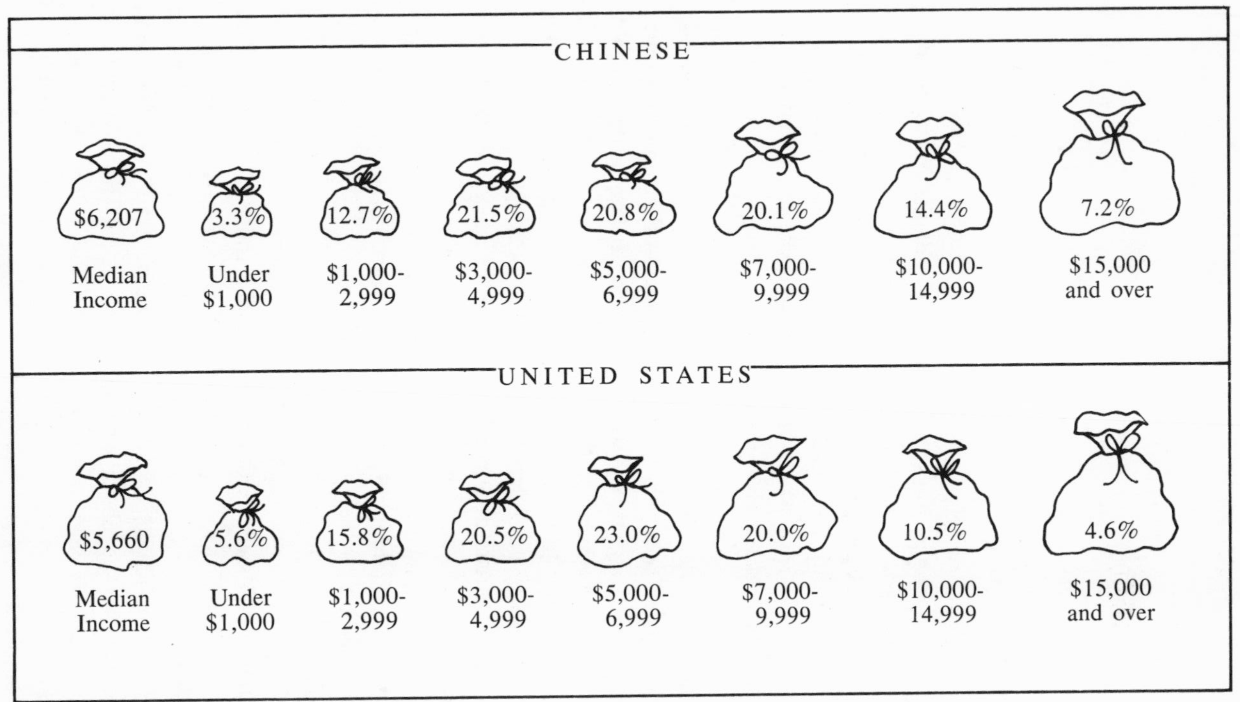

SOURCE: See Appendix, Table A–6

Figure 8-E

9

Chinatowns

"STEP right up, folks, step right up and this bus will take you to mysterious Chinatown, a little bit of Cathay right in the heart of downtown New York. Visit the Buddhist Temple where the heathen Chinese worship their gods and divine their fates from fortune sticks. Stand on the spot where fifty Chinese were murdered by screaming hatchet men of the rival tongs. . . ."

On and on chants the barker for the C——— Sight-Seeing Buses in Times Square, New York. His list of lurid and mysterious sights grows longer. Tourists from out of town—the timid, encouraged by strength in numbers; the adventuresome, seeking a thrill; the curious, enticed by promises of the exotic; the bold, sincerely believing that they are about to brave unknown hazards—all climb aboard the bus and away they go to Mott and Canal Streets.

As the tourists disgorge from the buses, they are instructed by the guides to hold hands as they file through the narrow, winding streets (who knows but some stealthy hand may reach out and grab one of them and pull him down into the reputed underground network of secret tunnels).

Such are the impressions of Chinatowns that the sight-seeing companies manage to impart to the American people. And they will continue with such tactics as long as the tourists' money keeps filling their coffers. For the two sight-seeing bus companies operating in New York's Chinatown, this means 2,000 fares daily and 2,500 on week ends and holidays. To keep this lucrative trade, the bus companies have no qualms about exploiting the peculiarities of the Chinese, fabricating tall tales about them, and re-enforcing the misconceptions held by the American public. Thus the Omaha-Nebraskan or the Springfield-Illinoisan experiences a momentary thrill of imaginary danger and goes home strengthened in his conviction about the intriguing evil Chinese, his strange customs, and peculiar habits.

Newspapermen themselves will admit that it is very convenient and easy to fabricate stories about Chinatown, and the more fantastic the yarn they spin, the more it excites public interest. Here is a frank confession from a reporter on how such stories once originated:

> "When the dog days come around and news is slack, the New York city editor calls to his desk the cleverest necromancer of pretty phrases on his staff and says to him:
>
> " 'Mr. Screamer, things are running pretty slow this afternoon. Do you remember that Bow Kun case up in Chinatown last fall? Well, it isn't settled yet. Get up there and get in touch with some of those On Leong highbinders and let's have a little color story. Let it run for all you can get."
>
> "Mr. Screamer being one who knows to a nicety the ways and carrying powers of his gifts of imagination, and who has, moreover, a subtle understanding of the psychology of the city editor, goes to the office 'morgue' or clippings cabinet, and gets down the envelope containing all the stories, the tragedies and comedies of Chinatown that have been written since that triangle of main streets off the Bowery first housed an abiding mystery. Mr. Screamer reads three or four of the most recent clippings of Bow Kun. Then the discerning reporter goes out to collect his thoughts on a walk up Broadway or over a tall celery vase with a beaded top, comes back to his typewriter and taps out a little color story, just such a one as the city editor wants—and the literature on the war between the tongs is enriched by one more contribution.
>
> "The imaginative reporter knows, the city editor who likes the story knows, that there is but one mustard seed of truth in all the garden of poppy fancies set forth in next morning's column. But both argue that the Chinatown cycle of myths is strong, else why the 'rubber neck' wagons that pound the night pavements of Pell and Mott Streets laden to the high poop with out-of-town folk bent on the pleasurable sensation of goose flesh and awful tremors? And ample permanent protection—what

> Constant Reader can write to the managing editor that this is all rubbish? So there you have an epitome of the New York Chinatown legend."[1]

In the face of these persistent prevarications, who would believe that no safer district is to be found in New York City than Chinatown? According to the Fifth Police Precinct, only one arrest for alcoholism was made in Chinatown over an eight-year period and none for murder or any major crime.[2]

When Charles Dobie set out to collect information for his book, *San Francisco's Chinatown*, no one was more surprised than he to discover that the "temples" were for tourist purposes only. In his book, he described how he climbed a long flight of stairs to the Chinese joss house one bright and early morning all prepared to take notes on the long stream of worshipers that came to do homage to the pagan idols and heathen gods. Instead, a locked door barred his entrance and a sign over the door read: "Open 8–10 in the evenings, For Tourists Only."

Shall I give away the secret of one of the "Buddhist temples" in New York's Chinatown? The original "temple" was located behind the cubbyhole post office on Mott Street, famous for being the smallest post office in the United States. The post mistress was also the "high priestess." When the cubbyhole post office relinquished this fame and bowed out to a modern enlarged post office, the temple closed down too. An enterprising chap seized upon this opportunity and erected a semblance of a temple in the back of his curio shop to attract sightseers to his store. A beaming, corpulent Buddha dominates the entire room. He was a product of expediency, slapped together with great globs of clay and plaster. In broad daylight, this deity would do no credit to its sculptor, but in the half-lit "temple" the smiling Buddha deceptively sits like a solid mass of strength and omnipotence for the throngs of curious sightseers day in and day out.

Much also has been written about Chinatowns describing their

[1] Robert Wells Ritchie, "The War of the Tongs," *Harper's Weekly* (August 27, 1910), pp. 8–10.

[2] "Chinatowns—Not East Not West," *The New York Times Magazine* (Dec. 15, 1946), p. 24.

Oriental architecture, depicting the festivities that go on during the week of Chinese New Year's, singing praises of the delicious food served in the restaurants, pointing out the peculiar foods, herbs, and drugs that are sold in the shops. But again, this is the Chinatown of the tourist—the shining façade which attracts and excites because it is different. Chinatowns did not come into being to lure the tourist dollar or to invite the stares and glares of the curious. Chinatowns grew out of vital and cogent needs of the immigrant Chinese.

Chinatowns are not peculiar to the United States. They are characteristic of all Chinese communities overseas. To every country where they have migrated, the Chinese have established these centers.

This is true also of other immigrant minority groups who invariably concentrate in an area that readily becomes identifiable as an ethnic enclave such as Little Italy, Little Tokyo, Greek Town, and the like. The first-generation immigrants are drawn together because of a common language and common customs, because they find themselves more comfortable in surroundings more similar to those found in the mother country, and because they can effect a more gradual transition into the new society. So it was with Chinatowns, except that Chinatowns had much more compelling reasons for being.

The cultural bridge between the United States and China was much wider than that between the United States and Europe. In dress, speech, attitude, religion, philosophy, and outlook the Chinese ways were radically different from the American. Then, too, the distinct and identifiable physical differences set them apart.

But added to these factors, the Chinese sought refuge within the boundaries of Chinatowns for their own protection from the persecution wreaked against them during the late nineteenth and early twentieth centuries. Later, the Alien Land Acts, forbidding Orientals from owning land, and other restrictive covenants prevented those Chinese who were ready to and wanted to move out from doing so. Thus mainly because of self-insulation and partly because of segregation, Chinatowns came into being.

San Francisco's Chinatown became a city within a city and sufficient unto itself. An invisible moat seemed to cut the Chinese off from the mainstream of American life just beyond the borders. From birth to death, a Chinese found his needs met within the enclave of an area ten blocks square. He lived a way of life as his parent remembered it back in the villages of Kwangtung Province.

Until a few years ago, San Francisco's Chinatown had its own telephone exchange, with a directory printed in Chinese and with Chinese telephone operators. English was quite unnecessary. If Jack Low wanted to speak to his Fourth Uncle, he picked up the telephone and shouted, "I'm Jack Low. Please put my Fourth Uncle on." There was seldom any hesitation on the part of the operator as to who was Jack Low's Fourth Uncle.

San Francisco's Chinatown boasts a 64-bed hospital, manned and staffed almost entirely by Chinese doctors and nurses. Founded in 1923, Tung Wah Hospital employs the latest in medical techniques and discoveries, but at the same time it will not scoff at certain herbal medicines that have been used with effective results for centuries in China. The hospital is especially popular with the Chinese who must be hospitalized because it serves Chinese meals. Those who are accustomed to their native fare find it especially difficult to adapt to a strange diet at a time when their appetites are on the wane and must be coaxed.

Not all Chinatowns are like that of San Francisco. In areas where the Chinese population is sparse, local residents may not even realize that there is a Chinatown in the vicinity. But for the Chinese, there is a street with a few shops, a restaurant or two, and rooms for the family or district association headquarters. It will be the place where one can stock up on Chinese groceries. It will be the place where a lonely soul can go to find others like himself seeking companionship. It will be the place where a fan-tan table or mah-jong table is set up on Sundays. It may be little else.

As the Chinese tried to side-step or avoid all contact with American governmental agencies, they formed their own organizations to provide some form of quasi-government that would set up rules and regulations, resolve differences between them, care for the needy and infirm, and act as liaison with the outside.

At the primary level of organization is the *fong*, literally a room or headquarters for people from the same locality, village, or district. Members come together to sit and chat, hail the new arrivals, exchange news and gossip, cuss each other in jest, or join in a game of cards or *pai-gow*. There are sleeping and cooking facilities for those who are temporarily out of work or for those from the same village or district who come from out of town. Generally, the relationship between members of the *fong* is characterized by close kinship.

The next step up in the organizational pyramid is the surname or family association. In this case, surname and family is synonymous, as everyone with a common surname presumably descended from the same ancestors. As mentioned previously, there are only 438 surnames in China for 700 million Chinese. Thus the number of Wongs, Chins, Lees, etc. is sizable. Notable also is the tendency of those with the same surname to congregate in the same city or locality in the United States. For instance, the Moys predominate in Chicago, the Lees in Washington, D.C., the Ongs in Phoenix, the Yees in Pittsburgh, and so on. Therefore the Moy family association wields heavy influence among the Chinese in Chicago, while the same is true for the Lee family association in Washington.

Because of their larger membership, family associations assumed wider functions than the *fongs*. There was room and board at the family association headquarters for members who needed it. If there was a death and the family of the deceased was poor and there were no kinsmen, the association would pay the funeral expenses. If a member was sick and did not know how to go about seeking medical help, an interpreter was sent to take him to the doctor. If there was a quarrel between its members, a panel of elders would sit and straighten out the differences. There was no force behind their decisions, only moral persuasion, but the decisions were generally accepted and adhered to. Always the members tried to keep a quarrel or difference within their own group, for to quarrel in public would constitute a serious loss of face. Once a year, around the time of Chinese New Year's, members with their families were brought together for a reunion at a sumptuous banquet.

Expenses of the associations were defrayed by assessment against male members of the families, for they were the ones who carried on the family name. Women and girls were not even listed in the family register.

A little further removed in the hierarchy of Chinatown organizations is the district association, which will accept for membership all those originating from the same district or county in China. Generally those who belong to the district associations do not have a strong family association in the city where they reside. For instance, the Fongs are numerous in Sacramento with enough members to organize a family association, but a Fong in Boston would find himself isolated except for the fact that he could then join his district association, which performs essentially the same functions as a family association.

With the Chinese Benevolent Association at the pinnacle of the organizational hierarchy, there is a departure on emphasis in kinship, family, or hometown. The Benevolent Associations in the various cities are formed by representatives from all of the Chinatown organizations including the chambers of commerce, women's clubs, the family and districts associations, the *tongs* and even the Chinese schools and newspapers.

The Chinese Benevolent Associations claim to be the supreme ruling bodies of the Chinese community in their respective cities. They presume to speak for the entire Chinese population of that city. In theory, all people of Chinese ancestry come under the jurisdiction of the Chinese Benevolent Association.

In New York City, forty organizations are represented in the Chinese Benevolent Association. Delegates to the monthly meetings are the presidents of the respective organizations. Dues are also assessed of the organizations, not of individual Chinese. The president is elected by these delegates and must be chosen for a term of two years. For every other term of office, a person from Toishan must be elected president. As pointed out previously, the Toishanese can demand the helm every other term because of their numerical superiority.

The office of the president of the Chinese Benevolent Association once carried great influence and great powers in Chinatown. As its chosen leader, he was the official spokesman for the entire Chinese community. He called meetings, initiated projects, settled disputes, organized celebrations, and presided at all public functions. In big cities such as Chicago, New York, San Francisco, and Los Angeles, these functions were for charity drives, China's Independence Day parade, reception of visiting dignitaries, and New Year's Day celebrations.

Each city has its own Chinese Benevolent Association, and each is organized and set up according to its own needs. For instance, in Honolulu, it is called the United Chinese Society. In San Francisco, this same organization is known by the English name of the Chinese Six Companies, although the Chinese name, *Chung-wah Kung-so*, is consistent. The Chinese Six Companies was the first of the Chinese Benevolent Associations founded by the Chinese for protection, mutual aid, and quasi-judicial purposes. At one time, the Chinese Six Companies even assumed consular duties, before China had formal representation through a consulate.

At this point, the story of Chinatown and the Chinese people would be incomplete without mentioning the *tongs* and their notorious wars, which were a disgrace and dishonor to the majority of the law-abiding and peace-loving Chinese. Let me hasten also to mention that the last of the *tong* wars took place back in 1931, and were it not for the repeated exploitation of the memory of those infamous wars by irresponsible journalists, gutter news-seekers, and mercenary tourist guides, whose tall tales give them their bread and butter, *tong* wars would have been relegated to the position occupied by the Indian massacres of the pioneer days.

The word *tong* itself means "hall." Freely translated, it means lodge or fraternal organization. It was a transplanted organization from China and not one founded upon the needs of the Chinese people in a foreign land such as the Chinese Benevolent Associations or the family and district associations. The first of the *tongs*, the Chee Kung Tong, was a secret society growing out of the Triad Society, whose primary aim was the overthrow of the Manchu Dynasty.

As the *tongs* did not grow out of a specific need, and for want of direction or purpose, they soon made prey of man's vices. The *tongs* developed into protection rackets for prostitution houses and gambling interests. For a "cut in the take," the *tongs* would provide protection against law-enforcement agencies or any person that threatened the disruption of their anti-social activities. It was the *tongs* that gave the Chinese a bad name.

But happily, *tong* wars are a thing of the past. For more than three decades, there has been no violence connected with *tong* activities. And the character of the tongs has changed too. Disputes between Chinese are generally given a hearing before the Chinese Benevolent

Association. Although there are no physical means or sanctions to enforce its decision, the pressure of opinion is generally sufficient to compel acceptance.

Today, the *tongs* do not even want to be called *tongs*. They know that the word has been blemished and tarnished by their former wicked behavior, and it does them no honor to be associated with such infamy. The On Leong Tong is now called On Leong Merchants Association and the Chee Kung Tong, the Chinese Freemasons. Their activities take on the character of a fraternal lodge as the word *tong* intended it to be. They are becoming more socially conscious of the welfare of the Chinese community and are beginning to take an interest in philanthropic activities.

The *fongs*, the family and district associations, the Chinese Benevolent Associations, and even the *tongs* were the cohesive, organizing forces that bound the Chinese people together. But as the conditions that gave rise to these Chinatown organizations gradually receded, the importance of these organizations also declined.

Nowadays the *fongs*, the family and district associations, maintain headquarters in Chinatown not to provide shelter or give aid to their needy sons, nor to provide interpreting service or settle disputes, but merely to stand as a symbol of common origin. What influence or importance they still retain is only with the older or first-generation Chinese. With the native-born, the student group, or more educated newcomers, these organizations mean nothing.

The native-born Chinese is familiar with the American setup. He has no language problem. He knows that if he is out of work he can collect unemployment insurance. If he is sick or injured, he can collect disability. If he should die, Social Security will help his widow and children. His personal and business relations are more apt to be with non-Chinese people and outside the sphere of any Chinatown organization. Any Chinatown organization he belongs to is more apt to be for social, cultural, or recreational purposes.

The student group and a great number of the recent arrivals come from different parts of China. They have no kinship or geographical ties with the more homogeneous groups from southern China. Their command of the English language and their education enable them to fit quickly into American society. They also disdain identification with the Chinatown Chinese.

Only the Chinese Benevolent Association in the larger cities can still claim some influence, but these, too, are losing their hold. The Chinese are no longer confined to the prescribed boundaries of Chinatowns. Social service agencies of the state and federal government have taken over many of the mutual aid and welfare functions once assumed by the Chinese Benevolent Associations and the family and district associations. The leaders number among the first or older generations, and they have not adapted their leadership to the change in status and conditions among the Chinese. They insist upon maintaining close ties with China and perpetuating a way of life as they once knew it—a way of life that is now extinct even in China.

So the functions of the Chinese Benevolent Associations have been reduced to the ceremonial—arranging celebrations for holidays and festivals and entertaining and feting special guests. Even as official spokesmen for the Chinese community, they seldom express the true sentiments of the majority any more.

In San Francisco, the Chinese Six Companies lost an important and revitalizing group from its ranks long ago. In 1904, a group of native-born Chinese-Americans decided that they could not accept the leadership of the first generation, whose interests and aims did not coincide with their own. Led by Walter U. Lum, Joseph K. Lum, and Ng Gunn, an organization called the Native Sons of the Golden State was founded. Its purpose was to provide leadership and direction for native-born Chinese who wanted to actively participate in and partake of their American heritage. It was dedicated to defending and securing for the Chinese the rights and privileges of his American citizenship.

Organized as a local chapter in San Francisco, the Native Sons of the Golden State soon branched out with chapters in Oakland, Los Angeles, Fresno, and San Diego. Chinese in other states began to feel the need for a similar organization and petitioned to set up local chapters. When the organization burst beyond state boundaries, its name was changed to the Chinese American Citizens Alliance to reflect a national rather than a state membership.

Chapters of the Chinese American Citizens Alliance, besides those mentioned above, are found in Portland, Chicago, Salinas, San Antonio, Houston, and Albuquerque.

The Chinese American Citizens Alliance has vigorously fought against every attempt in the past to disfranchise citizens of Chinese ancestry, to segregate Chinese children in the public schools, to apply discriminatory regulations against Chinese business, and to exclude or restrict Chinese immigration. Recently it was successful in halting production of a film depicting the Chinese as opium smokers in San Francisco's Chinatown.

Members of the CACA are active in American civic affairs and politics. Their custom is to invite candidates for public office to address their group and answer questions regarding their stand on the Chinese. By endorsing a candidate or by urging their members and the Chinese community to vote for or against a man, they try to utilize their votes effectively.

Membership in the CACA is by invitation only and is considered a recognition not only of that individual's personal achievements, but also of his ability and willingness to work for the advancement of his fellowmen. When I was invited to meet with the executive board on a visit to San Francisco several years ago, I noted that every man on that board was a college graduate.

More modern organizations with a wide variety of names spring up from time to time to meet the exigencies of the moment, but the compelling forces to band together for survival and mutual aid are gone.

I was brought up in Washington, D.C. We did not live in Chinatown, but my father went there religiously every Sunday afternoon. Sometimes the whole family went, and Father would drop us off to visit some family in the area, and he would go on to the *fong*, which was only a sort of dormitory setup with one room set aside as a sitting room. Father stayed there all Sunday afternoon, sometimes sitting, sometimes just standing around greeting the others who arrived, and "shooting the breeze." Many Chinese use the *fong* as their mailing address, and they would go in to read their mail from the home village. News about births, deaths, marriages, illnesses, political events, and even gossip was passed around, so that everyone was informed about happenings in the village in China.

The *fong* sponsored a *hui*, which in almost all respects served as a banking institution for the members. It operated on the principle of pooling of resources to meet immediate needs for funds for business or personal reasons. Those who elected to join the *hui* agreed to pay into the pool ten dollars per share for one hundred weeks for a total of $1,000. Members who needed current funds would bid for the weekly pool by submitting a written bid before 3 o'clock that Sunday. For instance, a bid might read 50 cents or 75 cents. This meant that the bidder was willing to pay 50 cents or 75 cents for each ten-dollar share, and the other shareholders only had to deposit $9.50 or $9.25 as the case may be for that week. High bid won and the successful bidder would receive the total pool deposited that week. Repayment was effected through his weekly deposits made either previously or subsequently.

In essence this was a cooperative banking system in which the members were both borrowers and depositors, but no funds were ever left on deposit. If no bids were put in for the pool on any particular week, the names of all the members who had not received a pool were thrown into the hat and one member was thus chosen to receive the pool at the minimum bid of 25 cents. Eventually every member received a pool. At the end of the hundred-week period, the *hui* was dissolved, and a new *hui* would be formed, possibly with different shareholders and their proportional interests.

The *hui* in effect served as a systematic savings method for the thrifty and as a source of credit for those who needed a lump sum in cash for business or other reasons. Few Chinese utilized the services of American banks.

Because my father was widely respected and trusted, he ran the *hui* for his village *fong* for many, many years. To the best of my knowledge, there was no formal organization or charter to this banking arrangement. Members who wanted to join merely signed up, and when enough members indicated an interest, the *hui* began. Bids were opened at 3 o'clock each Sunday and deposits made between 3 and 5. Members who could not make it down to Chinatown would call a relative at the *fong* or at a business nearby and arrange for the deposit to be made. Sometimes when a shareholder who had already received his pool defaulted in his payments, his nearest relatives or his guarantors would put up the money and get after the delinquent shareholder to pay up. He usually did, because the other shareholders were his own village people, and he could not risk their ostracism.

For two hours each Sunday, Father served as a banker. On other occasions, he served as one of the mediators when grievances and differences between members were brought before the *fong*. Typical cases were complaints against opening a laundry or restaurant too close to an existing one, wrangling over debts, problems with their base and origin in China but which could only be settled here because the family elders or heads were in this country, and once in a while, family quarrels.

I remember hearing one case concerning a wife who complained that her husband would not give her money to send to her aged father. The husband maintained that when a woman marries, her ties from her own family are severed and that her loyalties and obligations are entirely to her husband's family. The wife conceded that her father was not ill nor in dire need. She had two brothers to support the father. She merely wanted to send him some money as a token of her affection, and she felt she had an equal right to the family purse since she worked side by side with her husband in their laundry. The decision was made in favor of the husband. Chinese tradition maintains that a man is not financially obligated in any way to his wife's folks.

Of course this incident occurred in the 1940's, and I doubt if a wife has to fight publicly to spend part of the family income as she sees fit today. I doubt also if the *fong* still mediates any differences. The last *hui* sponsored by the same *fong* that I am speaking of dissolved in 1951. The Chinese have learned how to go to the bank and make deposits and borrow funds.

A revelation struck me when I went back to Washington, D.C. for a visit in 1957. Driving through 7th and H Streets one Sunday evening, I passed the length of Chinatown before I suddenly realized that the place was almost deserted. The faces that I did see on the street were not Chinese but Filipino. Ten years ago, I dare say most of the male members of the Chinese population would be found in Chinatown on a Sunday evening.

On reflection, I realized that my uncle and his sons had taken a drive out to Maryland in the family car. My cousin, whose family had recently joined him from China, was home playing with his new-born son. A girl friend and her husband were entertaining guests with a barbecue dinner in the backyard of their suburban Maryland home. My brother and his wife were sitting on the front porch. And I remembered how these men faithfully spent their Sundays in Chinatown a decade ago.

Family circles now provide the companionship and warmth formerly sought in Chinatown. Financial improvement and more knowledge of English enable the Chinese to seek entertainment elsewhere. Cars, once an unknown luxury among Chinese families, are now commonplace. Spacious houses and suburban dwellings make possible entertainment in the homes. Diversion can be found outside of Chinatown.

Segregation is no longer a factor in the perpetuation of Chinatowns. The social climate and the general attitude toward the Chinese have changed so rapidly in recent years that the Chinese actually encounter little or no discrimination in their choice of a place to live. In fact, only a small percentage of the Chinese in the United States live in Chinatowns, and the old-time residents have practically all moved away.

I am personally acquainted with a woman who brought up her brood of seven children in a four-room apartment on Bayard Street in New York's Chinatown. For thirty years, she occupied the same apartment and stubbornly refused to move to larger and more comfortable quarters elsewhere.

Money was not the problem. Her husband was a successful jeweler and could well afford a large house. The family definitely needed more room and privacy, but the mother felt comfortable in her old surroundings. Her friends were there. Her husband's business was there. It was convenient for her to shop. Knowing her, I thought she would be the last person to leave Chinatown. But in 1961, with most of her children grown up, married, and living in the suburbs, she, too, succumbed and bought a home in the suburbs near her children.

Have Chinatowns outgrown their purpose then? Will they soon fade from the American scene, In 1949, the late Rose Hum Lee, formerly head of the Department of Sociology of Roosevelt College in Illinois and a keen observer of the Chinese community in the United States, predicted the demise of Chinatowns.

In 1940, Professor Lee had found 28 cities with some area called Chinatown.[3] By 1955, Dr. Peter Sih, in a survey of Chinese churches for the National Council of Churches, found only 16 cities with Chinatowns. Professor Lee pointed out that many once-flourishing Chinatowns of the West have all but disappeared. She cited as examples the Chinatowns of Butte, Montana; Boise, Idaho; Rock Springs, Wyoming; and Denver, Colorado. These Chinatowns were founded by the miners and railroad workers back in the pioneer days of the West. When jobs in these industries gave out, the Chinese moved away.

Most Chinatowns are distinct enclaves and are generally found in the run-down slum districts of cities. In slum clearance plans, civic improvement projects, or expansion of private enterprise, the areas once staked out as Chinatowns are invaded or taken over all together. Chinatowns shrink, are overshadowed, or suffer demise. Honolulu's century-old historic Chinatown fell to the bulldozer in 1962 to make way for a cultural center.

> Philadelphia's Chinatown was seriously reduced in size when the city converted the main street of the ghetto into a thoroughfare leading into the Benjamin Franklin Bridge, thereby connecting Philadelphia with New Jersey. Later a slum clearance programme whittled away more of Chinatown; from an aggregation of a thousand, some two hundred Chinese remained. In the same manner, Pittsburgh's Chinatown was totally obliterated by the building of a modern express-way and the community succumbed to bulldozers, cement mixers and gravel grinders. Chicago's "Old Chinatown," located several miles north of the present one, could not stem the encroachment of business firms and a new site had to be selected. A large portion of Los

[3] Rose Hum Lee, *The Chinese in the United States of America* (Hong Kong, Hong Kong University Press, 1960), pp. 65–66.

> Angeles' Old Chinatown disappeared in the city's renewal programme.[4]

Does the demolition or relocation of these Chinatowns confirm Professor Lee's assertion that Chinatowns will soon be relegated to the pages of history? The answer would be yes if no large influx of new arrivals replaced the earlier generations who have outgrown the transitional stage. However, since 1957 over 40,000 Chinese have entered the country. These new immigrants must run the course of their own process of accommodation. They are replacing the former inhabitants of Chinatown and revitalizing it, but the tempo of change has speeded up.

Where Chinatowns were once static societies perpetuating a rural way of life known in the villages of southern China, the new immigrants are mainly from Hong Kong, where they have lived a pseudo-Western, urban way of life. Some of these newcomers came into the country under the various refugee programs. Some are family members of former immigrants being united with their families. All of them must have spent a year or more waiting for their visas in Hong Kong. They have had an ample diet of American movies. Most of them are modern and more Western in outlook than the former immigrants.

The women are more independent and no longer conform to the Confucian ideals. The new immigrants are more sophisticated and do not need to resort to the arrangement of a *hui* to meet their banking needs. They are more familiar with government services. Because they have not been threatened as a group from without, they have not had to stick together and work together as a unit. Communal organizations have no meaning for them.

Still the new arrivals continue to pour into Chinatown tenements vacated by the former immigrants. The presence and proximity of their own kind ease the shock of the trans-Pacific leap. In the enclave of Chinese faces and Chinese-speaking people, there is a sense of security that comes from the familiar.

The rent may be cheaper. Eating habits, already ingrained, may be preserved with the availability of Chinese groceries. Information may

[4] *Ibid.*

be obtained about employment opportunities. Even though some of the new arrivals may have skilled trades or professions, their first jobs may be in a Chinese enterprise in menial work. I know an accountant who washed dishes in a restaurant for more than a year. A tailor worked in a laundry. A school teacher found himself ironing shirts.

Strung around the rims of San Francisco's and New York's Chinatowns are many sportswear garment factories utilizing the labor of Chinese seamstresses. There are also bead factories. The Chinese women grasp eagerly at these jobs, which pay by the piece or by the gross. An aunt of mine works in a skirt factory that pays her 20 cents for each completed skirt. I gasped when she told me the rate, but I felt better when she told me she could average six skirts an hour.

In bead work, manufacturers farm out work to contractors who distribute it to women who work at home. Pay runs from $8 to $10 a gross, depending upon the complexity of the design. These wages must seem high at first to the new arrivals, whose thinking is still in terms of Hong Kong dollars, where the exchange rate is approximately H.K.$6 to U.S.$1. They also need the money to pay back the enormous expenses incurred for their trip. Of course working wives and working mothers raise family problems of their own, but these are more fully discussed in the chapter on the family.

Whereas Chinese immigration used to be a trickle, the non-quota provisions and liberalization of the immigration laws have raised the influx considerably. Instead of shrinking, the boundaries of the major Chinatowns such as the ones in San Francisco, New York, and Los Angeles are expanding. Formerly, New York's Chinatown was a solid cluster of eight square blocks bounded by Baxter and Canal Streets and the Bowery. The enlarged Chinatown is shaped more like a star, with the points extending along the lines of a single bus or subway fare.

New housing has also sprung up in Chinatowns. One of the earliest was the Ping Yuen Housing Project, which covers four city blocks along the northern border of San Francisco's Chinatown. These are modern apartment houses with Chinese architectual designs to conform with the Oriental setting of Chinatown. More units were added as the demand for these apartments increased.

In New York, the City Council proposed a slum-clearance program that would raze the entire Chinatown and rebuild it into a modern China City. New York wanted to retain its Chinatown as a tourist attraction, but some of the existing structures were more than a hundred years old. The streets were narrow, winding, cobblestone paths, barely wide enough for one car to squeeze through. The projected plans called for modern structures with Oriental architecture, but the merchants whose businesses would be temporarily disrupted during the rebuilding objected so strongly that the city government dropped its plans.

Since then, private builders have capitalized on the demand for better housing in Chinatown. Apartment buildings have sprung up in and around Chinatown—the best known of these is the Chatham Square project which departs from the traditional straight lines found in buildings and undulates like a writhing snake along Chinatown's southern border.

Other tall, narrow buildings are wedged in between dilapidated structures, utilizing whatever building space is available without thought for architectural harmony. Rentals in these new buildings are high. Housing could be secured at lower cost and in better surroundings elsewhere, but the newcomers eagerly snap up these apartments because they prefer to remain in Chinatown.

The word "ghetto" has been applied by many sociologists to Chinatowns, but in their reference, there is an implication that it is a place to climb out of or break away from. I must confess that from my superficial knowledge of sociology, I entertained these same ideas, and I felt that with lessening discrimination restricting the Chinese to a specific area of residence and with the acculturation of the Chinese into the larger society, it was natural and desirable for the Chinese to move away.

When I began to talk to Chinese from various walks of life about Chinatown, however, I found that even without physical attachment, there was strong sentimental attachment. Second-generation Chinese who had moved away confessed that if more desirable housing were available in and around Chinatown, they would prefer going back.

In one case, there was a seventy-year-old woman who had two sons with beautiful suburban homes. She lived first with one son and then the other, but the sons and their wives were away for most of the day at business. The old woman felt very lonely. In the end, she chose to live in Chinatown in a fifth-floor walk-up in a run-down apartment house, where she could be with her friends. This woman did not need money for living expenses, but she found employment in a garment factory sitting on a footstool cutting off thread ends as the seamstresses pulled the garments from the sewing machines. The wages were minimal, and a zealous social worker could make a case of sweatshop labor of it, but the woman was much happier than if she were wandering among the upholstered furniture on the carpeted living rooms in her sons' homes without a soul to talk to.

In an interview with Mr. Harold Lui, teen-supervisor of the Hamilton-Madison Houses, a low-cost housing project near Chinatown, I ventured a suggestion to him in a discussion of the emerging incidences of pre-delinquency behavior. I said that in meeting the problem of Chinese teen-age truants perhaps it would help if he advised the parents to move out of the area and remove their children from the environmental influences. Mr. Lui did not agree with me. He felt that anti-social behavior is a symptom of personal maladjustment. "It is mainly an individual problem," he said. "Some sail through their accommodation problems easily. Those who have difficulties need an identifying group more than ever."[5]

He cited several instances where he felt that living in Chinatown enabled bewildered teen-agers to overcome their problems. Living in a closely knit neighborhood, they found sympathetic and understanding listeners who had passed through the same stages. Buddies commiserated with each other and in doing so unburdened themselves. In time, these teen-agers straightened themselves out. If they were by themselves, he said, they might have developed indelible personality scars.

[5] On page 101 of his book, *The Newcomer*, Oscar Handlin brought out this same theory. He wrote: "Delinquency is more closedly related to failures of personal adjustment. There is no unanimity of opinion among students of the subject about the etiology of delinquency; but the most persuasive theories share a common view of the social situation of the delinquent. Whether the specific cause of breakdown be attributed to disrupted families, intergenerational conflict, personal anxieties and frustrations, or the influence of the peer group and the mass media, these explanations reveal the delinquent as an individual unsure of his own intentions and defiant of the authority that sustains values unacceptable or inadequate to his own life."

While Chinatowns are no longer the *sole* social and recreational outlet for the large majority of Chinese, wedding banquets, holiday celebrations, funerals, or the birth of a baby will still bring the Chinese back to Chinatown for the celebration. If there are no local Chinatowns to hold the festivities, they will go to one in a larger city nearby. A Worcester, Massachusetts, bridal couple held their wedding banquet in New York's Chinatown. A chartered bus brought the guests from out of town.

The restaurants are powerful magnets. During the week, the Chinese housewife may serve steak or roast, but comes Sunday and mouths will water for winter-melon soup, barbecued duck, crisp-skinned roast pork and other delicacies. Dinner in Chinatown may also be an occasion to entertain guests or get together with friends and family.

After a dance or poker game, a group or couple may head for Chinatown for a midnight snack. Restaurants in Chinatown cater heavily to Chinese clientele. More than any other reason, the Chinese love of good food will prolong the life of Chinatowns. If Chinese food is served at home, the basic ingredients must be purchased from Chinatown, for where else can one buy soy sauce, bean curd, dried mushrooms, snow peas, or bamboo shoots?

So while the men no longer hang around Chinatown all day Sundays, they still go there once a week or twice a month—if for nothing else, at least for groceries. Restaurants, laundries, and curio shops may find it more convenient to order their supplies such as rice and starch from Chinatown stores. For others, Chinatown is a handy one-stop marketplace, especially on Sundays, the only day off for a large number of Chinese. One can buy the groceries, pick up the mail, visit Third Uncle, drop by the doctor's office, see about a fifth partnership in that restaurant uptown, get some good food in the stomach, and maybe catch that latest movie from Hong Kong, all in the same vicinity. Even the bank and post office have hours on Sunday in Chinatown, and one doctor tells me that he seldom has patients on any other day except Sundays. He heads for home every night at six and is never troubled by night calls. But on Sundays, he is swamped.

"Don't your patients ever get sick during the week or at night?" I asked.

"If they do," he replied, "they manage to wait it out until the next Sunday."

Chinatowns have been a colorful landmark on the American scene. Cities with one have always used it as a tourist attraction. To heighten curiosity and make Chinatowns seem more exciting, a great many stories have been fabricated about these places. Even today, the tendency is to associate all Chinese in the United States with Chinatowns and to presume that whatever occurs in Chinatown may be taken to apply to all the Chinese in the United States at large. In actuality, only a small percentage of the Chinese now live in Chinatowns. Most have successfully found their niches in the larger American society. Those who live there are essentially newcomers, people with businesses or restaurants in the area, and old-timers who have not broken away.

In population and area, the larger Chinatowns have expanded, swelled by the increased numbers of immigrants within the past two decades. But the new Chinatowns are not like the old. Nor will they ever be unless we turn back the clock of history and re-create the conditions of yesteryears. The bonds that held the early Chinese together in Chinatowns are gone. Communal organizations have lost their leadership and their functions. The new Chinatowns will be characterized more as loosely knit ethnic neighborhoods with an artificially contrived Oriental atmosphere mainly for the sake of the tourist trade. Behind this façade, however, the true essence of Chinatowns will be found in the sense of identity and belonging they impart to the Chinese living beyond as well as within its borders.

10

The Chinese Family Transplanted

EDDIE Wang's father could not make up his mind whether to be irate or amused.

"Look," he fumed as he waved a note under my nose. The note was found propped up against the telephone in the hallway when we entered the apartment. "Read this, will you?" I took the note and read:

> Dear Pop,
>
> Gotta run back to school for the game. Need my black shoes for the dance tonight. Be a sport and polish them for me. Polish in upper drawer. Thanks.
>
> Eddie

"Why the very nerve of that boy! Asking me—his father—to shine his shoes for him! Why, it's utterly disrespectful! When I was a boy, I spoke to my father only when spoken to. I stood in his presence. I took him his pipe and his tea. I dared not disobey him. Nowadays, children have no respect for their parents," Mr. Wang wailed. "They do not pay any attention to the proprieties we observed toward our elders."

Yet, when Eddie came home, instead of sternly rebuking him or lecturing him, Mr. Wang treated the incident as a joke. To top it off, the shoes were shined and ready for Eddie in time for him to dash off to the dance.

That evening after dinner, I teased Mr. Wang about the shoe-shine incident. "It's your own fault," I chided. "You didn't reprimand Eddie for his disrespect. You even shined his shoes for him. I noticed that he didn't think it was anything out of the ordinary. To him, it was a perfectly natural request and you complied with it."

"What could I do?" lamented Mr. Wang. "Eddie was brought up in this country. The customs here are different. With us, a father was a god. The cardinal virtue was filial piety. In the United States, the emphasis is on an easy camaraderie between father and son. My problem is I was brought up under the old Chinese family system while Eddie is being reared under a totally different culture. Sometimes Eddie's actions appall me, but we enjoy a warm relationship that I never experienced with my father."

It is to Mr. Wang's credit that he has proved adaptable and pliable enough to recognize that he cannot import intact the standards of his upbringing from China to the United States. To this extent, the Wang family will not undergo the stresses and strains that such cultural changes exert upon a people transplanted.

For centuries, the nucleus of Chinese culture has been the family. To the Chinese mind, the word "family" has a much broader meaning than the American connotation of Poppa, Mama, and children. Family was more of a kinship group or clan.

Much has been written about the extended family system of China where many generations and their offshoots lived under one roof and under the domination of one patriarch or matriarch. Many social scientists have contended that the kinship family was more of an ideal, whereas the conjugal family was more of an actuality in China. Yet, the kinship family remained the model and the ideal for which most Chinese families strove for thousands of years.

The kinship family was not a mere penchant of the Chinese people for tradition. Rather, it was the product of social evolution, for the Chinese people met their economic, social, and religious needs in the extended family system.

In an agriculturally based economy, without the aid of technology, many hands were needed in a cooperative effort to cultivate the land and bring in the crops. A husband-and-wife team and minor children were hardly the optimal application of labor under this type of economic set-up.

Social service agencies and welfare programs operated in the public interest are a recent phenomena, but Chinese culture boasts a heritage of more than 4,000 years. Orphans, widows, the destitute, the sick, and unforeseen calamities have always been with us. Man has always met these misfortunes of life through collective efforts. The Chinese paid their "insurance premiums" by communal action through the family. The extended family system gave protection to all its members, and the larger the family the better able it was to cope with the contingencies of life.

Marriage was a family concern, not a private matter between man and wife. Choice of mates was based on considerations other than romantic love. The marital bonds were ironclad. Allowances were made for human nature so that a man could take a concubine or indulge in promiscuity without public censure. Women were not allowed such license, but once they had produced a male heir, their position in the family was secured, and they could not be cast aside.

Even man's longing for immortality, and his yearning for knowledge of the infinite was woven into the framework of the family institution through the practice of ancestor worship. The living were thus linked with the dead into infinity. The worst sin that a man could commit was to die without progeny and sever the family line. This led to the intense desire of the Chinese people for sons and more sons, not only to insure the family continuity, but to give a wider base to the collective system.

Females were relegated to a subordinate position on the male side of the family. Hence daughters were less desirable because they must be reared for the benefit of another clan. Once married, the woman identified completely with her husband's kin almost to the total exclusion of her own parental clan, except on feast days or special occasions. Births, weddings, funerals, festivals, and holidays were family celebrations and adequately met the recreational needs of its members.

Essentially, this was the Chinese kinship family as it has survived almost unchanged for more than 2,000 years. Its all-pervading influence into every sector of Chinese life adequately served the demands of a feudalistic society. But with the advent of modern technology, a shift toward industrialization, and contact with Western culture, the extended family system proved incompatible with progress and modernization.

C. K. Yang, in his book titled *The Chinese Family in the Communist Revolution*, stated that "K'ang Yu-wei, who led China's first organized modern reform in 1898, pointed out that the 'abolition' of the traditional family was a condition for proper performance of modern public duties. But his reform movement proved abortive. . . . Sun Yat Sen, the leading revolutionist to rise on the heels of K'ang's failure, sensed the same incompatibility when he urged the expansionism of 'familism and clannism' into nationalism."[1]

By 1919, so much of China's ills engendered by her forced entry into the world community of nations was blamed upon the family that the term "family revolution" was introduced into the consciousness of the public during the New Culture Movement or Renaissance, which started in 1917. Some of the objectives of the family revolution were a new role for women in the family as well as in society; freedom of social association between the sexes; marriage by free choice and love, not by parental arrangement; and greater freedom for the young.

In 1930, the Nationalist government in Nanking promulgated the Law of Kinship Relations, which incorporated many of the ideological objectives of the family revolution.

It remained for the Chinese Communists to shoulder the major portion of the blame for undermining the family structure, but as C. K. Yang pointed out: "This institution had been changing under constant stress and strain for the preceding three decades; and the Communist crisis, so far as the family was concerned, represented but a more drastic development of the same process."[2]

Although the family was the dominant institution permeating the entire social fabric of life in China, there were few families among the Chinese in the United States until after 1946. Both Chinese tradition and the American exclusion laws were responsible for this peculiar situation.

It was many years after the first Chinese set foot in Chicago, Illinois, that a feminine Celestial made her appearance, and the first

[1] C. K. Yang, *The Chinese Family in the Communist Revolution* (Cambridge, Mass., MIT Press, 1959), pp. 11–12.
[2] *Ibid.*, p. 18.

ladies to arrive were not the wives of the men they came to join. The wives had remained in China to tend the ancestral hearth while the husbands took for themselves concubines to accompany them overseas. In 1890, there were but a dozen families in Chicago. By 1920, this number had increased to fifty. A more recent survey showed only 350 families in the metropolitan Chicago area.[3]

Families meant women, and in 1890 there was but one Chinese woman to every 27 Chinese males in the United States. Even by 1960 the sex ratio of the Chinese population in this country was still disparately high at 133.1 compared with an over-all national sex ratio of 97.1.

With or without women, the men had no intentions of uprooting themselves from their ancestral homes. Only full-bodied young men emigrated. Their objective was a short-term one—to earn and save enough money to go back to China. The United States was viewed as the Mountain of Gold, and opportunities for economic betterment were powerful lures. If a Chinese saved enough passage money for another to join him, he seldom sent for his wife and small children. If there were sons, the man sent for them but not unless these sons were physically capable of working to help increase the family earnings. If there were no sons, the man sent for his brother or his nephew. As emigration to the United States was viewed solely as an economic proposition and a means of livelihood, the women did not participate.

This resulted in a bizarre form of marital arrangement called the *mutilated* family[4]—a family united in bond but dismembered physically. In other words, the Chinese men in the United States were family men without the presence of family members, which explains why there were four times as many married men as married women in the census of 1930. Invariably, a bride would be secured for the young man ready to embark on his journey overseas, so that he would have the responsibilities of a husband and father but none of

[3] Rose Hum Lee, *The Chinese in the United States of America* (Hong Kong, Hong Kong University Press, 1960), pp. 189 and 243.

[4] A term coined by Charles Frederick Marden in *Minorities in American Society* (New York, American Book Co., 1952).

the benefits, joys, and warmth of family life except for occasional visits separated by years of absence until, as an old man, he could permanently retire to China.

Chinese tradition was not the only bar to the reunion of families in this country. Eventually, the Immigration Act of 1924 made it practically impossible for a Chinese man to send for his wife and children. The Chinese were declared "aliens ineligible to citizenship" and thus could not be admitted as immigrants.

The mutilated family was the predominant form of family life (if it could be called such) among the Chinese in the United States until 1946, when several legislative acts opened a crack in the door to permit the reunion of some families. These were the War Brides Act and an amendment to the Repeal of the Chinese Exclusion Acts permitting wives of Chinese-American men to enter the country as non-quota immigrants. More than 8,000 men effected the entry of their wives before the War Brides Act expired on December 30, 1949. Additional thousands continue to bring in their wives and children under the amendment. (See Chapter 6.)

By this time, China had undergone nearly a decade of war and revolution. Many families who had overseas connections and who could afford the move were already uprooted from their ancestral homes and had fled to Hong Kong. The United States was just another step in the same direction.

The mutilated family refers more specifically to a situation in which the man was already married and probably had children living in China while he resided apart from them in the United States. A good proportion of the predominately male Chinese population in this country had no wives at all. Chinese women of marriageable age were few, and the difficulties encountered by the Chinese in the harsh interpretation of the immigration laws made re-entry an unknown risk, thereby condemning these men to a life of bachelorhood.

Liberalization of the immigration laws after World War II sent these men back to Hong Kong in droves to find themselves wives. Some of the men had been womanless for years. If they had emigrated to this country after attaining manhood, they were fairly well imbued, before leaving China, with the Chinese concept of family and of the role of women. Their quest for a bride generally conformed to the age-old pattern of getting their family elders to find a mate for them through a go-between or matchmaker.[5]

Concession was made to Westernization by having the man look over the prospective candidates for a wife. Sometimes it was prearranged that the girl walk through a certain street at an appointed time, and the matchmaker would point out the girl to the man. The most common arrangement was to have the man and girl meet in a teahouse in the presence of matchmaker and chaperones. If the man was favorably impressed by the girl, he would ask for a second and possibly subsequent meetings. Then he would ask the girl a few questions and elicit a few demure replies. Any proposal was made indirectly through the matchmaker or go-between.

A prospective husband from the United States was a much sought-after prize, and young and educated girls vied to marry a "guest of the Mountain of Gold." The man would be in holiday dress. No doubt he had saved and scrimped for many years for this important event, so he had money to spend. The magic word "America," however, was the attraction, and the man was the key that could open the gates to the land of gold. It seemed insignificant at the time to the girl that the man's background might be totally dissimilar to her own or that the man might be twenty, thirty, or even forty years older than she.

From the man's point of view, it flattered his ego to be able to marry a young, educated, and even pretty bride. In the atmosphere of Hong Kong, where women were plentiful and eager, the man chose his mate mainly on the basis of these attributes.

[5] The extent of arranged marriages among Chinese families in the United States is evident from a study made by Yuan Liang for his M.A. thesis from the University of Chicago in 1951, titled "The Chinese Family in Chicago."

Choice of Marital Partner	*Number of Families*
Own choice	20
Own choice with parental consent	23
Parent's choice with child's consent	13
Mostly parent's choice & matchmaker	11
Solely parent's choice & matchmaker	13
Total	80

Within the short span of a month or two or three, the couple would be married. The man would return to the United States and immediately file application for his bride's visa. This, in brief, is the way most of these trans-Pacific marriages were effected. Bride and groom hardly knew each other, but at least they had met and married by choice.

For the wives of the mutilated families and the brides of the trans-Pacific marriages the initial reaction upon arrival in the United States is shock. They are shocked to learn that the husband must wash other people's dirty shirts or prepare other people's meals to earn a living. They are shocked if the family living quarters are behind the laundry, above the restaurant, or in the crowded, dilapidated quarters of Chinatown. They are shocked at the heavy load of work both husband and wife must do. Separated suddenly from their family and friends and catapulted by jet from an Oriental environment to an Occidental one, they are confronted with the compound problem of accommodation and adjustment to their husbands and to their new life. The rainbow they had conjured up in their minds based on popular misconception of the United States vanishes, and their disillusionment is great.

Accustomed to a life of comparative ease made possible by the favorable rate of exchange from remittances and having enjoyed a modicum of social standing from their economic position, the wives of the once-mutilated families find life in the United States distasteful. They lament the absence of servants and leisure. They miss the mah-jong games and shopping sprees. In China, they held the purse strings and spent their remittances as they saw fit. Now their husbands control the family finances, and the wives find this restrictive.

Many of the wives had been separated from their husbands for as many as fifteen to twenty years. The young men they had married are now pot-bellied and bald, and they totter around the house in baggy pants and slippers. Most of the men are equally disillusioned. They left behind them blushing young brides, and their recollection of their wives remained unchanged until the wives step off the airplane in the United States. I was witness to reunion of a couple in their fifties at the Kennedy International Airport in New York. Husband and wife had not seen each other for more than thirty years. The couple had a grown son and grandchildren, and this was the bond that held them together.

When we met the wife at the airport, I saw a withered old woman with her hair tied up in a thin knot. The husband beside me gasped when he saw her. "How come she looks like that?" he asked. He turned almost as if looking for an escape. Then he repeated, "How come she looks like that?" One could see that his anguish was acute, but today, more than ten years later, this couple has kept their marriage intact. Each has accepted the other for what he or she is.

These older marriages, having survived the initial shock, generally settle into fairly comfortable arrangements in which both partners try to make the best of things. They are too deeply ingrained with family name and obligation, so that for one to forsake the other for personal happiness is uncommon.

The marriages that are undergoing the greatest strains are the more recent trans-Pacific unions characterized by a wide disparity in age, level of education, and upbringing between the partners. Men in their 30's and 40's with brides of 18 to 22 are very common. An extreme case was a laundryman in my neighborhood. He was 62. Having lost all trace of his first wife and children during the Sino-Japanese War, he went to Hong Kong after V-J Day and married an 18-year-old beauty. She accepted him because her family was poor. As a bride price, he had purchased for the girl's family a building in Hong Kong from which they could collect rent. The prospect of coming to the United States also influenced the girl's decision.

In Hong Kong, the man seemed affluent enough. In the United States, she discovered that he was a mere laundryman. She was eager to learn the language and wanted to go to school. He felt that there was no need for her to learn English. "I brought you here to work," he shouted at her one day, "not to go to school."

The differences between the old man and the young girl were much too great. The wife was very pretty, and she attracted the attention of other men who felt sorry for her. The old man was obstinate and unreasonable. A break-up was inevitable. One day the wife disappeared. The husband sold his laundry and his house in New York and retired to Hong Kong. The last I heard about him was that he had married another young girl.

The next time I went with my laundry into the shop, I met the new owner. He had youthful features, but his hair was entirely gray. I surmised that he was in his mid-fifties.

"Come in, come in," he greeted me. "Do you live around here? I want you to meet my wife, who has just arrived from China. She doesn't speak English. If it isn't too much trouble perhaps you can help her get around a little bit."

He led me into their living quarters in back of the laundry and introduced me to his wife. I must have gaped in disbelief. She, too, was a pretty young thing.

Rose Hum Lee found a surprisingly high divorce rate of 8.5 percent among the Chinese in the San Francisco Bay Area.[6]

In conversation with a practicing attorney in New York's Chinatown, I learned that the rate of divorce is fairly high in these trans-Pacific marriages.

"Usually it is the wife who initiates action for divorce," said Gene Chu. The girls from Hong Kong today are extremely modern. They are not like the old-fashioned wives from the villages. These modern girls are educated, and their ideas about the family and female status are quite Westernized. American movies and the urban influences of a city like Hong Kong have distorted their views about the United States.

"In China there is a saying for the women, 'Marry a chicken, follow the chicken. Marry a dog, live like a dog.' Modern Chinese women today don't subscribe to this. They want pretty clothes and a nice place to live. Most of all, they expect romantic attention from their husbands."

On the other hand, the men are quite out of tune with the changes that have taken place in China and in Hong Kong. They have retained their ideas about the family and the role of a wife as they knew them when they left China. They are wary about marrying American-born Chinese girls, thinking they are spendthrifts and too independent. They expect that one from China will be subservient, docile, obedient, and content to serve the husband and produce sons. They are stunned when events prove otherwise.

[6] "Established Chinese Families in the San Francisco Bay Area," *Midwest Sociologist* (December, 1957), pp. 19–26.

One wife gave her husband an ultimatum: "Move out of this dilapidated apartment by Tuesday or I get a divorce." Another woman sat in a television shop and refused to budge until her husband had purchased the set she wanted. Some use the man as an unwitting tool to effect entry into the United States. The schemer marries the man in Hong Kong and lives with him for a month or two. The husband returns to the United States and arranges for his wife to join him. Equipped with visa and passage, the woman comes to the United States but not to her newly wedded husband. By prearrangement with a former lover or some other person, she leaves her husband waiting in vain for a wife who will never show up.

The men, too, find themselves beset with ambivalent feelings about their marriage partners. On the one hand, they were brought up with a deep sense of family obligations, and their attitudes toward wifehood are predicated upon the satisfactory performance of the wife's role as a mother and manager of the household. On the other hand, they cannot help being influenced by the more glamorous and romantic notions of a wife as an alluring, attractive companion such as those depicted in films, in the press, and on television.

In the days of bygone China, these problems had been resolved by keeping the wife in her place in the home and compensating her with permanent status and standing. Socially acceptable outlets were provided for man's polygamous nature, so that in the institution of concubinage, the man could choose a second mate for her allure, or he could satisfy himself without being furtive in his visits to the sing-song girls in the tea or wine houses. But in Western culture, these outlets are denied the men, creating their share of unresolved frustrations.

The reunion of long-separated families, an almost mass importation of brides from Hong Kong, and the roles brought on by cultural differences created many unusual situations in the establishment of families among the Chinese in the United States. By and large, however, the Chinese are still imbued with some vestige of the traditional customs and attitudes regarding the family, and they look upon its continuity as their primary obligation.

In spite of the stresses and strains borne by both husband and wife in the transition, the Chinese family usually remains intact. Discord and unhappiness are generally turned inward toward the self and are reflected in a higher suicide rate rather than in divorce statistics. The suicide rate among the Chinese in San Francisco is four times greater than that for the city as a whole, and it is predominantly the women who decide to end it all. Suicide has been the traditional form of protest for Chinese women who find life unbearable within their matrimonial bonds.

The divorce rate is also kept low in that some wives are not sophisticated enough to seek a legal severance of their marriage. They merely run away and form another union by the *de facto* act of cohabitation.

As mentioned previously, China-born men are prejudiced against native-born women as wives, and the feeling is mutual. Conversely though, many American-born men have taken China-born brides from sheer necessity, since intermarriage or bachelorhood were the alternatives. These marriages present their peculiar set of problems, chief among them the barrier of language and the differences in cultural background. But in general, American-born men, brought up with a different attitude toward women, are more considerate and more accommodating, so that these marriages on the whole are happier than ones in which the husband is China-born and the wife is Americanized. When both spouses are native-born, the family pattern approximates the American norm.

With such a variety of factors influencing the family among the Chinese in the United States, the structure, the hierarchy, and the pattern of living vary accordingly. Rarely does one find the extended kinship family operating as a unit within the same abode. The family pattern is conjugal, consisting of husband, wife, and children, and occasionally aged parents.

In the strictly first-generation family, the father is the undisputed head of the household. He makes the decisions, manages the finances, and expects unquestioned obedience from both his wife and children. If the wife and children are recent arrivals from China, but the father has lived in this country for some years, he is their contact and link with the outside world. Though his English be broken and his knowledge of American ways shallow, still the family is entirely dependent upon him in such daily occurrences as going to the store for food and clothing. As their dependence upon the father is great, his authority is respected.

The wife, to all appearances, occupies a subordinate position to her husband. But the scarcity of women and the fact that the main livelihood of the Chinese is small service enterprises in which the wife is also a working partner, she quickly assumes a status higher than her traditional role in China. Her share in keeping the family unit going is invariably greater than her husband's, for she is also expected to assume the entire burden of housekeeping and child-rearing as well as help in the family business. The wife is usually the first to rise in the morning, and she will be rinsing diapers and mopping floors long after the labors of the husband have ceased. It follows then that the women will be given a greater voice in making the decisions that affect the family. The husband may hold the purse, but more likely than not, the wife will decide how its contents will be spent.

In Yu-Chen Liu's study of the Chinese in Portland, Oregon, there was substantial agreement among the respondents, including the wives, that authority should be vested in the head of the family (meaning the husband), but in specific instances where major family questions were to be decided, 13 out of the 23 wives conceded that they made most of the decisions.[7]

In the story of *Chinatown Family* by Lin Yutang, Mrs. Fong is an excellent portrayal of the typical Chinese woman migrated from China. For ten years, Mr. Fong lived in a dingy laundry in a basement where each day had been a repetition of the preceding one in monotonous procession until Mrs. Fong's arrival. With a few feminine touches, she managed to transform the laundry into a warm and cozy home.

Mrs. Fong did not want her husband to stay in the laundry business. She preferred operating a restaurant instead. The idea was never put into words outright. It was merely suggested once or twice, but under her direction, the activities of the whole family became geared to this purpose.

[7] Yu-Chen Liu, "Interaction Within Chinese-American Families in Portland, Oregon, Resulting from Cultural Differences," unpublished Ph.D. Dissertation (Oregon State College, 1951), p. 288.

Nyuk Tsin Kee, an illiterate peasant woman of James Michener's novel *Hawaii*, is another excellent characterization of the influential behind-the-scenes role that Chinese women play. The husband had contracted leprosy and was banished to Kalawao, a leper colony whose inmates were abandoned to their own resources against the elements and the lawlessness of the doomed survivors. For most lepers, the banishment was tantamount to a death sentence. Of her own free will, Mrs. Kee chose to accompany her husband to Kalawao. To defend her own honor against the lepers, Mrs. Kee had to kill the bully who terrorized the colony. As a result, she was feared and respected.

After the inevitable death of her husband, Mrs. Kee left the leper colony when medical examinations showed that she had not contracted the disease. She returned to Honolulu to reclaim her five sons whom she had left in the care of good Samaritan Hawaiians. By sheer hard work, resourcefulness, endurance, and innate intelligence, Mrs. Kee put them through school and endowed them with qualities that enabled them to become a financial *tour de force* on the Islands.

With the exception of the highly educated or the more modern city-reared girls, the China-born wife is more reserved, more reticent in her relationship with her husband. She remains in the background. She does not accompany her husband to Chinatown unless it is a family outing. She does not hire a baby sitter so that she can take in a movie with her spouse. All the children go along too. There are few expressions of intimacy between husband and wife in front of the children. The parents must be dignified in composure and behavior to command respect from their children.

Among the older couples, the husband does not refer to his wife by name, and the same is true with the wife. They may not address each other directly until after the arrival of the first-born. Then husband and wife are known to each other as "So-and-so's father" or "So-and-so's mother," inserting the name of the first-born.

To strangers, the husband will introduce his wife as my "inside person" or "my woman." Sometimes she is not introduced at all. She may be in the same room pouring tea for guests, but her presence may be ignored.

In her dress and behavior toward her husband, the China-born wife makes little display of sexual attraction. Their marital life is confined to the privacy of their bedroom. Rarely does one see a Chinese man kiss his wife in public. Even with native-born girls, any demonstration of affections or emotions is inhibited because of their upbringing and family influence.

A wife who is more Chinese-oriented will make do with the basic necessities, considering it her primary duty to be thrifty. One with Western ideals wants a decent home and furnishings. She wants to keep up with the fashions, and she dresses to be attractive for herself and her husband. The China-born woman, once married, feels that her position as wife is secure and that there is no need to bid for her husband's attention by decking out in fineries and frills.

The native-born or more Westernized Chinese wives have adopted many of the American ways, but they also retain a large measure of the Chinese ways.

In the United States, marriage is for the fulfillment of man and woman. Evidence of this is seen in the fact that in 1950, 48.3 percent of all American families had no children under 18 years of age although this percentage dropped to 43 percent in 1960. In China, marriage is for the procreation of children, and the family is the post-natal womb that cushions and protects the child, nourishing him into adulthood.

In English a common form of salutation is "good luck." In Chinese, one says, "May you be blessed with many sons." According to the old Chinese scale of values, a man's stature rose in direct proportion to the number of sons he sired, and a woman's status was naught until she had produced a son. The more sons, the better, because sons meant the continuation of the family line and the assurance of honor, respect, and support in old age.

Although this traditional desire for many children has been filtered through the sieve of Westernization, the size of Chinese families in the United States is larger than the American.

In a study of 181 Chinese-American families, Beulah Ong Kwoh found that when both parents were born in China, the median number of children in the family was 6.2. When both parents were born in the States, the family averaged only 3.2 children. Taken together, the median number of children per family was 5.5. Among the 181 families, 17 had eight children, 12 had nine children, 4 had ten, 1 family had eleven, and another had an even dozen.

Other researchers who have made surveys of Chinese families in different parts of the United States have come up with varying averages of the size of the Chinese-American family. Homer Loh's study of 81 Chinese families in Philadelphia showed the average number of children per family to be 4.7. In her research of the New York Chinatown area, Ching Ho Liu found the average number of children in the families of Chinese children surveyed to be 4.4, compared to 2.89 in the Caucasian families. In data secured from interviews and study of another 50 families in Portland, Oregon, Yu-chen Liu did not average out the number of children per family, but in several of her case histories, there were families that had eight to ten children. But then, some had only two.

Rose Hum Lee wrote that after the turn of the century, first-generation Chinese families averaged 6.4 persons per family whereas native-born Chinese families averaged 4.5 persons. This was a decrease of two persons per family in one generation. As Americanization proceeds, the size of the Chinese family shrinks. Still, it is larger than the American average of 3.65 members per family.

In the strictly Chinese family, the parent-child relationship predominates over the husband-wife ties. The family is geared to raising the child. In turn, the child owes total commitment to the parents. Filial piety or loyal devotion to the parents is the primary commandment to all Chinese no matter how old an offspring may be, no matter how exalted a position he may hold, or how large a family he, himself, may sire. The son's first obligation is to his parents. The daughter's first obligation is to her husband's parents.

A story that best illustrates the order of familial obligation is about a man who did not have enough food to feed his family—a wife, a son, and an aged mother. There was only enough food to keep three persons alive until the harvesting of the next crop. If the meager rations were further divided, the entire family would perish. The man came to the agonizing decision that he must kill his son to preserve the family. He consoled his wife by saying, "We can always have another son, but I can never have another mother."

When he went out to dig his son's grave, his spade uncovered a pot of gold placed there by the gods who rewarded him for his filial devotion.

In the small, tightly knit American family, the child completely identifies with his parents until he attains maturity. A close, warm relationship is encouraged between parent and child, but when the child is about to enter the adult world or when he forms his own conjugal family, he is admonished to cut loose from his mother's apron strings. Leave your parents and cleave unto your wife, says the Bible. Marriage counselors condemn interfering in-laws, and wife or husband is advised to establish primary rapport with the spouse.

This abrupt about-face is a negation of the offspring's life experiences up to that point, whereas there is continuity for the Chinese offspring. A man considers his mother's wishes above that of his wife's, and instances of the man ordered to beat his wife because she was irreverent or disobedient to his parents are quite common in Chinese folklore.

In families where parents and wife lived under one roof, the man sent his remittances from the United States not to his wife, but to his parents, and they would dole out an allowance to the wife. In turn the same honor, obedience, and sacrifice were exacted from one's own children. Parental authority was absolute. The parents commanded and the children obeyed. Children were not consulted about things that affected their lives. They were just told what to do. No back talk was tolerated. To a large extent, strict parental authority persists in the Chinese-American family.

In two delightful autobiographies by Chinese-Americans, *Fifth Chinese Daughter* by Jade Snow Wong and *Father and Glorious Descendant* by Pardee Lowe, the authors tell what parental authority meant in their lives. Jade Snow Wong said that even at the tender age of five she had learned the meaning of discipline without understanding the necessity for it. "A little girl never questioned the commands of Mother and Father, unless prepared to receive painful consequences."

Pardee Lowe wrote of his mother: "She knew only too well how to wield the wrong end of a pliant bamboo duster. With this Rod of

Purification, she directed our lives, and we became, as our Chinese friends put it, 'model children who had partaken generously of parental instruction.' "

When Chinese children misbehave, the children themselves are not blamed. Onlookers do not say, "What naughty children!" Rather, they say, *"Mo kao fen"* or literally "no training." In other words, the parents are to blame. They have been derelict in their duty toward their children.

Discipline is strict and punishment immediate in the Chinese household. Most Chinese parents never heard about the psychological theories of indelible scars left on a child's personality from corporal punishment. As Jade Snow Wong relates of her childhood, "Teaching and whipping were almost synonymous." Harold Lui sums up his childhood experiences with these words: "There was never any question of right or wrong. If my parents disapproved, it was wrong."

The Chinese child is taught that when he does wrong, it is not a personal matter between himself and his conscience; he brings dishonor and shame upon his family and his loved ones. They, too, share in the disgrace and must make amends to repair the family honor. In an incident described in *Coronet* magazine, a small Chinese boy accidentally cracked a barbershop window playing ball. Of course, the boy's father paid for the window and apologized for his son's carelessness, but the very next day, the barbershop had an unusual number of Chinese customers. Word of the family embarrassment had spread to the boy's relatives, and they came from all parts of the city to make amends by patronizing the barbershop.[8]

Much misinformation has been printed about the upbringing of Chinese-American children. Take the letter that was printed in Frances Story's column in *Newsday*, a Long Island, New York, daily, that read:

> Chinese children are ruled through love and affection, not fear. . . . Spankings for the little ones, corporal punishment for the older children are practically unknown. Emphasis is on making the child feel loved, protected and appreciated. Parents

[8] Conniff, J.C.G. "Our Amazing Chinese Kids," *Coronet* (December, 1955), pp. 31–36.

do not exact obedience, but they set a good example. What's more, absentee fathers are almost non-existent. . . .

From the experience of Jade Snow Wong, Pardee Lowe, Harold Lui, and myself as well as those of hundreds of families that I am personally acquainted with, nothing could be further from an accurate description of the Chinese-American child's upbringing than these assumed Freudian and Geselian ideals.

A Chinese baby may be cuddled and fondled, showered with kisses, and rocked to sleep in his mother's arms, but as the child grows older, the mother gradually withdraws her expressions of love. She refrains from hugging or kissing him. She rations her words of endearment or consolation, shoving him firmly toward independence and maturity. Emulation of adult behavior is encouraged. The mother does not invite confidences or direct talks and discussions. She commands and decides what is best for the children, and the children are expected to obey. Disobedience is not tolerated and corporal punishment is freely meted out.

The father is even more distant from his children. His work may keep him away during the day, but as most Chinese families in the United States operate small service enterprises, the likelihood is that home and business are in the same place. If the father clings to the old Chinese tradition, he may be all the more strict with his children for fear that American influence may diminish the effect of his teachings.

In his doctoral dissertation, Milton Barnett wrote this description of the Chinese father:

> In his relations with other members of the conjugal group [the father] holds a position of superordination. His authority ought not be (and seldom is) questioned. He expects obedience from his wife and children. He is the purveyor of advice, the disciplinarian, and conversely, is held responsible in the community for the conduct of his children. . . .
>
> In practice, however, this description does not hold up. The Cantonese family head in New York is too involved making a living to carry out the obligations, and for that matter, even the privileges derived from his father status. The long hours devoted

> to work and the possibility of having to live away from home during the work week limit contacts with his children. In this respect, there is no differentiation to be made between worker and business man. Men in both categories keep the same hours. . . . Unlike the village situation where the family members all participated in the economic enterprise, farming, business enterprise in modern urban America does not encourage maintenance of the family as an economic unit. The circumscribed nature of most Chinese businesses does not reward concerted family cooperation.
>
> . . . Many are the complaints that the fathers are too involved in business affairs to spend time with or pay attention to their children.
>
> Even the dinner meal, when the family group has congregated, will be skipped by the father who eats instead with his employers or co-workers. Fathers are described as cold, unreceptive and undemonstrative. The absentee or quasi-absentee father tends to insist, all the more, that others reciprocate toward him in a manner more befitting the ideal definition of the subordinate child status.[9]

Chinese parents think they can maintain their authority if they are careful to keep a certain distance from their children. I once went to the airport to meet a relative arriving from China who had been separated from her mother for more than ten years. When the mother came to the States, she had to leave her daughter behind because she could not obtain a visa for the girl. The day the mother set foot in this country, she had worked with singleness of purpose to be reunited with her daughter.

At long last, the daughter was granted a visa. On the day of her arrival, I went with the mother and an American friend to meet the plane. We were witness to the mother-daughter reunion after ten long years of separation. When she came up to her mother the daughter greeted her with one word: "Ma." The mother smiled and replied, "You have come." All around us people were hugging and

[9] Milton Barnett, "Alcohol and Culture: A Study of Drinking in a Chinese-American Community," unpublished Ph.D. Dissertation (Cornell University, 1953), pp. 244–246.

kissing each other, squealing with joy and delight. The contrast caused our American friend to nudge me and whisper more in the tone of a question than a remark, "Isn't she thrilled to be reunited with her daughter?"

No one denies that parental love is universally intense and enduring, but Chinese parents tend to stand aloof from their children lest their children lose respect for them. To maintain this respect, Chinese mothers and fathers discourage the warm and intimate relationship idealized in American families. The father never tries to be a friend to his son, nor the mother a big sister to her daughter. There is never the informal comradeship or intense emotional feeling between the Chinese parent and child as there is in American homes. A parent is the authority that demands obedience, and authority must maintain its dignity.

One writer, Hwuy Ung, was very critical of this autocratic parent-child relationship in his book, *A Chinaman's Opinion of Us.* He wrote: "With us, a father is god; his children his slaves. . . . The obedient mind of a son would not be that of a slave, but of one who freely yields it in a sense of justice and a feeling of affection."

Miss Ching Ho Liu, disagreeing with Hwuy Ung, defends her opinion in her dissertation titled "The Influence of Cultural Background on the Moral Judgment of Children." Miss Liu writes: "Filial piety involves love and identification with the parents. With love and identification, one obeys; at the same time, one may have the inner freedom which eliminates fear and apprehension. If one is not fearful, one is free to think and act without subservience to rules and regulations."

In her study of 52 Chinese and 52 Caucasian children at Public School 23 in New York's Chinatown, all the school teachers remarked that the Chinese children are better behaved, more obedient, and more self-reliant. She discovered that corporal punishment was used freely, and it was usually the mother who meted out the punishment.

It was her contention that "The Chinese children are given more responsibilities and less freedom of action. But in spite of a more limited sphere of outer freedom, the children actually learn how to behave within the limited framework, and with more responsibilities they seem to develop a more mature concept of normative judgment.

It might also be conjectured that the child's somewhat restricted daily routine makes it easier for him to become familiar with a norm of action."

One phase of filial piety generally lost in the parents' emphasis on exacting obedience and respect is that for the child to develop character and virtues, the parents must, of necessity, be the primary models. To demand that the child be industrious, the parents cannot be shiftless. To command respect, the parents must deport themselves accordingly. How many times have parents refrained from infractions because of their youngsters' eyes trained upon them?

Character building is also a continuous experience. In the United States when little tots are bounced on their mothers' knees, they are taught nursery rhymes like "The Cow Jumped over the Moon," "Little Boy Blue," "The Owl and the Pussy Cat," and other fanciful ditties. Upon examining an American first-grade reader, one is apt to find a text like this:

> John and Jane live in the city.
> John and Jane live in a house.
> The house is on Maple Street.
> John and Jane like to live in the city.

In so far as I can remember, my Chinese readers were always used as a vehicle for moral training. My son's first primer starts out with these two lessons:

> At home I obey my parents.
> At school I obey my teachers.
> In school
> Respect the teacher
> Love your schoolmates.

Ballads and songs sung to children are more akin in theme to Aesop's Fables or to fairy tales like *Cinderella* and *Beauty and the Beast*, in which the wicked are punished and the good rewarded. The upbringing of a Chinese child is geared to a larger extent upon character building, both at home and in the school. He is taught that forbearance, patience, and sacrifice are virtues and that self-interest must be subordinated to the larger good, whereas the American child is encouraged to give free expression to his own personality in a very permissive atmosphere.

In sum, the parents will provide the children with a strong moral base, but for answers to specific problems such as: What courses should I take in high school? How am I going to get permission to go on the moonlight cruise? How can I get a suede jacket like the one Fred has? Should I get my military service over with first, or should I wait until I am called? Chinese-American children must seek their own solutions and make their own decisions, with the older children blazing the trail and smoothing the path for the younger ones to follow. As a rule, if the parents were strict in forbidding the oldest daughter to date a young man without being engaged to him, they will have yielded considerably by the time dating becomes an issue with the younger girls.

The normal Chinese-American child brought up in the United States may be expected to chafe under the strict discipline imposed upon him, not so much because he is restricted but mainly because he has a comparison in his American friends. He sees an easy informal relationship between American parents and their children. He sees their permissive attitude. And like all little boys and girls, he is apt to wonder: "If Johnny can do it, why can't I?"

But conflict generally does not arise until the child is aware of the difference, usually when he is thirteen to fourteen years of age. At this age he visits the homes of his schoolmates. The world of books unfold to him. Movies, television, magazines, and newspapers extol the romanticism of boy-meets-girl, leisure-time fun, hobbies, fashions, comradeship between father and son, the satisfying warmth of a mother who is kind, understanding, and gentle instead of one who is stern, distant, and old-fashioned.

The child opens his eyes and sees two people different from the parents whom he was taught to obey and look up to without question. He sees them perhaps as uneducated, unable to speak the English language fluently, working at lowly manual labor, stubbornly clinging to traditions they knew in China, and unwilling to adopt the modern viewpoint. He is even a little ashamed of them.

This is a trying period for the Chinese boy and girl, coming at a time of adolescence when physical changes compound the problem to cause much unhappiness. In their autobiographies, both Jade Snow Wong and Pardee Lowe wrote of their adolescent rebellions against parental authority, and I dare say it is common to most second-generation Chinese-Americans.

A young girl wants to go to a dance sponsored by the church (no such extreme as a school dance, a night club, or a dance hall). The parents forbid it because they consider it immoral and unmaidenly for a young girl to allow herself to be held in a man's arms in a public place. A young lad wants to go on a camping trip with his schoolmates. He is not allowed to go because he is needed at home, and camping is considered idle play. A young man must learn to be industrious. Sister would dearly love to have that cute little frock in the store window, but she dares not ask her parents for the money. They will say her home-made dresses give her the warmth and protective covering required of clothes. Styles and frills are immodest and unnecessary. Older brother wants to buy a car. Heaven have mercy! Has this son been raised to be a spendthrift?

These are typical differences of opinion between parents and child, each grounded in his cultural background. The parents feel that their culture and their teachings are being threatened, undermined, and replaced by demoralizing behavior which, in the Americanized eyes of the child is perfectly innocuous and normal.

The child in disagreement with his parents will at first try reasoning with them, but the parents, shocked that their decisions are being questioned, refuse to listen. Here, again, another barrier prevents full communication and lucid explanation. The child, though he may speak enough Chinese to be able to understand the ordinary expressions used in everyday living, cannot express himself clearly when it comes to phrasing principles and ideas. He flounders and thrashes about, knowing well in his mind what he wants to say in English but finding himself at a total loss when he must express the same idea in Chinese.

The recourses opened to the child are to submit to his parents or defy them, but his defiance is tempered by the disciplined life he has led, and he must decide whether the issue is important enough for him to rebel. As pointed out previously, the Chinese child scores high in moral judgment, and when his rebellion is well-aimed, the parents gradually yield their ground.

An example is seen in the case of Mei-fang, who wanted to go to college. Her father opposed on the grounds that girls do not need a college education. Besides, he was getting old, and it was his duty to see that Mei-fang was entrusted to the care of a husband. Believing he was acting in her best interests, he refused to underwrite any of her expenses if she insisted upon going to college.

But Mei-fang won a scholarship and got an odd job on campus. Seeing he was defeated, the father threatened to disown her if she persisted in disobeying him. The conflict between father and daughter lasted nearly a year, during which time Mei-fang sought the advice of her minister and teachers. Finally convinced that she was doing no wrong in defying her father's wishes, she left for college. The father was enraged, but his anger softened in time. A year later, he was boasting to relatives that his daughter was *in college*.

One type of accommodation between parent and children is described by a third-generation daughter, age 19:

> We conform to many of the Chinese customs in little things such as serving tea with two hands on the cup or saucer, respecting all people older than ourselves, taking small steps and not being boisterous, using certain phrases at certain times, but in the larger things such as marriage and divorce and in the treatment of our own children, we young people refuse to conform.[10]

In more instances than not, as the child matures in outlook he eventually concedes that the parents may not be such ignorant clods after all. In his usual ability to see situations in a humorous light, Mark Twain wrote: "When I was a boy of fourteen, my father was so ignorant I could hardly stand to have the old man around. But when I got to be twenty-one, I was astonished at how much the old man had learned in seven years."

A young bride in Portland, Oregon, learned her lesson the hard way. As is the custom in China, the bride must kowtow and serve tea to her mother-in-law at the wedding feast, at which time the mother-

[10] Norman Haynor and Charles Reynold, "Chinese Family Life in America," *American Sociological Review* (Oct. 1937), pp. 630–637.

in-law places a gift of money wrapped in red paper or a gift of jewelry for her daughter-in-law in the empty cup after she has sipped her tea.

The bride, hoping to make things clear from the very beginning that she was not going to be a subservient daughter-in-law, refused to kowtow or serve the tea. When the guests looked for the tea ceremony, they learned of the bride's refusal. Their immediate reaction was to criticize the bride's parents for failing to teach their daughter the proper manners, and the bride found her husband's relatives turned against her.

Another young lad told me he listens with respect when his parents speak now. Once his opinion of them was that they were work horses, ignorant bumpkins who did not know how to enjoy life. Matriculated at the University of Rochester, Calvin saw his American schoolmates picking up their dates by car and going places on weekends, whereas he usually went home and helped his father and mother in the restaurant. When he broached his parents on getting a secondhand jalopy, they gave him a long lecture on industry and thrift, telling him how he should use his spare time for his studies instead of running around.

For quite a while, Calvin was very unhappy. He moped and complained and even wished a little that he had not been born into a Chinese family. Shortly afterwards, he learned what happened to the boy he envied most. Out on a joy ride with his date and another couple, he had swerved off the road and plowed into a tree. When the broken bodies were brought back to campus, Calvin's eyes were opened to his parents' viewpoint.

In families where the parents are native-born, the parent-child relationship is not so patriarchal or so formal, but neither has it given way to the degree of permissiveness characterized by the American family. Upon reflection, though the parents themselves may have strained at the leash and rebelled against the strong control exerted over them when they were youngsters, they realize in their maturity that children's characters must be molded and their excesses restrained. Thus they are prone to be more strict than lenient. They demand respect but not unquestioned obedience. They seek a warm rapport with their children, with the inevitable loss of some dignity and authority.

Each year, while more than a million youths find their way into trouble with the law, American authorities, school officials, parents, law-enforcement agencies, and scientists have noted the conspicuous absence of Chinese children among the offenders. A municipal judge of New York City wrote to *The New York Times* to say that not in seventeen years on the bench had a Chinese teen-ager been brought before him on delinquency charges. The judge queried his colleagues and found that they, too, had never seen a Chinese teen-ager hailed before their court on any charges of depredation, narcotics, speeding, burglary, vandalism, stick-up, purse-snatching, or mugging.

Astonished by their own discovery, they checked with Chicago and San Francisco, where the judges confirmed their findings.[11] In further substantiation of the low incidence of juvenile delinquency among Chinese children, the Juvenile Aid Bureau of New York City reports that in 17,000 cases handled by the Bureau, only 12 involved Chinese, and these were for minor infractions such as marking a wall with chalk.[12]

In two school districts of Portland, Ore., and Seattle, Wash., where 71 to 90 percent of the students were Chinese, the rate of juvenile delinquency was markedly below that of adjacent areas.[13] A study undertaken by the California State Department of Correction revealed that out of 1,600 youth under custody, only one was Chinese-American.[14]

This commendable record brought praise by Congressman Arthur Klein of New York who read it into the *Congressional Record* on July 29, 1955.

Why do the Chinese children not succumb to the same evil influences that tempt their schoolmates and playmates? Why are they not affected by the same environmental forces that lead American youth astray? What factors in the Chinese upbringing enable parents to nurture their children into upright, law-abiding youths?

In probing into the backgrounds of Chinese children, social scien-

[11] "Why No Chinese-American Delinquents?" *Saturday Evening Post* (April 30, 1955), p. 12.

[12] Barnett, *op. cit.*, p. 215.

[13] Haynor and Reynold, *op. cit.*, p. 636.

[14] Alvin Rudoff, "A Study by the California State Dept. of Correction," Sacramento, California.

tists found that the more common causes of anti-social behavior do not apply. Chinese children have more than their share of crowded, antiquated living quarters in Chinatown or in the cheaper rental areas of large cities. As a visible minority group they suffer economic and social discrimination. As marginal individuals, they straddle the fence between two cultures with resulting personal and cultural conflicts. With the majority of Chinese, the family income is never sufficient to cover the increasing needs of large broods. In families that were mutilated, the mothers and sisters lived in China while the fathers were both parents to the sons.

Certainly the lot of the Goon family of Portland, Maine, was not an easy one. In 1940 Mr. Goon died, leaving his widow with eight children and a small hand laundry. By dint of toil, courage, and endurance, Mrs. Toy Lien Goon raised her family. In 1952, in recognition of the success of her efforts, she was chosen America's Mother of the Year. She went to Washington, D.C., to accept her title from Mrs. Truman. At that time, her eldest son was a doctor. The second son operated a radio and television store. The third son was studying law at Boston University. The fourth son was graduated from MIT and was teaching in Troy, New York. Her fifth son was in the Navy. Of her three daughters, the eldest was married and employed by the federal government. The second daughter helped her mother at home while preparing to go to college that fall. The youngest daughter was still in high school continuing in the footsteps of her brothers and sisters by maintaining a straight-A average.

In a *Reader's Digest* article of March, 1944, T. E. Murphy describes a Hartford, Connecticut, family. To shield their brood of nine children from mocking, name-calling rowdies ganging up on them, Goon Mah and Wong Shee had to move from San Francisco to Boston to Hartford, where they finally found they could live in peace and harmony with their neighbors. The Mahs, too, operated a small hand laundry. The family income was always low, and the parents worked long, hard hours to keep the children clothed and fed. At the time the article was written, the oldest son, George, had almost finished his work for a Ph.D. in organic chemistry at MIT when he was called into the military service of his country. The two oldest daughters, Gladys and Margaret, were trained nurses. Kenneth was in the Army

Air Force. Harold was working his way through pre-medical school at the University of Chicago. Alice held a responsible position in a war industry. May helped her father in his business, and the two youngest boys, still in high school, had newspaper routes.

Although a large share of the credit for the low incidence of juvenile delinquency among the Chinese may be attributed to the family within the context of the old Chinese culture—the Chinese child learning early to respect authority and operate within the acceptable standards of society—there are other contributing factors. Until the recent liberalization of the immigration laws, there were few Chinese families and consequently few Chinese youths. As was pointed out in an earlier chapter, the Chinese kept to themselves and lived under their own code of rules and regulations. Any deviant behavior was handled within the community by the family elders, and the parents were called to task if the children got into trouble. A silver-haired lady who had already passed the half-century mark in age made this point doubly clear when she explained, "Even if I, at my age, did something wrong and got in the courts, Chinese people would be asking, 'Who's daughter is she?' "

The children were always kept busy. About a fourth of the children in the vicinity of New York's Chinatown attend Chinese school following American school from 5 to 7 P.M. daily. Homework and chores leave little time for mischief-making. Another cultural heritage—the Chinese love of learning and respect for scholarship—causes the parents to spur their children on to higher academic achievement. Therefore children have to work harder at their studies.

The Chinese go to great lengths to keep their "dirty linen" within the family walls. They regard it as a serious loss of face when the parents cannot keep an offspring in line or if a family quarrel becomes publicly known. Aunts and uncles, brothers and sisters, cousins and even distant kin exert great pressure upon the party or parties to adjust their differences or mend their ways. Even when trouble in a family is common knowledge throughout the Chinese community, there is a great deal of reluctance to reveal it to outsiders.

In recent years, however, evidence of creeping pre-juvenile delinquency behavior has become apparent. At the first, the Chinese dismissed the incidences and refused to believe their ears. "Impossible," they said. "Not our children." If they were concerned, they went home and tried to keep a tighter rein on their offspring by more stringent rules and sterner punishment, but somehow, these methods were not as effective as they used to be.

Increasing reports appeared in the Chinese press about unruly boys, truants, vandals, and gang fights in the Chinatowns of Honolulu, San Francisco, and New York. At teen-age dances the boys come in groups, dressed in tight levis, sporting Beatle hairdos, and toting their own beer supply. The skirts of their chicks are halfway up their thighs. It is hard to believe that these are Chinese boys and girls although they are no different from American boys and girls their own age.

An extensive survey was published by the Community Service Society in 1962. Written by Stuart Cattell, an anthropologist who had made a two-year survey of the health, welfare, and social organization of New York's Chinatown, the survey was supposed to determine whether the facilities of the welfare agency could best be utilized elsewhere in the city. Instead of curtailing its services, Mr. Cattell's report resulted in the Community Service Society expanding its operations and establishing a Chinatown branch. A synopsis of the report appeared in *The New York Times* and the *New York Herald Tribune,* bringing to public attention that festering problems beneath the surface threatened to erupt into problems of larger proportions.

"Incredible," I protested to Stuart Cattell. "Your sample is invalid. You are using information taken only from the files of those who have come to you for help. It's like counting the number of sick by the number of patients in the doctor's office."

"The very fact that there are patients in the doctor's office speaks for itself. Why do you and the rest of the Chinatown leaders with whom I have spoken refuse to accept the findings of this survey?" retorted Mr. Cattell. "I know. You don't want it to be true. You hope it isn't true. But hiding your head in the sand is not going to help matters.

"What makes you think that Chinese youth, exposed to the process of Americanization and the conflicting values of East and West can escape what the Irish children went through, what the Italian children went through, and what the Puerto Rican and Negro children are going through?

"Yes, the Chinese children have had an excellent record to date because there were so few Chinese youth to speak of, and these were confined to the Chinese community and isolated from the larger American society. Now that there are more Chinese children going through the integration process, some disorganization and demoralization are inevitable. The important thing is to recognize this fact and take steps to cope with the situation."

I sought out Father William Mulcahy of New York's Chinese Transfiguration Catholic Church. Seated at his desk, Father Mulcahy slowly spun around in his swivel chair and gazed wistfully out of the window.

"Four years ago," he drawled, "I do not recall any serious incident of juvenile delinquency involving any Chinese boy or girl. Chinatown was proud of its orderly, obedient, and respectful children. Newspapers and magazines wrote articles about the absence of juvenile delinquency among Chinese youths. Judges and policemen were in consensus about the low incidence of infractions of the law among the Chinese.

"Last Saturday, right across the street from this window, a gang fight took place. Not a fist-fight or squabble as all healthy boys are inclined to engage in; it was more of a gang rumble. A group of young toughs drove by in a car. They jumped out and attacked another group of boys idling in front of that store. The boys, taken by surprise, were badly beaten. The young toughs jumped back into the car and sped away.

"No, you didn't read about it in the papers. The boys who were beaten up were immediately trundled off to their homes. The toughs who sped off had already fled the scene. Sure, everyone knew who they were, but nobody talks."

Father Mulcahy continued, "The Chinese community is undergoing a tremendous upheaval at a rapid pace. The social controls of the old Chinese society are no longer effective. I have worked with the Chinese people practically all of my life both in China and in this country. I speak to them in Chinese. In my ministry here, I have come to devote a greater and greater percentage of my time to family counseling."

The portentous signals were not entirely ignored by the Chinese people. Young professionals and the more dynamic Chinatown organizations are genuinely concerned. For instance, in New York, the Chinatown Planning Council was organized to discuss and formulate plans for dealing with the situation. Among its more energetic members are a psychiatrist, a settlement house social worker, a mental health consultant with the New York City government, a lawyer, a public health nurse, a doctor, and businessmen. The group met with the local police precinct patrol workers, with the Chinese Benevolent Association, and with the *tongs* to get funds and space in the association buildings for recreational activities. Unselfishly, this group of dedicated and highly qualified professionals set up a clinic and offered their services free after their regular working hours to individuals who seem in urgent need of psychiatric aid or counseling.

I asked the group for their comments on the juvenile delinquency problem.

"We really don't have a juvenile delinquency problem yet," said Harold Lui. "What our offenders exhibit today, in the jargon of social work, is pre-delinquency behavior, such as truancy, staying out late at night without parents' permission, hanging around in groups, and getting into bad company.

"I am working on the case of a teen-age boy now. His mother and father called me on the phone and told me what a bad boy he was. 'He doesn't come home,' they wailed. 'He won't listen to us. He plays hookey. You must help him.' "

Harold Lui made an appointment to speak with the boy. When he went to the home address, the father invited Lui to dinner. The bad son, it turned out, was merely starved for someone to identify with. He was at the adolescent stage, trying to free himself from his parents' control and even his sister's maternal ministerings. In Harold Lui he found someone he could look up to and talk with. He was so eager to please and so afraid of incurring Lui's displeasure that he would do almost anything Lui asked of him.

The very fact that the Chinese children are rebelling openly causes much consternation among the parents. The encouraging sign is that the parents are sufficiently concerned about their children's welfare.

Gene Chu, an attorney who was born and raised in New York's Chinatown and who is practicing law there, contends that the social environment is not what it used to be. "Lately I have had a few cases where I had to defend some pretty tough kids in court," he said. They got into trouble fighting some Puerto Rican gangs that came into Chinatown."

Patrolman Mario Frieda sides with these "tough" kids. He looks upon these gang fights in a different light. "They *should* fight back," said he. "I get annoyed when the Chinese children just stand there and take it. Others go to great lengths to avoid a fight. Perhaps if they fought back more often, outside gangs will not come in to bother them." In this respect, Patrolman Frieda's viewpoint reflects his Italian-American background. He has studied sociological and psychological theories of gangs, but he prefers to take the practical and realistic approach to dealing with teen-agers.

Patrolman Frieda works with the Youth Council of the 105th Police Precinct which takes in an area in lower Manhattan covering three to four large minority groups—the Delancey Street section of Jewish immigrants, a large Italian population, all of Chinatown, and a recent influx of Puerto Ricans.

As a member of the Youth Council, Patrolman Frieda arranges sports and social activities for the youth in the area. He gives talks and shows films such as those on drug addiction. He visits schools and makes court appearances. He works with the groups in the Police Athletic League program.

"I have been in police work for thirteen years," said Patrolman Frieda. "In all these years I have not seen the name of a single Orthodox Jew (they are identified by their beards and their skull caps) on the police blotter on a juvenile delinquency charge. The Chinese run a close second. Chinatown is very much concerned about the behavior of the younger generation, a few of whom are playing truant, carrying knives, loitering, shooting off fireworks, and committing petty thievery. But in comparison with other groups it is nothing. The Chinese children are good kids."

The shades of opinion as to whether the Chinese youth will undergo the same demoralizing process as other minority groups on their path to acculturation varies, depending upon whom you speak to. There is consensus, however, that the authoritarian control which the family once exerted over the children has slackened. The garment, the costume-jewelry, the food-packing industries that have sprung up around Chinatowns are taking more and more women out of the homes, and the mother has always been the central figure in the discipline and character molding of the Chinese children.

"It is those Hong Kong teen-agers who have come over here and spoiled our good name," assert the native-born Chinese-Americans. They are the trouble makers. They think they are better than we are and refuse to accept jobs in the restaurants, laundries, and groceries. They are not used to work because their families just cashed the remittance checks sent to Hong Kong by the fathers. They have been living in a polyglot city like Hong Kong, which is not Chinese and not Western.

"They don't do well here in school because they have difficulty with the language, and they can't get decent jobs for the same reason and because of their stuck-up attitudes. They just hang around Chinatown and idle their time away."

There is a large grain of truth to this assertion. The mass of recent immigrants did embark from Hong Kong, where they had been living for many years. Though the population of this Crown Colony is predominantly Chinese, the way of life is cosmopolitan. American influence in recent years has been so great that commonly heard British expressions such as "lift" and "petrol" have given way to "elevator" and "gasoline."

In its commercial dominance in the Far East and in its continuous contacts with the West through the stream of foreign ships that call at the port, Chinese culture has long been diluted in Hong Kong. American movies are especially popular with the Colony's residents, sometimes making their debut overseas before they are seen by American audiences. Impressions of life in the United States are gained largely through these reels of celluloid shot in a world of fantasy and make-believe.

A youth in Hong Kong once begged me to help him come to the

United States. "Do you have a trade?" I asked. "What kind of work can you do? Before you apply you must have a guarantee of a job offer to insure that you do not become a public charge."

In all naïveté, the young man replied, "I want to be a movie star!" Would such a one as he be willing to wash dishes or deliver groceries after he arrived in the United States?

On the other hand, the China-borns blame the native-borns for the disintegration of family discipline. The native-borns are accused of challenging the authority of their elders, of not learning how to speak Chinese, and of being devoid of Chinese culture. The contention is that native-borns are responsible for most of the trouble. A study by Rose Hum Lee, late professor and head of the Department of Sociology at Roosevelt College, titled "Delinquent, Neglected and Dependent Children of the San Francisco Bay Region" and published in the *Journal of Social Psychology* of August 1952, seems to corroborate this.

From information supplied by the Juvenile Court of San Francisco, Professor Lee found that of 170 delinquency charges against children of Chinese ancestry between 1943 and 1949, 145 were committed by native-born males and 18 by native-born females. In comparison, only 5 foreign-born males and 2 foreign-born females had police records against them. However, the figures for this period pre-date and preclude to a large extent the huge influx of teen-agers who immigrated to this country after 1946. Moreover, delinquent behavior was no cause for consternation prior to 1960.

Professor Lee's study revealed that most of these cases resulted from: (1) cultural conflict between parents of foreign or mixed nativity and children of American birth; (2) the fact that most of these children came from broken homes; and (3) the longings of these children for self-expression. The children themselves provided illuminating insight toward a solution to their problems. They confessed that they did not know where to seek guidance, counsel, or sympathetic understanding when they thought their parents had failed them.

My own thoughts are that it is not the nativity but the individual background of the person or family involved. The fact remains that the Chinese family in the United States has undergone modification to reflect, for better or worse, the conditions in this country. In the process, some disorganization is inevitable.

In its new form, the family has shrunk in size. The extended kinship family is rare. Family stability has been shaken up by the peculiar situations created by the reunion of mutilated families and the mass importation of brides. Husband-and-wife relationships have been altered by the freedom and higher status accorded women. Parental authority, once absolute, has been undermined by comparison with more permissive attitudes in American families. Symptoms of the younger generation's protests are showing up in anti-social behavior.

Considering that the Chinese family has been battered by wave after wave of new ideas, the shock of physical transplantation from one continent to another, the process of integration into American life, the learning of a new language, and the acceptance of different roles by the members, it has survived the storm well.

11

Laundries—A Haven and a Prison

AT the first meeting of the United Nations in New York, China's chief delegate to the fledgling international organization had gone to visit a friend in the Hotel Ambassador. Preoccupied with the heavy burden of state matters weighing on his mind, he absent-mindedly rang the wrong door bell. A lady appeared at the door and without a word thrust a bundle of laundry into the astonished ambassador's arms. Before he could protest, the door had banged shut.

Standing with the bundle of soiled clothes in his arms, the ambassador was at first startled and puzzled. Then it dawned upon him that the lady had mistaken him for her laundryman. He rang the door bell again and explained.

At one time or another, most Chinese in the United States can recount a similar experience of being taken for a laundryman or a restaurant man. A personal experience I remember very clearly occurred when my family was moving into a brand-new housing project. When completed, the project would have housed over a thousand families, and a large shopping center was being built within the project.

As we dragged our belongings up the walk to our new home, a neighbor dashed out to greet us. "I'm so glad this housing project will have a Chinese laundry," she gushed. "I've always taken my husband's shirts to a Chinese laundry. When will you be opening up?"

The neighbor had not stopped to think. She had just presumed that we, being Chinese, would open up a laundry in the new shopping center. She was quite disappointed when we told her it was not our intention to open any laundry. Yet, before many weeks had passed, a sign in the window of a store in the shopping center-to-be announced the coming of a Chinese laundry along with the ubiquitous supermarket, drug store, delicatessen, and hardware store.

It was perfectly natural for the ambassador or any other Chinese man to be mistaken for laundrymen. For more than half a century, the predominant occupation of the Chinese in the United States *was* the laundry business. In 1920, the U.S. census gave a breakdown of the occupational distribution by specific type of work. At that time, 30 percent of the Chinese employed were engaged in laundry work. Ling Liu in his book, *Chinese in North America* (1949), estimated that there were 10,000 laundries, 4,300 restaurants, and 2,000 groceries operated by the Chinese in continental United States. Rose Hum Lee found that of the 669 business enterprises operated by the Chinese in Chicago in 1950, 430 were laundries, 167 were restaurants, 21 were groceries, 30 were general merchandise stores, 10 were food manufacturing concerns, and 11 were gift shops.[1]

In New York, the Chinese-American Restaurant Association's *Twenty-Seventh Anniversary Issue* published in 1960 reported on Chinese business enterprises within the city. These included 2,646 laundries, 505 restaurants, and 144 other businesses.

The United States census no longer gives a clear-cut breakdown of the number of Chinese engaged in laundry work. Those who work for wages in laundries are included in the broad occupational classification of "Operatives and kindred workers." Those who own and operate their own laundries are included with "Managers, officials, and proprietors," but the large proportion of Chinese within these two categories supports the premise that laundry work is still an important livelihood of the Chinese people. However, the numbers are dwindling rapidly.

Table 11–1 gives a percentage comparison of the Chinese by major occupational group for the years 1940, 1950, and 1960. Note the continuing decrease in the "Managers" and "Operatives" categories.

The Chinese have also been strongly identified with restaurants, but this line of work merits separate discussion and will be dealt with in the following chapter. On the West Coast and in the South, a large number of Chinese own and operate grocery stores, some of which

[1] Rose Hum Lee, *The Chinese in the United States of America* (Hong Kong, Hong Kong University Press, 1960), p. 266.

TABLE 11-1

Percentage Comparison
Major Occupation Groups of the Chinese
Years 1940, 1950, and 1960

Major Occupation Groups	1940	1950	1960
Professional, technical	2.9	7.2	17.9
Farmers, farm managers	1.3	1.2	0.6
Managers, officials, proprietors	20.4	20.1	12.7
Clerical workers			6.6
Sales workers	11.3	16.2	13.8
Craftsmen	1.2	3.0	5.2
Operatives	22.4	17.4	15.0
Private household	6.1	2.6	1.0
Service workers	30.1	29.2	18.0
Farm laborers	2.6	1.4	0.4
Laborers	1.7	1.7	1.3

SOURCE: U.S. Census

have expanded into giant supermarkets. The professional class has made the greatest gains of all. From 1950 to 1960, the percentage rose from 7.2 to 17.9. (See Chapter 8.)

The Chinese did not go into laundry work by choice. The fact that so many are engaged in this line of work is peculiar to the Chinese in the United States. The more traditional occupations of Chinese emigrants in other lands are peddler, trader, or businessman.

The first Chinese who came to the United States started out as miners. They branched out into farming, manufacturing, and building railroads. The anti-Chinese campaign led by Dennis Kearney succeeded in whipping up such a frenzied hatred of the Chinese that employers who may have preferred hiring Chinese labor were intimidated or prevented from doing so. The Alien Land Acts kept the Chinese from owning farms. Unions kept them out of organized trades. Prejudice effectively cut them out of the labor market. Persecuted and harassed, the Chinese could not find jobs. They were compelled to rely upon their own resources.

They soon discovered that the scarcity of women in the frontier lands placed a high premium on performance of essential domestic duties. "Women's work" like washing, ironing, and cooking went begging at exorbitant wages. The detachable hard shirt-fronts and rigid collars worn by the men in those days cost $8 per dozen to wash, starch, and iron. On top of that, there was often a wait of six to eight weeks for one's laundry to come back from the Hawaiian Islands where they were shipped off to be washed. An alternative was to give the clothes to the Mexican girls, who washed them in the lagoon. This method, however, was often disastrous, for these washerwomen banged the shirts on the cobblestones, and after a few bangings, there was very little shirt or collar left.

So when the Chinese were barred from the gold mines in the hills, they found an equally lucrative gold mine in the city. To open a laundry required practically no capital or investment. All one needed was a scrub board, some soap, an iron and ironing board, and a laundry business was launched.

Most of the laundries were one-man enterprises or kinship arrangements, each laundry taking in only as much as it could handle. Location or frontage of the business was of little importance because the laundryman would collect and deliver, an advantage to both customer and laundryman alike. Therefore, rent and expenses were low.

In this kind of self-employment, there was no need to go and ask the white man for a job or to compete with the white man on an unequal basis. Nor did the white man mind the Chinese doing this type of "women's work." By 1880, more than 7,500 Chinese in San Francisco were earning their rice over the wash tub and ironing board.

When the Chinese began to disperse eastward, they found the laundry business equally suitable to their situation. In setting up laundries, they did not have to seek out jobs in established industries or incur the risk of heavy capital investment. They would canvass a neighborhood, seek out a low-rent location, and be in business.

Compare their lot with the Yugoslav immigrants whom Louis Adamic wrote about so vividly in his book, *Laughing in the Jungle. Crying in the Jungle* would have been a more appropriate title, for despair, hardship, and disorganization marked the lives of the newly arrived immigrants from Yugoslavia, who generally sought employment in the construction companies or mines in Pennsylvania. Employment depended upon seasonal fluctuations and the whims of the construction bosses. Strikes and layoffs meant uncertainty of income, insecurity of job tenure, hunger, and want. Human dignity is trampled when a man must grovel for work, and the Yugoslav's solace in drink only compounded his problems. Yet each succeeding wave of newcomers headed for the same mines and steel construction companies and met with the same experience as their predecessors.

Can one conjecture about the course of Negro history in the United States if the Negro had not remained so dependent upon the white man for a job or livelihood? A century after he has been constitutionally unshackled from the chains of slavery, he has not managed to free himself from the white man's economic oppression. Some headway has finally been made within the last ten years, but can it be denied that the Negro was generally the last hired and first fired? He has been given the lower-rung, menial jobs and not permitted to rise above them, so that his pride and ambition have slowly dissipated.

How much frustration, indignation, hurt, and abuse must have been spared the Chinese by their self-insulation! They were independent and self-sufficient. They were free from the insecurity of unemployment, cutbacks, layoffs, and business cycles. They answered only to themselves and their customers, and when these were satisfied, they did not suffer the pangs of hunger. Their fortunes depended upon their own initiative and efforts, and the Chinese were resourceful and hard-working.

No one implies that laundry work was less menial than that of janitor, ditchdigger, field hand, miner, or construction gang, or that the Chinese managed to pull themselves up the occupational scale through laundries. The main differences were that the Chinese owned and operated their own businesses, or they sought employment from their own people. Income and work depended more upon one's industry and initiative. Prejudice was one step removed from the immediate satisfaction of one's daily food and wants. But most important of all, the Chinese were spared the degradation of the human spirit—apathy born of a sense of futility.

Today, laundries still provide the ideal economic solution for many first-generation Chinese. If only a scrub board, iron, and ironing board were needed to go into business in 1870, capital investment does not amount to much more today. The scrub board may be obsolete, but most laundries do not do their own washing. They sort the clothes and send them out to be washed at what is known in the trade as a "wet-wash." The wet-wash trucks make the rounds of the various establishments, pick up the soiled laundry, wash it in huge mechanized plants at night, and return it the next morning, cleaned, but damp dried.

The shirts are then starched, dried, and ironed. Most laundries do their finishing by hand, but some make use of shirt presses and mangles. With laundry machinery, two to three times the amount of work can be completed in the same amount of time, but other factors offset the advantages. Machinery is costly and requires mechanical know-how to maintain, operate, and repair. The laundry becomes more of a plant than a service enterprise, calling for increased personnel and payroll. There must be enough business in constant and sufficient volume to make efficient use of the machinery. Besides, shirts put through the shirt press can never compare with one finished by hand.

To combine the demands of modernization and at the same time preserve the traditional characteristics of the Chinese laundries, the wet-washes offer a finishing service along with their washing service. For the wet-washes—already huge mechanized plants—it is relatively simple for them to add shirt presses and mangles. The huge volume collected from many laundries assure efficient use of the machinery. Individual laundry operators are thus spared the heavy cost in investment in washing machines, dryers, and presses. When business is slow, the operator will finish most of his work by hand. When the work load is heavy, he sends out a portion to be finished by the shirt presses.

Many families now rent store fronts where the wife collects, sorts, and wraps up the parcels. The work of washing and ironing is sent out to the wet-washes and shirt presses. These "collecting stations" are used as a means to supplement the family income while the husband works at another job. Thus, in many respects, laundry work has two advantages. (1) It is a haven against the vicissitudes of the labor market, and (2) the requirements needed to operate a laundry were easily met by the Chinese.

Most Chinese, however, do not view laundry work so objectively.

The daily routine of a laundryman is characterized by long hours, hard work, monotonous repetition, and loneliness. More often than not, he is the lone operator, and his shop is on a side street. The only people he sees are his customers, who bring in their parcels and reclaim them when they are finished. Until recent years, few men had their families with them. Exclusion laws and subsequent immigration restrictions were responsible for the enforced separation of these men from their families.

Up until recent times, the average Chinese laundryman, though insulated against the other occupational disadvantages previously mentioned, regarded his work as something akin to a self-condemned sentence. He came to the United States to better his economic position. He came with rosy dreams of how easy it would be to amass a modest fortune and retire to China to enjoy the fruits of his labor. Most prospective immigrants have little idea of the kind of life that the Chinese in the United States undergo and the kind of work that they do. What impresses the people back home is the bank roll that return emigrants bring back, owing to the favorable rate of exchange of the United States dollar for Chinese currency. And the name *Gum Shan* or Mountain of Gold, from the days of California's Gold Rush, has persisted in coloring the imagination of the Chinese who look upon the United States as a land of get-rich-quick opportunities.

The biggest shock to newcomers is the lowering of their status here. In their home villages in China, the overseas Chinese were highly regarded. Steady remittances enabled their families to live in comfort and above the station of the ordinary farm families. The wives and children of the emigrant families lived a life of comparative ease, for their income arrived in the mail from abroad. They did not have to go to the fields or work in any other manner. There was enough time and financial resources for the children to go to school. Actually, families of the overseas Chinese in Toishan were the genteel leisure class. Few of the emigrant families in China ever wondered about the hard work behind the remittance checks from abroad. The checks came regularly and when magnified by the favorable rate of exchange, the sums seemed considerable.

In social prestige and economic status, families of the overseas

Chinese occupied the upper-middle stratum. When the emigrant returned home for a visit, he generally had money to spend. What most people did not know, however, was that it may have been his entire life's savings. He would bring gifts for his relatives and friends. He would build a new house. He might have come home to marry off a daughter or get a wife for his son. The wedding feasts may have set him back a thousand or two, but sumptuous feasts were expected of him, and he gained a tremendous amount of face and prestige thereby. The overseas Chinese gave generously to the support of schools and charity, and evidence of this was conspicuous. Is it any wonder then that the overseas Chinese were mistaken by the people in China for rich men by village standards?

Can you imagine the immigrant's dream of coming to the Mountain of Gold only to find himself doing other people's dirty clothes? The disillusionment at first is a traumatic experience. Here is the reaction of one newcomer, who used to be a practitioner of herb medicine in Hong Kong:

> I had no idea that we Chinese have to work so hard like this in this country. The very first day, I had to begin to work. What is hard for me is to get up so early—5 o'clock in the morning—as I have not been accustomed to that in China. In China, life was easy for me. I usually slept until 9 or 10 o'clock as I pleased. In case a patient came to see me, I took it easily and slowly. I had only a few cases a day. I had plenty of time for recreation. In the evening, I went to a show or a tea-house with friends. What a comfortable life it was!
>
> Now it is different. I have to work all day long.
>
> That is right. If I had known beforehand that this is the way I would have to toil I would never have come here. I would rather have stayed with my family and be poor.
>
> Oh, I don't know. When I heard about a chance to go to America, the hardships just didn't occur to me. All I got excited about was to take the chance in going to America.
>
> Now I am here, I begin to feel America is work, work, work. It is nothing to get excited about.
>
> I have learned to iron now. I am doing three or four shirts

> an hour. That is very slow I am told. But will soon do better. After all, ironing is difficult work. It is only manual labor.[2]

This young fellow tried to get away from laundry work by practicing herb medicine in Chinatown but found that he could not earn a living at it. He worked for a year in a restaurant but eventually returned to the laundry, resigned to the hard work and drudgery.

Another man expressed his opinion of laundry work:

> People think I am a happy person. I am not. I worry very much. First, I don't like this kind of life. It is not a human life. To be a laundryman is to be just a slave. I work because I have to. If I ever stop work, those at home must stop eating. . . .
>
> I am not an old man yet, but I feel old. How can a man feel good when he is forced into an occupation he doesn't like.
>
> But I get used to it. After you are at it for so many years, you have no more feeling but to stay on with it. You can't get rich but you don't have to worry about money as long as you can work.[3]

This last paragraph sums up precisely the attitude of the Chinese toward laundry work. At the same time, it reveals why the Chinese persist in it. Newcomers go into the line of work that their relatives or sponsors are engaged in. By the time they manage to pay back the expenses incurred in bringing them to the United States, laundry work has become a habit; or inertia, indifference, or resignation causes them to accept it. Many continued in laundry work because it spared them the ordeal of job hunting. Others looked upon it as a stop-gap measure. They kept thinking that their sojourn in the United States was but a temporary interval in their lives although this "temporary interval" often stretched into twenty, thirty, or forty years.

This unrealistic attitude served as an anesthetic to deaden their frustrations. At any rate, few Chinese laundrymen looked upon their work as a business or career. They accepted it as necessary to earning

[2] Paul Siu, "The Chinese Laundryman, A Study in Social Isolation," unpublished Ph.D. Dissertation (University of Chicago, 1954), pp. 140–141.
[3] *Ibid.*, p. 159.

a livelihood. They knew it was almost impossible for them to compete with the white man for a job. And they made little effort to lift themselves above their imposed status. All their hopes were concentrated upon the day when they could accumulate enough from their labors or make a quick killing at the gambling table to enable them to return to China, there to enjoy an elevated status and a more comfortable life.

Events beyond their control lifted them out of their lethargy. Southern China was overrun by the Japanese in 1937 and occupied until 1946. At that time, most of the Chinese in this country still had their families in China. Not once did any of them waver in their faith that the enemy would be driven from their homeland. They worked even harder to give to the anti-Japan fund, and their contributions to the war effort are acknowledged.

After the war, many rushed to go home, but before many years had lapsed, the tide reversed. Once again, China was torn apart by civil war. The Communist take-over was complete by 1949.

Meanwhile the United States had relaxed somewhat its immigration restrictions against the Chinese, enabling many to bring their families to this country. Reunited with their families here, and entertaining no illusions about retiring to China under a Communist government, they were forced to re-evaluate their outlook on life in the United States.

Where they had once regarded laundry work solely as a means of livelihood—as a drudgery to be endured for the sake of the rice bowl—closer scrutiny revealed an economic sphere in which an enormous reservoir of good will existed for the Chinese. It was also a sphere which the Chinese pretty well dominated. If laundry work is hard, monotonous, and repetitious, so are typing and filing, driving a bus, or standing in an assembly line.

Washing and ironing clothes may be low in status, but status in many respects is relative to income and earnings. Scholars may be esteemed in China, but the frayed cuffs of the university professor have been the butt of many a joke in the United States.

Income from laundry work is not in the upper brackets, but neither can it be considered paltry. According to the *Statistical Guide to New York City* put out by the Department of Commerce in 1961, factory wages averaged about $85 a week. When I asked the owner of a "wet-wash" how his wages compared with this figure, he threw his head back and roared with laughter.

"Let me put it this way," he answered. "If I paid my men only $85 a week, they wouldn't work."

Mrs. Foon Ma changed her attitude toward the laundry business when she realized that it netted good financial returns. Mrs. Ma came to the United States just before Pearl Harbor. In China, she had enjoyed a brief period of comfort and ease as the wife of a "guest of the Mountain of Gold," a term applied to Chinese in the United States. Then her husband managed to arrange for her to join him, and she was equally eager to come to the fabulous *Gum Shan.*

But the Gum Shan of her dreams was not the *Gum Shan* that she found upon arrival. Her home was in the back of the laundry, where she cooked, slept, and kept house. When she was not at her domestic duties, she was expected to help with the laundry work. Soon the children began to arrive, one after the other, almost at regular intervals. But care of the children did not excuse her from her share of the work in the laundry.

Mrs. Ma was also lonely, for their laundry was in a suburb, far from Chinatown. Besides Chinese women were few, so that it was difficult to make friends. Her brood of children and their care had sapped much of her youth and energy. She was tired and worn-out from pounding an iron each moment she could spare from her domestic chores. She was sick—sick and tired of the life she endured. She blamed it all on the laundry.

Looking around her, she saw that American women kept beautifully furnished homes. Their children played in enclosed yards with borders of pretty flower beds. Their husbands had jobs in an office or at a factory. The wife did not have to work alongside the husband. He brought home the pay check for the wife to spend. Mrs. Ma sighed and pined in envy. Her frustration, her hatred of the laundry, and her accumulated fatigue brought on a neurotic condition. She developed ills and pains for which there was no physical cause. She went to doctor after doctor, and when they gently reproved her for being a hypochondriac, she would accuse them of trying to hide the severity of her illness from her.

At home she chided and nagged her husband, begging him to sell the laundry and get a job like the husbands of her American neighbors. Finally, to keep peace in the family, the husband sold the laundry and got a job in an aircraft factory starting at $75 a week. With the proceeds from the sale of the laundry, he bought a little bungalow for his wife, which she decorated and kept with loving care. Simultaneously, all her ills and pains disappeared.

Each morning, Mr. Ma went off to work at the factory, and each evening he returned. Each Friday he handed his wife the pay check from which he deducted his car fare, lunch money, and allowance. Mrs. Ma was a frugal woman, but she could barely stretch the pay check to cover their necessities, and there were so many things she wanted for the house. Somehow the money just disappeared although every effort was made to tighten the purse strings. Mrs. Ma became alarmed when she saw their bank account built up in previous years from the laundry business dwindling rapidly. She experienced pangs of guilt when she sent her husband off each morning to his labors while she, accustomed to a day crammed with chores and work, felt idle and useless.

One evening she announced to her husband and children that she had found an empty store in a good location and that she was going to open up a laundry. The news was incredible. The family refused to believe that Mrs. Ma, who had hated the old laundry with every inch of her five-foot-four frame, who used to sneeze and cough every time she came near the laundry but felt perfectly well away from it, was going to open up a laundry of her own free will and choice.

Mrs. Ma was not joking. All by herself she signed the lease and opened up for business. Her husband kept his job at the factory, and Mrs. Ma kept their pretty little bungalow with its lawn and flower beds. Every morning at eight she went to work and every evening at seven she closed the doors of the laundry and went home.

If business was slack, she did most of the work. If business picked up, she sent to the shirt presses what she could not finish within her working hours. Now her day is full but not harried. She can look forward to an evening in a comfortable home with her husband and children. Her attitude toward laundries is changed, but so is her relationship to the laundry. Once it was her master, dominating the twenty-four hours of her daily life. Her working hours were six in the morning until ten or eleven at night. There was no escape from the work because it was always staring her in the face. And it seemed such a shame to send the work out when she was sitting in the laundry anyway. Nowadays, Mrs. Ma closes the door of her laundry at seven and heads for home, dinner, and rest. Comfortably settled in an upholstered chair, she is not apt to get up and tramp several blocks back to the laundry to do the odds and ends that plague one's mind when the work is in plain sight. Now under her control, the income from the laundry has relieved her of financial worries.

Lee's case also shows a second insight into the laundry business. Lee grew up in a laundry. His father had been in this country for more than thirty years. All during this time, the father had held to his goal of returning to China with singleness of purpose. At the end of World War II, he was one of the first to board a ship for Hong Kong.

To his eldest son, Lee, he offered the laundry which had brought him a steady income through the ups and downs of America's business cycles and which had enabled him to bring up his family of five children.

But Lee would have none of the laundry. He had seen his father toil from six in the morning until ten at night. He knew how the muscles ached from standing at the ironing board wielding a ten-pound iron all day. As his father bent over the hot iron on hot summer days, his sweat poured. And Lee still remembered that he felt a little ashamed when asked about his father's occupation at school. No, the laundry was not for him. Besides, he was well-educated and experienced in other lines of work.

Lee had a university degree in radio and electronics. His service in the Army had given him valuable experience as a member of the Signal Corps. Back from the wars, he had gone off to Alaska to set up radio stations in the remote outposts of the chilly wilderness. After completion of that job, he readily found employment at the airport directing the landing and take-off of planes by radar.

Surely Lee had led an exciting and interesting career in a line of work in which he was well trained and well qualified. His pay was not meager, but somehow, he felt that life was just one long wait for the next pay check. One day, he chanced passing by the laundry that had once been his home and dropped in for a visit. The long absence made him see the laundry in a different light. He saw possibilities and potentialities that never crossed his mind before. Ideas sprouted from the familiar surroundings where he had spent the major part of his life. Before he left, he sounded out the owner on the possibility of a sale.

The owner took the offer as a joke. Had he not bought the laundry from Lee's father because Lee did not want it? Besides, Lee was an educated man with a professional job. There was no need for him to revert to the manual labor of washing and ironing other people's dirty clothes, Half in jest, he accepted Lee's offer. Imagine his surprise when Lee showed up in earnest with the legal papers, cash, and witnesses to document and legalize the sale.

Under Lee, the laundry took on a new character. Whereas the building had once been a small shop with living quarters on the second floor and a huge backyard of grapevines and rose bushes, it was converted into a mechanized plant with roaring washing machines, dryers, shirt presses, and mangles. A fleet of trucks pick up from many individually owned laundries, both Chinese and Caucasian, throughout the city. The soiled laundry is disgorged onto conveyor belts where it is sent to the second floor, sorted, and tagged. From there the laundry goes down yawning chutes to the ground floor where it is washed, pressed, and bundled and put back into the trucks for delivery.

In other words, the laundry is a mechanized assembly-line plant operated by a man who applies the same engineering know-how and managerial ability as is applied to any number of small manufacturing concerns. This laundry is a far cry from the one Lee knew as a little boy, and his income greatly exceeds what he could earn as a salaried engineer.

A paradox developed many years later when Lee was offered an attractive position by a former classmate to work with him on an exciting project connected with the space program. By then, Lee felt that he could afford to forgo the better financial remunerations from the laundry and permit himself the personal satisfaction of working with the challenging new venture of conquering space. The problem was to find a buyer for his laundry.

He approached a number of people who could operate such a huge plant, but they did not want it. There seemed to be a social stigma attached to the idea of being a laundryman. Many would have liked to buy the laundry, but the complexities of maintaining the machinery, financing the business, and meeting a large payroll deterred them. Lee was stuck with the mammoth he had created.

From both of the examples cited above, we have seen some change in the attitude of the Chinese toward an occupation which they had staked out for themselves, but which they considered an inferior, menial job. That vestiges of this attitude still remain is evident from the rapidly declining numbers engaged in this line of work and the reluctance of the native-born Chinese to follow it. Yet, the laundry business has not been the affliction that the great majority of the Chinese think it is.

Laundries eased the Chinese over a period of intense antagonism. It insulated them against even greater ills that may have befallen them if they had to compete in the open labor market. It provided the Chinese with a modest but steady, continuing income. It was a business that required few skills, little capital, and a minimal understanding of the English language to operate.

However, for those Chinese who have not had a chance to view the laundry business more objectively or to look at it from another angle as Lee or Mrs. Ma did, laundry work is still a drudge to be endured for the sake of the rice bowl.

12

Restaurants—A Natural Inclination

ON a good-will tour to Russia in 1896, Li Hung Chang, viceroy and foreign minister of China under the Empress Dowager, decided to return to China by way of England and the United States. When he sailed into New York harbor, he was greeted with the appropriate artillery salutes and escorted from the dock by the Sixth Cavalry to the Waldorf Astoria for his five-day state visit. On the second day, President Cleveland came to pay his respects, followed by most of the other leading citizens of the nation.

The world-renowned kitchen and chefs of the Waldorf Astoria were ready to serve Li all manner of delicacies, and although he was invited to sumptuous feasts and banquets, he would partake of nothing but the food prepared by his own cooks. When his inquisitive hosts asked him what he was eating, he replied, "chop suey." They were invited to sample the food. A few mouthfuls were enough to convince them why Li Hung Chang chose it above the banquet dishes of his hosts. News of the incident spread and quickly established the popularity of chop suey, resulting in the subsequent sprouting of Chinese restaurants.

Another version of how chop suey was introduced to the American palate takes place under humbler circumstances. Back in the Gold Rush days of California, there were many eating places maintained by Chinese miners, who insisted upon having their own food. Most unexpected, however, was the large white patronage that these Chinese eating places attracted. Each week as Saturday rolled around, miners from the surrounding hills would swarm into San Francisco to replenish their supplies, seek momentary diversion from their hard labor, and get a few solid meals under their belts.

It was very late one Saturday night when six husky, hungry miners knocked on the door of one of these eating places. The place was closed because the food was sold out. The proprietor tried to explain this to the miners, but they would not listen. They were hungry. They wanted something to eat, and they were not in a mood to look for another restaurant. Afraid of what the miners could do to his place if they were not fed, the proprietor scurried about trying to dig up something with which to feed them. With scraps of meat and vegetables, he concocted a platterful, which he set before the miners.

The miners attacked the food with gusto and praised it as the best they had ever tasted. They wanted to know the name of the dish, so the proprietor said, "chop suey," meaning a miscellany. From that day on, the miners coming into the restaurant insisted upon chop suey and nothing else.

Chow mein, the other staple dish of Chinese restaurants, was also born of an incident in the United States. There is a counterpart to chow mein among Chinese dishes, but the two bear faint resemblance. Literally, chow mein means fried noodles. As served in Chinese restaurants in the United States it consists of some kind of meat or shrimp, bean sprouts, onions, and celery served over a generous portion of crisp, deep-fried, golden brown noodles. The noodles give the dish its crunchy flavor. The origin of the crisp fried noodles characteristic of American-style chow mein is attributed to a cook who dropped some noodles into a pot of deep fat by mistake. The noodles emerged crisp and golden brown. Being a frugal man, the cook served them to his customers anyway. Chow mein's popularity was thus established and is more popular than ever today.

So we see that chow mein and chop suey, supposedly Chinese foods, are native American dishes. Neither is served in Chinese homes nor in restaurants in China although their widespread reputation has established their identity.

Restaurants follow laundries as the second most important type of business for the Chinese in the United States. The grocery business trails a far third and is one of the major enterprises of the Chinese in some southern and western states.

It is natural that one of the main occupations of the Chinese in the

United States should be the restaurant business. Aside from the popularity of chop suey and chow mein, the Chinese themselves are especially fond of good food.

> Pleasure in food has been synonymous with Chinese culture way back into Chinese antiquity, in fact into recorded time. It should be said . . . that as one of the few dependable joys of human life, the Chinese, in a practical sense have as much respect for food as for learning or religion. The Chinese love of good food is an important element in their conversation. They share with the French a preoccupation with cookery, and both races love to speculate upon, exchange opinions about and anticipate its pleasures. Scholarly essays on the culinary art permeate the whole of Chinese literature and Chinese poets sing of food as the Occidental poet sings of love. . . .
>
> In Chinese food, we sense qualities which stem directly from those centuries of progress and devotion to art which through many dynasties upheld their world supremacy. They were experimenters. They learned the value of many roots and herbs and other growing things. . . . They performed miracles in alchemy of reciprocal flavors, of principles of mixtures, of delicate combinations.[1]

The Chinese in the United States have been accused of lowering the American standard of living because they subsist on white rice and salt pork. If necessary, they *may* subsist on such a diet, but they will never do so by choice. The Chinese love good food and will not spare the expense to please their palates as well as to satisfy their hunger. By choice and by tradition, the Chinese eat only the best available. For example, chickens are purchased at the live poultry market instead of from the supermarket because the flavor of non-eviscerated chickens deteriorates when they are stored over any length of time. Similarly, Chinatown stores buy their meat freshly butchered. Refrigerated meat, they insist, loses much of its flavor. Fish, shrimps, lobsters, and crabs must be swimming in water, and that is the way they are usually sold in Chinatown shops.

[1] Ramiel McGehee, "Fit for a King." *The Merle Armitage Book of Food* (New York, Longmans Green & Co., 1939), p. 7.

In a later chapter when we see that the Chinese have adopted most of the material traits of the American way of life, we see that food habits still remain strongly Chinese.

If chow mein and chop suey are not Chinese dishes, then what is the real Chinese food? What do the Chinese in the United States eat at home?

By Chinese food, I refer more to manner and style of cooking and serving rather than to any difference in the basic foods themselves. However, the Chinese do enjoy many wonderful foods that Occidentals have not learned how to cook or to eat. Historically, because of the scarcity of food, every source was combed for edible morsels. The water was cultivated almost as carefully as the land. Seaweeds, lotus seeds, lotus roots, and water chestnuts are water crops. Other unusual foods are bean curd, bean sprouts, a fungus known as cloud ears, bird's nest, shark's fin, and bamboo shoots.

The average Chinese-American—unless he has ready access to a large Chinatown—cannot include these ingredients in his daily diet. He utilizes the meats and vegetables readily obtained in this country and cooks them Chinese style.

For instance, Westerners usually cook string beans by boiling the beans with a little water, adding salt, pepper, and butter to taste. The Chinese, on the other hand, cook string beans a little more elaborately.

I cannot give you a recipe according to the Western format, in which the measurement of ingredients and the method of preparation are exact and precise, for herein lies the difference between Western cooking and Chinese cooking. The former can be reduced, in effect, to a science; Chinese cooking is an art. A Chinese cook finds it difficult to tell how he prepares a dish. He does little measuring, if any. With a dash of this and a shake of that, he relies mainly upon his sense of taste to tell him when the flavor is just right. The flame, the cooking time, and the texture of the food must all be taken into consideration.

Here is one method of cooking string beans:

Slice thin about three ounces of pork. Braise the pork in a little oil in a frying pan until brown. Slice and add half a medium-size onion and a stalk of celery. These are mixed in with the pork and braised so that the flavor of the onion and celery blends with that of the pork.

Turn up the flame. Stir in three-fourths of a pound of string beans that have been stringed and cut into bite-size pieces. Add seasonings of fermented bean curd, salt, and a little soy sauce. Put in just enough water to keep the food from burning. Lower the flame slightly. Cover the frying pan until the water boils (about two minutes). Cut the heat off immediately and turn the string beans into a serving dish. The entire cooking process takes less than five minutes, as it is done over a high flame and intense heat. The vegetables are cooked but still green and crisp. Little of the vitamins and nutrients is lost because of the short cooking time and small amount of water used.

The basic food for all Chinese meals, of course, is boiled white rice served in individual bowls and eaten with chopsticks. At the usual family meal, there are three to four courses of vegetables, meat, fish, or soup. In addition to variety in kind, there must also be variety in method of preparation. If one dish is braised, the others will be boiled, fried, roasted, or steamed. But a meat dish is never exclusively a solid hunk of meat, nor is a vegetable found in its solitary state. Meat may be cooked with mushrooms, bamboo shoots, water chestnuts, or other vegetables to add to the flavor and texture of the dish. Vegetable dishes are usually cooked with a thinly sliced meat to highlight the flavor of the bland vegetables. The delightful quality of Chinese food is due in part to the clever combination of flavors and aromas.

The diet of the middle-income Chinese family has been found to be one of the best balanced and most nutritious in the world. It contains little or no sugar or sweets and is heavily weighted on the side of vegetables, which are rich in minerals and vitamins. Meat is used but sparingly to highlight the flavor of other foods. Diet-weary Americans have often observed that there are few overweight Chinese, and Dr. Ancel Keys, originator of the K-rations for troop survival during World War II, recommends Chinese food for heart patients and calorie-counters.

The fastidious attention of the Chinese to food made him a natural for the restaurant business. When the eating places that the Chinese had set up for themselves soon attracted large numbers of outsiders, the Chinese realized that here was a profitable business enterprise well suited to their temperament.

There are fewer Chinese in restaurants than in laundries because restaurants require larger capital investment, more facility in the English language, and managerial ability to buy and serve food appetizing and appealing to the eating public. Operation of a restaurant is much more complex than operating a laundry. Even the humblest of chop-suey joints cannot be a one-man operation like a laundry, for even if the cook doubled up as dishwasher, he could not very well dash out to the dining room and serve as waiter, bartender, and cashier at the same time.

Capital investment in opening up a restaurant can be substantial. The eating public demands more than good food well prepared. It wants atmosphere, comfort, and good taste in design and decor. Recently, Lum's, an old established and well-known restaurant in New York City near 57th Street, spent over $100,000 to redecorate. Establishing a new restaurant costs more, and the trend is toward more lavish and luxurious decors drawing upon authentic Chinese architectural designs, furnishings, and works of art. The Empress in Manhattan is done in the style of a fifteenth-century prince's palace in the Forbidden City in Peking.

Location for a restaurant is of paramount importance, and this means high rental and operating expenses. This kind of capital outlay makes it difficult for many Chinese to set themselves up in the restaurant business as sole proprietors, but once a restaurant is established, it employs other Chinese as cooks, dishwashers, waiters, headwaiters, and bartenders. The number of restaurants owned and operated by Chinese may be small in comparison with the number of laundries, but the gap between the number employed in restaurant work and laundry work is not as great as it seems.

Before World War II, when job discrimination kept many a well-qualified young Chinese-American from entering other occupations or pursuing a professional career, the enterprising ones managed restaurants or became waiters or bartenders. They were the ones who met the public. Their fluency in the English language and their American upbringing enabled them to provide their patrons with gracious and hospitable service. Many an American diner has discovered to his surprise that his waiter held a college degree.

The cooks and dishwashers came from the ranks of the immigrant group. In the kitchen, their unfamiliarity with the English language was no handicap. Having been brought up in China, they were imbued with the appreciation and reverent love of good food, so they were better suited to its proper preparation.

The Chinese look upon restaurant work as a notch above laundries. Kitchen work is dirty work, but cleaning a duck and barbecuing it into a succulent dish is more creative than finishing shirts cut along the same lines, day after dreary day. And in restaurants, the problem of loneliness is not as acute, for there invariably is someone else to talk to.

The frustration lay with the younger men, many of whom were well qualified for other types of work. These young men despised any association with laundries but the only other occupations open to them at one time remained in waiting on tables or bartending. Few had the capital to become sole owners or managers, for ownership was more likely to be a pooling of the savings of many partners. Before World War II, native-born Chinese youths who wanted to stay in this country had little choice. They were confined to restaurant work. The more enterprising ones rolled up their sheepskins from colleges and technical schools and went back to China, where they hoped for a more promising future.

We know that social changes since then no longer restrict the Chinese to their two or three types of traditional occupations. With the restrictions removed, the better-qualified, the ones without language handicaps, the more courageous ones, ventured into other lines of work and were quickly followed by others when their efforts did not meet with rebuff. Into the vacated jobs in the restaurants stepped the influx of immigrants admitted after the repeal of the Exclusion Acts.

Surprisingly, many young men and women who hold good positions in commercial and professional capacities elsewhere go back to restaurants on week ends to supplement their income. Now that they are not exclusively confined to restaurant work, they need no longer disdain it. Offhand, I can name an architect, a vice-president of a finance company, a welder in an aircraft factory, a medical student, and a dental student who work regularly over the week ends as waiters or headwaiters in various Chinese restaurants.

Another group of Chinese revised their attitude toward the restaurant business too. These are the intellectual and political refugees who once held high office in China. Although lucky enough to escape with their lives and their savings, they came to this country faced with the grim prospect of having to start all over again, perhaps at the bottom.

At first, these *émigrés* disassociated themselves from the "overseas Chinese," whom they looked down upon as laundrymen and restaurateurs. When they began to look around for means of earning a livelihood or investing their capital, they found that restaurants can yield a good living and handsome returns. Some opened restaurants outright. Others invested capital in going concerns. The Cathay Garden in White Plains, New York, is owned and operated by Li Han-wen, former governor of the Province of Kwangsi.

Chinese restaurants have also undergone drastic change. Once they might have been chop-suey joints consisting of a few tables and chairs in a store front, serving the few staple pseudo-Chinese dishes of chop suey, chow mein, egg foo yung, and fried rice. Now even the most modest Chinese restaurants must take into account the sensitivity of their patrons to cleanliness, service, and atmosphere.

In recent years, restaurants in the United States have become big business. Families are making it a regular habit to eat out once or twice a week. The increasing number of working wives and mothers contributes to this trend. Expense accounts, more leisure time, and the restless urge of the American people to "go out" all help to push up the volume of business. Money spent on food and drink served outside the home amounted to seventeen billion dollars in 1960. A poll once showed that among the foreign foods served in restaurants, Chinese food is the second most popular, being nosed out only by Italian food with its reigning favorites, spaghetti and pizza pies.

Chinese restaurateurs are well aware that the American eating public is becoming more sophisticated. Waiters are encountering more and more requests for the "authentic" Chinese food. Cantonese lobster, barbecued spareribs, shrimps with lobster sauce, sweet and sour pork, and won-ton soup are now regularly featured on the menu in Chinese-American restaurants. But some patrons who have lived or traveled to the Far East or who have been introduced to a higher realm of the Chinese cuisine by gourmet friends ask for five-flavored duck, bird's nest soup, bitter melon with beef, thousand year eggs, stewed sea cucumbers, fish maw steamed in herbs, and a great variety of other dishes. As previously mentioned, there are few edibles that the Chinese have not learned how to prepare in an appetizing manner.

To cater to this sophisticated demand, Chinese restaurateurs are trying to bring in well-known chefs from Hong Kong, or they are sending their own chefs to Hong Kong for training. Sou Chan of New York's well-known House of Chan sponsored the entry of twenty of Hong Kong's best chefs under the Refugee Relief Act. These chefs were readily granted first-preference visas, generally reserved for those with special skills and knowledge urgently needed in the United States. Sou Chan has also set up scholarship funds at Brooklyn College and Columbia University in restaurant management.

Dining in Chinese restaurants can be made a much more pleasurable experience if the patrons would try or ask for some of these tasty Chinese dishes. The large majority of Chinese restaurants in the United States serve the southern Chinese food or what is generally known as the Cantonese cuisine. China being so vast, there are regional differences in food, but Canton has long held the title as culinary capital of China. There is a popular Chinese saying, "Live in Soochow, eat in Kwangchow (Canton), die in Wuchow." Freely translated, it means Suchow is the most ideal place to live in because of its excellent climate and scenic beauty. Kwangchow or Canton offers the best in food. And Wuchow produces a fragrant lumber used in making exquisite coffins. The Cantonese cuisine ranks first, even with the fastidious Chinese.

Unlike most restaurants where the food is generally prepared beforehand and kept hot on steam tables, Chinese restaurants cook each dish to order. Your lobster is still alive at the time you give your order, but fifteen minutes later, it will appear piping hot on your table. Much of the flavor of the vegetables depends upon their color and crispness, which are lost if the vegetables are cooked and allowed to stand for any length of time. Dishes that require long cooking time like Peking duck or stews should be ordered in advance.

My suggestion to the uninitiated in Chinese food is to tell the manager or headwaiter your likes and dislikes in food and ask him to make up for your approval a menu from appetizer to dessert. On the spur of the moment, he may be limited to what he can readily prepare, so it is best to call ahead of time, give him the number of persons to be served, and specify the price limit. Most chefs will be flattered and pleased to prepare some of the more unusual dishes for you although it may involve much more work.

Few people are more knowledgeable about national cuisines and fine food than Silas Spitzer, food editor of *Holiday* magazine. On a gastronomical tour of the Far East and the South Pacific in 1965, he and his wife, long-time devotees of Chinese food, anticipated with gustatory pleasure their arrival in Hong Kong—the Mecca of gourmets in the Far East.

During the time they were in Hong Kong, they sampled food from the "unspoiled little places with lots of local color" to the plushiest restaurants accustomed to catering to the highly discriminating palates of world travelers. After six days of experimental dining, Silas Spitzer was asked how Chinese food in Hong Kong compared with the American version. He concluded:

> A forthright judgment after only six days may seem presumptuous. Still, writers' necks were made to be extended. My firm opinion is that for every first-rate Chinese restaurant in Hong Kong there are at least ten in New York or San Francisco as good or better. And there are sound reasons for this.
>
> Oriental restaurants on our side of the Pacific enjoy a great advantage. They are able to draw upon the national superabundance of meat, fish, vegetables and other produce. They can utilize the latest ideas in equipment, storage, and transportation. But in Hong Kong it is a miracle that restaurants do so well with the little they have. Many of them, in spite of their limited resources, are masters of the intricate "conversation piece" dish that is rarely served elsewhere. But the economic and geographic handicaps are insurmountable. My feeling is that the poetic and imaginative Chinese cuisine available is today at its best in the United States.[2]

[2] Silas Spitzer, "Dining in the Far East," *Holiday* (December 1965), p. 107.

If you are ever in or near one of the large seaboard Chinatowns like those in San Francisco, Los Angeles, or New York, you may find it an exotic experience to take tea in one of the teahouses. Tea is, of course, the national drink of China. It is prepared fresh each morning, kept in a tea cozy, and drunk warm or hot throughout the day.

Chinese tea is different from the Ceylon or black Indian tea generally served at American tables. The essential difference lies in the meticulous care and tedious labor expended in the planting, picking, and curing of Chinese tea to insure perfect fermentation. In the curing and firing process, every leaf must be opened by hand four times, each time after the leaves are passed over a charcoal fire, with the result that a great deal of the injurious tannic acid is turned to sugar. The success of Chinese tea is well known. Only its leaf keeps its strength after successive brewings. Chinese tea has the largest percentage of the stimulant theine and the least amount of poisonous tannin.[3]

There are many kinds of Chinese tea. Oolong and Po Nay are black teas. Iron Goddess of Mercy is a red tea. Jasmine, Water Nymph, Dragon Well or Fragrant Petals are green teas. Chinese tea may be used over and over again. In fact the aroma and fragrance of the tea does not come out until the second or third brewing.

In China, a favorite pastime is to go to the teahouses, which is done at all times of the day. There, teahouses not only fulfill a social function; they are actually places where most professional and business activity take place. Chinese firms seldom maintain elaborate offices where business transactions are brisk and formal. The Chinese prefer to go to the teahouses, sit over a cup of tea, select a few pastries or tidbits, and seemingly chat about everything but business. But before the patrons leave, hundreds of thousands of dollars may have changed hands, or a marriage may have been arranged between the son and daughter of the two parties.

In the United States, teahouses do not assume the functions of those in China as places of business transactions. Rather, they are patronized for the dainty pastries known as *dim sum*. Literally

[3] John S. Thomson, *The Chinese* (Indianapolis, Bobbs-Merrill Co., 1909), p. 130.

translated, *dim sum* means "touch the heart," or in American slang, "hit the spot." Most of the *dim sum* are bite-size pastries made of meat, shrimp, fish, or lobster wrapped in paper-thin dough and steamed. The sweet pastries like the egg tart are baked, and the turnip patties are fried. Whether steamed, fried, baked, or barbecued, the making of these delicacies calls for culinary artistry and skill. When properly prepared, they are a gourmet's delight.

Actually, Chinese restaurants have become an integral part of the American melting-pot culture. A small item in a guide book to Germany for American tourists confirmed this. The guide book listed the usual tourist spots—historic places, religious shrines, museums, and night clubs. At the very end were these words of comfort to the American away from home:

"If you get homesick and lonesome for an American face and some American talk, go to the Shanghai Cafe. Owned and operated by two Chinese-American GI's who stayed here after the war, the Shanghai Cafe is the main hang-out for Americans in West Berlin."

13

Many Roads to Heaven

THE Reverend Hung was sound asleep in the Church House on 11th and L Streets, N.W., in Washington, D.C. It was 2 A.M. in the morning and the Reverend was a heavy sleeper. But the sharp clang of the telephone beside his bed woke him with a jerk. Before his hand reached out to grab the receiver, he was already up and dangling his legs over the bed. A phone call at this hour of the night could only mean a call for help.

"*Fai-loy, fai-loy*," moaned the voice at the other end of the receiver. "Come quickly, come quickly."

No name was given—nor an address. The Reverend Hung traced the call through the operator and quickly placed a call for an ambulance. In a few minutes, he was out in the dead stillness of the night, heading for a laundry twenty-odd blocks away.

Having arrived to find the ambulance waiting, he gave orders to force the door. Inside, they found Liu Pon, age 40, doubled over and contorted with pain. Liu was rushed to the hospital. An hour later, he was wheeled from the operating room, minus his appendix.

Liu Pon knew the Reverend Hung, pastor of the Chinese Community Church, by sight. He had spoken to the Reverend when the latter had come to his laundry in a fund-raising campaign to build a church. Liu had given $5.00. He had never been to the services at the Chinese Community Church, although he had gone regularly to the Baptist Church on H Street near Chinatown for two years right after he came to the United States. That was before the Chinese Community Church came into existence.

At the Baptist Church near Chinatown, Liu had learned his few words of English. Without those two years of Sunday School English lessons, Liu would never have had the courage to open and operate his own laundry. How could anyone operate a business without some knowledge of the English language?

Liu managed to get along with the fundamental phrases taught him, but often he felt the lack, the poverty, of his knowledge of English. Then he would regret that he had not continued with his Sunday School English lessons. But this hindsight did not take into account the fact that Liu was young and fun-loving at the time. Sunday was his only day off from the drudgery and toil of the week. He wanted to go to Chinatown, to meet his friends and relatives, to relax and laugh and enjoy himself—maybe get a few thrills at the gambling tables. So Liu was content to learn a few essentials and quit the English classes.

Many times he had thought of picking up his studies, but inertia led him to rationalize. He was too old now to get anything through his thick skull. People would laugh at him if he sought to go back and study English. Oh, it was all right for a new arrival to go to Sunday School; they were foolish if they did not. But Liu had been here for nearly twenty years. No, it was no time to go back to Sunday School classes.

Liu worked in his shop alone. He could order his laundry supplies by phone, but this was seldom necessary as salesmen called regularly. He could tell a customer if his laundry was ready and other routine business connected with the laundry, but he knew that in an emergency he would be completely lost. That is why he always hung the number of the Chinese pastor above the phone along with the telephone listings he frequently used. That number gave him a sense of security. In time of need, he could always dial that number for help.

There was no sense in listing the numbers of the fire department, the doctor, or the police station. He would not have been able to make himself understood. All he needed was the pastor's number. This sense of security was shared by many Chinese who reasoned along the same lines. The Chinese pastor's phone number is always handy above the phone although they may never have met the pastor or been inside his church.

In 1955, a comprehensive survey was conducted by the National

Council of Christian Churches on the impact of the Chinese church on the Chinese population in the United States. They found a rather gloomy picture—statistically.

According to the survey, there were 62 Protestant Chinese churches in the United States mainland and 4 in Hawaii at that time. By Chinese churches, we mean those essentially Chinese in membership and dedicated mainly to serving the Chinese community. These churches generally have a Chinese pastor, but sometimes an Occidental minister leads the Oriental flock, although he is generally assisted by a Chinese pastor.

Of the 62 churches, 29 were in the one state of California: 8 in San Francisco, 4 in Oakland across the Bay, 5 in Los Angeles, 4 in Sacramento, and 8 in other cities of the state. Two churches were found in Portland, Oregon, and one in Seattle, Washington. In the Mountain Region, 2 churches were found in Arizona and 1 in Denver, Colorado. The South had 8 churches, of which 3 were in Texas. The Midwest listed 5; New York City had 6; Philadelphia 3; and 5 were distributed throughout other cities of the eastern seaboard.

The most active denominations working among the Chinese were the Southern Baptists, the American Baptists, and the Presbyterians.

Of these Protestant churches, 12 were self-supporting with a full program, 26 were mission-aided, depending on some denominational home mission board for financial support. Fifteen Chinese churches were missions, leaning heavily or entirely on denominational boards for support. These missions generally are limited in program by a small membership and a minimum budget. Seven Chinese churches were self-supporting with a limited program. These independent churches may not be churches in the usual sense of the word. Some are just store-front meetings or home meetings where a group of Chinese gather to worship or find fellowship. Membership is unstable and fluid.

The average membership of the Chinese church was placed at 155 members, and the annual budget at $5,260. This compared with 406 members for the average American church at that time. A rough estimate placed the number of Chinese who belonged to Protestant churches at approximately 9,500.

A more encouraging note was that 13 churches reported an increase in membership by 86.7 percent from 1940 to 1950. The total Chinese population increased 51.8 percent for the same period. In one year, from 1951 to 1952, the same churches grew 9.9 percent.

To look at the statistics—the formal membership of a church, the number of churches, their annual budgets, even their regular programs—is misleading in judging the place of the Christian church among the Chinese. This is evident from the story of Liu Pon. As of 1966 there are approximately 275,000 Chinese in the United States. I dare say that directly or indirectly, closely or remotely, the Christian church touches a large majority of these Chinese—but not necessarily in the same sense that the average person expects a church to serve.

To understand this anomaly, we must delve a little into the background of the Chinese attitude toward religion. To the average Occidental, or for that matter, to most peoples inhabiting this globe, religion is a powerful gripping force. It is an intense, emotional, personal, cohesive, unifying experience. It is the central axis around which cultures evolve and revolve. This very nation was founded upon Christian Protestantism, and it still professes to stand upon a solid foundation of Christ's teachings.

Religions have had their place in the Chinese culture, and they have left their marks, but the average Chinese views his religions with a much more detached point of view. When he needs his gods, he will make the proper offering and prayers. At other times, they are left alone; to the Christian or Moslem, however, God is a continuous experience. To the Chinese, his gods are as much dependent upon him as he is upon the good will and favor of the gods. If the proper offering of food, clothing, money, and other necessities are not burnt in sacrifice on feast days, the gods will go hungry and be ill-clad. To the Christian or Moslem, God is omnipotent. Blessings emanate from God and are bestowed upon man, never the reverse.

> The Chinese attitude toward the supernatural and religion contrasts sharply with that of the American Christian. The cultural anthropologist points out that it is natural for the more emotional, self-centered and competitive American to embrace a monotheistic God and an evangelistic approach to religion. His

> one God is good; any other is false or evil. The monotheist cannot compromise with evil; he must eliminate the false and the bad. No such dichotomy of good and evil exists for the Chinese; if propitiated correctly, all spirits will be good to men. The Chinese polytheist calls on his gods for practical purposes; the Christian must wage a constant war on evil in order to be good. The polytheist has a temporary allegiance to any god who can help him but is irretrievably committed to none. The Christian has but one God and owes him all allegiance. The Christian, working toward salvation, believes in a doctrine of "saved souls", the Chinese with many gods has little interest in any except as they might make the fate of either the living or dead more amenable. . . .[1]

In sum total, the Chinese take a practical view of religion. It has been said that Confucianism, Taoism, and Buddhism are the three great religions of China. Confucianism, which has molded Chinese culture for the past two and a half centuries, is not a true religion but a body of ethics. Confucius is not considered a god. Taoism, though full of mysticism, stressed a moral and ethical way of life. Buddhism, too, underwent metamorphosis in China. A Chinese may be a Confucianist, a Taoist, and Buddhist at one and the same time. Often one temple will house images and tablets of many deities, and worshippers may offer prayers and incense to all.

This polytheism is difficult to comprehend for a person who has been brought up to believe in an only God. He looks upon such beliefs as primitive, uncivilized, and insincere whereas to the average Chinese, all religions are good as long as they teach man to be good and ethical. To believe in one religion is not to exclude the other, and insistence upon such exclusion only tends to antagonize rather than convert him. That is why the Chinese will accept Christianity for its teachings, but not for its dogma. They believe in praying to the Christian God if such prayers will bring its rewards.

The Chinese does not believe in exhibiting his religion for appear-

[1] "The Chinese in the U.S. and the Chinese Christian Church," National Council of Christian Churches (April 1955), p. 7.

ance's sake. Religion is a private matter, not a social badge. Yet, if it serves his purpose to go to the Christian church, he will go. He will take advantage of the English classes offered on Sundays. He will take advantage of the fellowship found in the church among his own people. He will accept the multiple services offered by the church such as help with registration, immigration procedures, interpreting facilities, and so forth. He will call upon the pastor in hour of need because he is sure that his need will be met. In fact, he has even come to expect these services from the Christian church, for to him the church is synonymous with service.

On his part, the average Chinese in the United States, young or old, believes in the profound goodness of the Christian church. Chinese parents encourage their children to go to church and Sunday School. Those here a long time urge the newcomers to go to Sunday School. At fund-raising time, the Chinese who has never stepped inside the Chinese church will make a contribution. Some contend that a Chinese is ridiculed and ostracized by his own people if he is baptized or if he joins the church. I do not believe that is true. A Chinese Christian may be regarded as a little bit more strait-laced, more puritanical. Others may hesitate to crack dirty jokes or suggest a trip to the brothel when he is around, but that is not social ostracism.

A book entitled *Orientals and Their Cultural Adjustments*, published by the Fisk University in 1946, corroborates my own observation. This volume is a collection of interviews, life histories, and social-adjustment experiences of Chinese, Japanese, and Filipinos of varying backgrounds and lengths of residence in the United States. Seven of these life histories involve Chinese. Of the seven Chinese cases, four of the Chinese interviewed mentioned the Christian church and the part it played in their lives. When they were in a dilemma, they sought the church. When they needed help, their first thought was of the church.

Liu Pon never figured in the statistics of any Chinese church. Yet he was indebted to the church for the fundamental knowledge of English he possessed. He was indebted to the church for his very life, not to mention the sense of security he continually enjoyed by having the pastor's number always handy.

How are these intangibles to be gauged? There are no yardsticks, no numerals, no scale to measure the weight, the influence, or the place of the Christian church among the Chinese in the United States.

But some church leaders are apt to ask, "Are we interested in converting the Chinese into Christians (Western interpretation of the word) and saving their souls, or is the church to be a charitable service organization?" At this point, I must revert to my Chinese sense of logic and reasoning. Is the church more concerned about the fate of souls in heaven or is it more interested in helping their members to attain fuller and better lives on earth? And now to be typically Chinese, I must quote Confucius, who answered when he was questioned about the immortality of the soul: "We do not know about life, how shall we know of death?" And to be downright practical about the whole thing, the Christian church will never make any headway among the Chinese except through social services. The church has already gained an inroad through these means. It has merited the respect and confidence of the Chinese. The battle for their souls is more than half won.

Dr. William Speer, the first Protestant pastor to minister to the needs of the Chinese in this country, immediately recognized the avenue of approach. Dr. Speer had served as a missionary in China and was conversant in the Cantonese dialect. When the Presbyterian Board of Foreign Missions appointed Dr. Speer to open a mission in San Francisco in 1852, he opened a dispensary in conjunction with the mission, for he was a trained physician. His successor initiated evening classes for the study of English. During the persecution of the Chinese and the anti-Chinese riots in the early days of California's history, the church and clergy gave protection to many Chinese and spoke up for them. This was the foundation that the pioneers in mission work made. It was a strong foundation.

Because of the heavy emphasis on service to the Chinese community and because the Chinese approach religion from an entirely different cultural frame of reference, the Chinese church in America, to be effective, must adapt itself to the group which it seeks to serve. The worst attitude that the church could adopt is to assume a haughty and lofty air of superiority, contributing to the support of the Chinese churches, teaching in the Sunday Schools, and otherwise rendering service for the express purpose of raising the heathen Chinese above his false gods. The Chinese are a proud people. Nothing will antagonize them more quickly than belittling their ways of belief and thinking.

One of the ministers interviewed expressed his opinions freely on the attitude of Caucasian church workers toward the Chinese traditions:

> Both the ______ and ______ churches are dominated by their Caucasian workers, who are aggressive in denouncing the Chinese traditions and culture. This does a great deal of harm, not only to the program of the other churches which seek to preserve all that is valuable in Chinese philosophy and culture, but to the inner security and integrity of the young Chinese Americans themselves. . . . The youngsters cannot help but absorb some of the white man's contempt of their ancestral wisdom and tradition, and thus the home is broken into two—the old and the young.[2]

Many foreign mission boards as well as the American people were shocked at the treatment meted out to the missionaries by the Chinese Communists. According to the American way of thinking, the missionaries had made great personal sacrifices to go among the Chinese and preach the gospel. They felt that the missionaries had gone with only the purest purposes in mind. They pointed to the schools, the churches, the dispensaries built and maintained by the mission boards. But for all their zeal, they went with a haughty air of arrogance, not only for the heathen's religion, but also for his ways of life. Some never learned the language of the people among whom they had lived for twenty years, yet their purpose was to communicate the goodness of their God.

Most of the missionaries never adopted the native dress or lived among the people whom they had come to convert. Pearl Buck wrote about the lives of the missionaries in China in her autobiography, *My Several Worlds*. Each summer this foreign colony went up into the mountains to a resort reserved exclusively for the white man where the air was pure and uncontaminated by the sweating masses of

[2] *Ibid.*, p. 61.

humanity who could neither afford to nor were allowed to enjoy the breezes of the upper atmospheric strata.

Ida Pruitt in her book, *Daughter of Han*, the life story of a servant woman, Ning Lao Tai-Tai, tells how a British woman missionary insisted upon calling her servants "bond servants." They would correct her by pointing out that they were hired by the month or year and were free to come or go at will and were not indentured, but she paid no heed. She continued to call them bond servants, a term deeply resented by even such humble folk as the servant class.

The reason why the Communists have had such wholehearted support behind the ouster of the missionaries is that the resentment against the missionary group was so widespread. The cry against the white man was: "Take away your guns and your missionaries." Missionaries were classed with guns!

But it is not within the scope of this book to dwell upon the missionaries in China. Nor can one make the generalization that all missionaries were of the same hue, for personally I have known many who were the epitome of self-sacrifice. This side of the ledger is well balanced too. My point is these incidences reveal the resentment of the Chinese toward any disdain for their customs or their culture.

The Christian church among the Chinese in the United States is cast in a different light. In China, the missionaries were the minority, while in the United States they belong to the majority group. As such, they are judged purely within the confines of their church activities. Such factors as the language, dress, and personal conduct of those who seek to spread the gospel are extraneous.

One of the most beloved of Christ's workers among the Chinese is the Sunday School teacher or *Sien-sung Po*, which means lady teacher. Of course there are men among Sunday School teachers, but most are women. *Sien-sung Po* is definitely one of the fixed and most important institutions among the Chinese in the United States.

If an immigrant comes to the States in his teens or in his twenties (and most of them do), he is marched right off to the Sunday School for English lessons, because as a rule he must work during the week and cannot attend regular school classes. This presents an excellent opportunity for the church to win adherents to the faith—an opportunity that has been sadly overlooked by church leaders, for the manner in which these newly arrived young boys and young women are welcomed and made to feel a sense of belonging to the church determines the length of their stay with the Sunday School and their future attitude toward the church.

Either the young arrival is assigned a *Sien-sung Po* for private instruction, or he is assigned to a class with other young men or women at more or less the same level of English understanding. Then, in addition to verses from the Bible, the *Sien-sung Po* uses as a text a simple vocabulary builder of common everyday English words and phrases.

Most new arrivals manage to stick with the Sunday School lessons for at least a year or two because plain common sense compels them to reason that an absolute minimum of English is essential for their livelihood in this country. During this time, most of them develop a deep affection and respect for the *Sien-sung Po*. Reverence stems from cultural training—respect and honor one's teacher second only to one's parents. Affection derives from the devotion of the Sunday School teachers. Though the pupil may drop out of Sunday School, the relationship between teacher and pupil may be a lifelong one. In many, many instances, I have seen older men, some in their forties or fifties, who had never been back to church for twenty years or more, remember their *Sien-sung Po* at Christmas time with a card or a gift.

Speaking personally, I feel that my Sunday School teacher, Miss Gertrude Barber of Washington, D.C., was one of the most important guiding influences in my life. Miss Barber was more than a Sunday School teacher. She did not confine her interest to mere teaching of the Bible and its tenets. Miss Barber took a personal interest in every one of her eight girls, all of us about the same age and with similar interests. She took us shopping and taught us how to select and buy. She organized picnics and swimming parties for us, paying the expense out of her own salary as a government clerk. Once in a while, she took us to a movie.

I do not think my relationship with Miss Barber was unique. My sister also had a Sunday School teacher, Mrs. Hannah Dorn, equally dedicated and devoted to serving the Chinese people. She did the same things for my sister and her other pupils that Miss Barber did for me, and Mary Banta, who served for more than fifty years with the True Light Lutheran Church in New York City, has become a legend among the Chinese community. The story of her services among the Chinese people in New York is typical of the devotion, love, and dedication of the whole group of *Sien-sung Po*.

That is why I maintain that the Christian church has made a tremendous impact upon the Chinese in this country—statistics to the contrary. Often the church is the main social organization where the younger generation can go. That is why the Chinese church membership is made up predominately of young people and children. The American-born Chinese have little, if any, ties with the family associations, the Chinese Benevolent Associations, or the *tongs*. On the other hand, they do not feel entirely at ease among Caucasian groups. More often than not, they are excluded from the social activities and organizations of their white neighbors. That is why they need the Chinese Christian church—an organization which is theirs, where they will not feel self-conscious, where they can seek out other young people of their own race and customs for fellowship, where they will find a wholesome atmosphere and a healthy outlook on their marginal status.

Some critics will advance the argument that the Chinese Christian church tends to retard assimilation of the younger Chinese. With other Caucasian minorities, this argument has much validity, but with the Chinese, their physical differences will always set them apart as foreign. The American-born Chinese may be entirely American in speech, dress, customs, thinking, and loyalty. He may be completely adjusted to American culture, but he will not be entirely accepted among the American community as one of their own kind. He needs people of his own race to round out his feeling of belonging and security, and if the Chinese Christian church can provide this sense of security in a healthy, religious surrounding, its existence is well justified.

So far, I have described the Chinese Christian church almost wholly as a social service agency. This is far from the facts, because as a transplanted institution, the Christian church and its methods of spreading the gospel has had to make its adjustments. In actuality, the Chinese church is a multi-purpose organization with its ultimate aim of winning religious converts to the fold of the Christian God, but en route, it is also dedicated to rendering services in the fields of education, physical and moral development, social welfare, and recreation.This is a big job, but the churches have done admirably well considering their many, many handicaps and barriers.

All of the churches have regular services on Sundays. At times the services are held in the morning, but more often they are held in the afternoon to better accommodate the laundry workers, who stay open Sunday mornings and who must tidy up for the week end, and the mothers who have young children to dress and feed before they leave the house. Church-going among the Chinese women as with American women is quite a social occasion. It gives them a chance to get out of the house once a week, to meet and chat with other women, as well as to get dressed up in their finery (a strong tonic for female morale). Sermons are often preached in both languages—Chinese followed by a brief summary in English, or vice versa. As church membership is shifting more and more toward the younger people, English has become the predominant language employed in church services and activities.

The "typical" Chinese minister was born in China, is in his middle forties, speaks Chinese and English, is a graduate of a college or seminary, is theologically conservative, is highly dedicated, and is more Chinese than Western in his outlook and thinking. Few native-born Chinese heed the call to the ministry.

A Caucasian minister is handicapped with a Chinese congregation unless he can speak the dialect and appreciate the Chinese attitude toward religion. The True Light Lutheran Church in New York, a well-established church with one of the largest Chinese congregations, has traditionally had a Caucasian minister although he is assisted by a Chinese pastor.

A Chinese minister does not mean, however, that the channels of communication are wide open. It was pointed out that there are many dialects of the Chinese language. Whereas most of the Chinese in the United States speak the Toishan dialect, few of the ministers do. They generally speak Cantonese, a dialect similar enough to Toishanese to be mutually comprehensible. Difficulties arise if the minister is Mandarin-speaking or if he is a native-born Chinese-American who speaks little or no Cantonese.

The Chinese minister plays an ambiguous role. He is a connecting link between two cultures. As a Christian minister he is expected to preach and adhere to a code of standards that evolved from Western civilization. He cannot, however, disregard the practicalities of Chinatown life or a cultural heritage that antedates Christianity.

In the National Council of Churches survey mentioned previously, ministers were asked what were their favorite topics for sermons and from what sources did they draw most of their illustrative material. Most ministers replied that their illustrative material came from Biblical stories and verses, but many also drew from Chinese history, philosophy, and literature. Frequent reference was made to those two great sages of China, Confucius and Lao Tze, upon whose teachings much of Chinese civilization is built. This may seem sacrilegious to the Western mind, but is perfectly compatible to the Chinese mind.

Ministers were asked to check the following topics treated in sermons during the past year: gambling, race relations, temperance, parent-child relations, corruption in government, social welfare, public housing, and so forth. It is interesting to note that not many ministers preached on gambling, one of the most deeply rooted problems among the Chinese. On the other hand, many checked temperance as a sermon topic, though drinking is almost never a vice among the Chinese. The absence of gambling as a sermon topic is conspicuous not only from the survey but also from talks with church-going Chinese. One reason advanced for this is that gambling is such a favorite pastime with the older generation upon whom the church must rely for financial support and cooperation. Any attack against gambling would antagonize this group, making it difficult for the church to carry on its work.

The most frequently mentioned sermon topic was parent-child relationship, with race relations and social welfare tied for second place. Differences and conflicts between parent and child have been one of the most disturbing and pressing problems of the younger generation Chinese in the United States. It deserves a great deal of attention, and the minister who can counsel wisely in this respect, directing his sermons not only at the younger generation but toward the parent generation as well, will have given substance to the importance of religion.

Other sermon topics deserving special attention and treatment are: careers, employment opportunities, adjustment and acculturation to the American way of living, marital and family difficulties, and education. To know and gain comfort and release for a troubled soul is the magnetic power of the spiritual side of religion. Social services will attract an attendance at church, but it is the effectiveness of the sermons that will win the converts to Christianity.

In addition to church services and Sunday School, the Chinese churches carry on many other activities. Some sponsor teen-age fellowship groups. Some have young men's clubs or women's organizations. There are church suppers, outings, annual picnics, dances, competitive sports, bazaars—as wide a variety of activities as one will find in a generously supported Caucasian church.

In answer to the question "What are the major needs of the Chinese Protestant churches in your city?" the answer was almost unanimous that the greatest need was for trained leadership. Trained leadership means Sunday School teachers to serve in the roles mentioned above, as well as Chinese men and women conversant in the Chinese language to give counsel and guidance and to impart spiritual inspiration. The time and energy of one man, the minister, is definitely limited. Some of the ministers do not speak or understand Chinese, whereas others do not speak or understand English. Twenty-seven out of the thirty-three ministers interviewed were born in China. Four were Caucasians. The language barrier is decidedly a setback to full communication and full rapport between the shepherd and his flock. If the minister could depend upon a group of helpers to reach out to the diverse elements among his fold, the influence of the Christian church would be increased considerably.

Unfortunately, the Chinese churches are constantly losing their best young men and women to Caucasian churches. Boys and girls, nurtured in the bosom of Chinese churches, grow up, finish school, get married, and move away from Chinatowns. If their faith is strong, they seek a more spiritually challenging atmosphere in their neighborhood churches. By so doing, they move closer to the cultural norm of the larger American society and through the church gain acceptance among their neighbors. In fact, therefore, the number of Chinese Christians is greater than the sum total of the Chinese church membership. The result of this continuing process is desirable, but it is a heavy toll upon the Chinese churches when they cannot draw upon the services of this group capable of rendering assistance and leadership.

Only one or two of the ministers polled in 1955 mentioned their inadequate building facilities for religious or recreational work or the meager budgets that must be stretched to the breaking point. This is not to say that there is no need for better facilities or more funds. Imagine running a church with a full complement of recreational, social, and educational services on an average budget of $5,260 per year! And this included the pastor's salary. (Present-day budgets are not much higher.)

For many of the Chinese "churches," services are held in borrowed quarters, store fronts, private homes, and other makeshift places. Needless to say, such places of worship are not the most inspirational for meditation, worship, or communion with God. Room and facilities for recreation and social gatherings are equally lacking. In Chicago, with a Chinese population of 6,000, the only recreation area in Chinatown was an empty lot donated by a merchant. In Washington, D.C., the Chinese Community Church owned an old brick house. Services were held in the living room, and when attendance was heavy, seats were placed in the dining room, where worshippers could hear but not see the pastor. The only recreational area was the converted garage and backyard of the house. Thanks to the ceaseless efforts of the Reverend C. C. Hung, this building was torn down in 1956 and a modern, new church, adapted to the needs of its members, was erected. In spite of their cramped, makeshift space or quarters, the Chinese churches have improvised admirably and carried on a heavy load under tremendous odds and handicaps.

One of the most important adjuncts to the Chinese church is the Chinese language school. Invariably, the school is sponsored by the church, although in some of the larger Chinese centers the Chinese

Benevolent Association assumes this responsibility. A good example is the Hip Wo School, sponsored by the Chinese Methodist Church of San Francisco. Years ago, the Reverend T. T. Taam began teaching Chinese classes in the basement of his church. Today, the Hip Wo School classes go as high as the twelfth grade or the equivalent of a high school. It is the most advanced Chinese school in the continental United States.

Chinese school is generally held after regular public school hours from 4 to 6 P.M. or 5 to 7 P.M. daily and from 9 A.M. to 12 noon on Saturday mornings. This makes for a long school day for Chinese children who must keep up with their public school work as well as their Chinese studies. But most Chinese parents want their children to know something of the history, culture, and language of their ancestors. This knowledge was especially important when even the native-born Chinese had to seek a livelihood among their own people. Without some rudiments of the Chinese language, a person would be at a decided disadvantage.

Although conditions have changed today, and a knowledge of Chinese is no longer absolutely essential, the general consensus among the ministers polled is that the Chinese language should be retained among Chinese-Americans. So within the Chinese churches, Sunday School is utilized to teach English to immigrants from China, and Chinese school is held for the benefit of the American-born Chinese. Usually the Chinese minister is the teacher or principal of the Chinese school.

According to the Chinese mind, the most perplexing thing about the Christian religion is the number of denominations, each believing in the superiority of its own creed. As a result, Chinese churches dependent upon outside support must follow the dictates of the parent church and claim to be Methodist, Congregationalist, Presbyterian, or what not. They fight for, and lure away, members from each other. Instead of cooperating, they compete. Instead of unity, there is dissension. Church funds, if pooled together, might be put to work much more effectively. Parceled out among the denominations, their strength is diluted.

I am sure there are valid reasons for some division according to locality, make-up of the congregation, and so forth, but to concentrate in and around Chinatown and split along denominational lines is to dilute the powerful influence and impact that the Christian church could wield among the Chinese.

In answer to the die-hard denominationalist of the parent church who feels that only through his sect can its principles and beliefs be perpetuated, let me reveal the secret of one Chinese minister who has served in three Chinese churches, once as a Baptist minister, once as a Methodist, and is now a Congregationalist.

The Catholics, too, have their missions or churches working to propagate the faith among the Chinese. Francis L. K. Hsu, a learned student of Chinese culture, writes:

> Catholicism with its many saints, its complex rituals, and its priestly hierarchy which possesses the power to forgive, comes closer to the traditional Chinese approach to religion than does Protestantism. Even the Catholic purgatory, in which the punishment of the dead may be alleviated by the good deeds (including religious devotion) of living relatives is similar to the Chinese version of hell. To the Chinese mind, all this appears more logical than what Protestanism offers—relatively simplified rituals, no secondary supernatural beings, and an emphasis on direct communion with God. My guess is that, in so far as the Chinese take to Christianity, the great majority will continue to be Catholic rather than Protestant, and that the Protestant converts will tend to be Episcopalian rather than Unitarian.[3]

Although Chinese propensity may be toward Catholicism, two major factors in the United States work against it. First, the United States is a predominately Protestant country, so that being a Catholic means being a member of another minority. In striving for social acceptance, greater status value attaches, therefore, to being a Protestant.

Second, in the early history of the Chinese in California, the most vociferous group to oppose the Chinese was the Workingmen's Party, whose members were mainly Irish and southern European. Both of these strongly Catholic groups worked actively for Chinese

[3] Francis L. K. Hsu, *Americans and Chinese—Two Ways of Life* (New York, Henry Schuman, 1953), pp. 260–261.

exclusion, and neither was inclined to admit the Chinese into their religious fold. Any Catholic effort to evangelize the Chinese was isolated and minor.

Old St. Mary's Church on Stockton Street in San Francisco was one of these first efforts. Established in 1854, it is situated in the heart of Chinatown and has the largest Chinese membership of any church in the United States. St. Mary's has its own parochial school as well as a Chinese language school and evening classes in adult education. Mass is said in both Chinese and English.

The Transfiguration Catholic Church in New York City is unique. It is located in Chinatown, but it is also the parish church for the Italian community adjacent to Chinatown. Of its 2,000 parishioners, about 700 are Chinese. The priest, an Irishman and former missionary in Hong Kong, speaks fluent Cantonese. One mass on Sunday is delivered in this Chinese dialect.

The Chinese look upon this as their church, and the Italians consider it theirs. In spite of continuing efforts to get the two groups to mingle and join each other in fellowship meetings and social activities, the two groups remain separate. Somehow, this cleavage has not interfered with the spiritual aspect of church-going for either group.

Catholic efforts to evangelize the Chinese may have been belated, but its spectacular record in Philadelphia and Chicago points to its vigor and success in winning adherents.

In 1939, Archbishop Paul Yu-pin of Nanking paid a visit to Cardinal Dougherty in Philadelphia. It was natural for the Archbishop to inquire how many Catholics could be numbered among the residents of Chinatown. The answer: Not a one!

Both churchmen were shocked by their revelation and both were spurred to action. Through their efforts, the Chinese Catholic Church of Philadelphia was established. Two years later, the church numbered 200 members with a 95 percent attendance.

The church is located in Chinatown. For those members who live beyond this area, a brightly colored bus picks them up and sends them home. For the children, the church operates a parochial school and supplements its English courses with studies in Chinese history, language, and literature. The gaily painted bus gathers the children from the various sections of the city and delivers them home after classes. When not in use for church and school purposes, the bus is put to use for sight-seeing trips, visits to shut-ins, and recreational purposes. At all times during the week the bus, which has become a familiar trademark, can be seen cruising through the streets of Chinatown on its various missions.

In Chicago, the late Cardinal Stritch recognized the need for the Chinese to have their own church and designated St. Thérèse Catholic Mission as the parish church for all Chinese in the Archdiocese of Chicago. He placed the church under the Maryknoll Fathers because he wanted the parish to be directed by missioners who had seen service in China and could speak the Cantonese dialect. Today, St. Thérèse has close to 1,000 parishioners out of an approximate population of 6,000 persons of Chinese ancestry in Chicago.

Catholic ranks among the Chinese in the United States are growing not only because of the increased effort by the church, but also because a large number of the recent immigrants from China were already converted in Hong Kong or Formosa. Catholic missionary work in these places has traditionally been greater than Protestant efforts. One Catholic churchman related that the church goal for converts in Hong Kong was 25,000, but the actual number of converts has long ago exceeded that figure and now runs to the six figures rather than five.

Since 1952, the Catholic church has actively aided more than 1,000 students to come to the United States on scholarships, and it has also rendered incalculable service to refugees and immigrants in facilitating their entry into the United States. The Chinese are not unmindful of these benefits and services and in gratitude will give lifelong devotion to the church.

14

The Chinese Get into the Best Places

"PREJUDICE?" asked Richard Lee, a tall handsome young man of twenty-nine, responding to my question. "Sure, there must be some bigoted people around, but if you mean have I ever encountered evidence of it, no.

"I was brought up in a small town near Boston, Massachusetts, one of ten children. My parents operated a laundry. Our playmates, our schoolmates, our neighbors were all Caucasians. Sure, I participated in extracurricular activities, plenty of them, and I have a wonderful memory of my school days. So did my brothers and sisters. Actually it was harder for us to get along with other Chinese children when we went to Boston for an occasional visit to Chinatown.

"After high school, I was drafted into the Army. For physical reasons I was discharged. I went back to school and got myself a college degree. I've traveled a lot and met a lot of people. I don't feel that people have been unkind to me because I am Chinese. It is up to me to make the overtures. After all, every place you go, the people are already settled. They have their circle of friends, their way of doing things, and their way of thinking. If I want to join them, it's up to me to break the ice.

"Yes, I've held jobs and I've owned a business, and I can't truthfully say that my being Chinese has meant anything one way or the other. My business partner is a Caucasian. I go out occasionally with Caucasian girls. If I marry one, ours will be the first mixed marriage in the family, but I see nothing against it."

Richard's personal experiences enable him to look at the race relations problem from a very healthy point of view. He grew up in a Caucasian neighborhood where he did not encounter any prejudice. He lived a way of life that was more American than Chinese. He, himself, is a very personable young man. He is well educated and well adjusted. He is not inclined, therefore, to think that every slight, every unkind remark, every refusal can be attributed to prejudice. But he also happens to be living in an era of unprecedented prosperity. The Big Depression was before his time. The unemployment rate at the time of this writing is less than 5 percent. In some of the industrial areas, the rate is as low as 2.5 percent, and the labor shortage is acute.

Richard is living in a period when it is quite unfashionable to exhibit any expression of prejudice. The Civil Rights Movement has resulted in employers actively recruiting members of minority groups. Children are bussed from distant points so that schools can be integrated in practice. A Catholic has been elected President. Politicians in large metropolitan areas look first at the color of a man's skin not to reject him but to get him to run to balance the ticket.

The social atmosphere now is different from the days, say, when Pardee Lowe tried to get his first job as an office boy in San Francisco. The time was around the mid-1920's. Pardee had just finished a course in American history, and Thomas Jefferson's ringing phrases on the equality of men were fresh in his memory. That words and deeds did not mesh had never occurred to him, but his youthful naïvete did not last long. In his book, *Father and Glorious Descendant*, he wrote:

> The next summer, my thirteenth, I decided to go to work during vacation. I needed spending money badly for my first term in high school. Father applauded this show of independence until I informed him that I intended, if possible, to become an office boy in an American business firm. Then he was seized with profound misgivings. "Would they hire you?" Father inquired.
>
> "Why shouldn't they?" I replied, with overwhelming self-confidence. "See!" I pointed to the Sunday editions of the *San Francisco Chronicle*. "I can hold any of these jobs. . . ."
>
> Blithely one sunny July morning, I went forth job hunting, well-scrubbed, wearing my Sunday suit and totally unaware of the difficulties that confronted me. In my pocket were ten clipped

> newspaper advertisements, each one, I thought with a job purposely made for me.

Almost at once, Pardee began to sense that something was wrong. When he was finally admitted to an inner office at Richard and Mathison, a bond house, he thought for a minute that his suspicions were not justified, but . . .

> There it was. On Mr. Royal's lean, smooth-shaven face was the same look of incredulity that I had once noticed on Mr. Brown's. But only for a moment. For he suddenly reached for a cigarette, lit it and looked at me quizzically, while I hopped on one foot and then on the other.
>
> "Young man," he said, "I understand you would like to work for us? Well then, you'd better tell us something of yourself."
>
> "Why, of course," I said, "of course." And impulsively I told everything, my boy-scout training, and my desire to earn my own keep during the summer.
>
> Mr. Royal seemed visibly impressed. When a faint smile replaced his frown, I stopped fidgeting. I fully expected him to ask me to come to work in the morning. Therefore I was appalled when he told me that he was sorry, but all the jobs were taken. It never occurred to me that our interview would end like this.
>
> My face fell. I hadn't expected such an answer. To soften the blow, Mr. Royal added that if I filled out an application he would call me if there were any openings.
>
> I filled out the application under the unsympathetic eyes of the information girl, and stumbled miserably out of the office, vaguely sensible of the fact that there would never be any opening.
>
> The feeling was intensified as I made the round of the other nine firms. Everywhere I was greeted with perturbation, amusement, pity or irritation—and always with identically the same answer. "Sorry," they invariably said, "the position has just been filled." My jaunty self-confidence soon wilted. I sensed that something was radically, fundamentally wrong. It just didn't

> seem possible that overnight all of the positions could have been occupied, particularly not when everybody spoke of a labor shortage. Suspicion began to dawn. What had Father said? "American firms do not customarily employ Chinese." To verify his statement, I looked again in the newspaper the next morning and for the week after, and sure enough, just as I expected, the same ten ads were still in the newspapers.[1]

In the social climate of that day, neither education nor qualifications counted when it came to getting a job. The mere fact of being Chinese or non-white meant that one never got a chance to get a foot in the door. In 1928, the Stanford University Placement Service stated:

"It is almost impossible to place a Chinese or Japanese of either the first or second generation in any kind of position, engineering, manufacturing or business. Many firms have general regulations against employing them; others object to them on the grounds that the other men employed by the firms do not care to work with them."[2]

This statement was made roughly forty years ago. If the hands of the clock were turned back another forty years to the late 1880's, the position of the Chinese in the United States then was practically insufferable. The noted historian James Bryce wrote in his classic work, *The American Commonwealth*:

The Second Constitution of California of 1879 "forbids all corporations to employ any Chinese, debars them from the suffrage by thereby attempting to transgress the 15th amendment to the Federal Constitution, forbids their employment on any public works, annuls all contracts for 'coolie labor,' directs the legislature to provide for the punishment of any company which shall employ Chinese, to impose conditions on the residence of Chinese and to cause their removal if they fail to observe these conditions."[3]

In placing the above passage in its perspective, one should not

[1] Pardee Lowe, *Father and Glorious Descendant* (Boston, Little Brown & Co., 1943), pp. 143–146.
[2] Eliot G. Mears, *Resident Orientals on the American Pacific Coast* (Chicago, University of Chicago Press, 1928), p. 200.
[3] James Bryce, *The American Commonwealth* (New York, The Macmillan Co., 1927), p. 439.

fail to note that this was the supreme law of the state of California. Charles F. Marden in his book, *Minorities in American Society*, elaborated on other discriminatory legislation aimed at the Chinese:

> Acts discriminating against the Chinese, imposing special taxes on them and prohibiting them from entering the state were passed by the California legislature in the 1850's and 1880's. Opposition to the Chinese was manifested also in city ordinances which attempted to reach the Chinese indirectly. For example, "San Francisco had a laundry ordinance imposing a license fee as follows: on laundries using a one-horse vehicle, $2 per quarter; two horses, $4 per quarter; no vehicle, $15 per quarter. The Chinese laundries commonly used no vehicle. It was made a misdemeanor for any person on the sidewalks to carry baskets suspended on a pole across the shoulders—a typical Chinese practice." And because the loss of a queue was a disgrace to some Chinamen, the so-called "queue ordinance" was especially perturbing to them. It "provided that every person convicted of a criminal offense should have his hair cut to a length of one inch from his head."[4]

Oscar Handlin, Pulitzer-Prize-winning scholar and authority on immigrant minorities in the United States, commented on how the Californians, in their intense prejudice against the Chinese during this period, were willing to undermine the entire structure of human rights, international obligations, and Constitutional guarantees upon which this nation was founded. He wrote:

> The Workingmen's delegation brought in a series of anti-Chinese propositions of which the most important were as follows: Aliens should not be allowed to hold property; Chinese should not be allowed to trade, peddle or carry on any mercantile business, no person not eligible to be a citizen should be allowed to settle in the State; and any person encouraging such should be fined; aliens ineligible to citizenship should be prohibited from bearing arms, giving testimony in the courts in

[4] Charles F. Marden, *Minorities in American Society* (New York, American Book Co., 1952), p. 161.

> cases involving white persons, from fishing in the inland waters of the State and from employment on public works; a per capita tax of $250.00 should be levied on each Chinese immigrant.
>
> These propositions were remarkable not only for their display of rancor and ignorance, but for their total inapplicability to the problem to be solved. Their tone is inhuman in its disregard of the common rights of men, as well as of the protection guaranteed to the Chinese under the Burlingame Treaty. At least two-thirds of them were on their face violations of the Federal Constitution and several had been passed and declared invalid in previous years.[5]

With the turn of the century, public furor died down somewhat, but it brought no improvement. In 1906, Alien Land Acts in Washington, Oregon, and California, aimed at divesting both the Chinese and Japanese of their land holdings and preventing them from purchasing new parcels, were passed. The Acts forbade persons ineligible to citizenship to own any interest in agricultural lands by purchase. Even if the land were inherited, such aliens were compelled to sell and take only the proceeds from the sale. Alien title to agricultural lands were defeasible by the state and good against all individuals. The Acts made it difficult even for the American-born Asiatic child, who was by birthright a citizen of the United States, to own agricultural land.[6]

It seems, therefore, that the pattern of prejudice and discrimination against the Chinese has progressed from wretched to tolerable to good. One could surmise that the trend is for the better, except that we already know from Chapter 2 of this book that the American attitude toward the Chinese has come full cycle. The cordial reception tendered to the Chinese at first and the warm sentiments of the Western pioneers toward the hard-working, adaptable, and pliable Chinese gave way to an abrupt about-face when these very same traits caused them to pose competition to the white man's livelihood.

It has long been apparent to students of psychology—the science

[5] Oscar Handlin, *Immigration as a Factor in American History* (Englewood Cliffs, N.J., Prentice-Hall, Inc., 1959), pp. 170–171.
[6] Mears, *op. cit.*, p. 187.

of human emotions and behavior—that prejudice is without logical or rational base. In his book, *The Nature of Prejudice*, Gordon Allport asked:

> Why do so many people admire Abraham Lincoln? They may tell you it is because he was thrifty, hardworking, eager for knowledge, ambitious, devoted to the rights of the average man and eminently successful in climbing the ladder of opportunity.
>
> Why do so many people dislike the Jews: They may tell you it is because they are thrifty, hardworking, eager for knowledge, ambitious, devoted to the rights of the average man and eminently successful in climbing the ladder of opportunity. Of course, adjectives applied to the Jews may be less laudatory. . . .
>
> The fact that prejudiced people so readily subscribe to self-contradictory stereotypes is one proof that genuine group traits are not the point at issue.[7]

In warding off prejudice, in minimizing it, or in learning to live with it, minority groups have adopted their distinctive ways of dealing with the problem. One way is to fight back and try to gain a foothold in the dominant group by resorting to belligerency, eliciting public sympathy, and threatening the use of force, riots, and aggression. The Jews and Japanese are typical of the groups that react in this manner. They will aggressively attack any attempt to deny them equality. When California tried to segregate Japanese students in the public schools, Japan threatened war, and California backed down. When a Jewish friend of mine felt he had been slighted because he had not been invited to a party, he crashed the affair, made sure that his presence was noted, and left. But the gains obtained in this manner evoke deep feelings of resentment and hostility.

Another way, formerly employed by Negroes in dealing with racial prejudice, was to submit—in other words—to know one's place and keep to it. If the front seats of a bus were reserved for whites only, the Negro did not sit in the front even though the back seats were fully occupied. If the wash rooms were marked "white" and "colored"

[7] Gordon W. Allport, *The Nature of Prejudice* (Reading, Mass., Addison-Wesley Publishing Co., 1954), pp. 189 and 195.

the Negro meekly went in the door marked "colored." If the Southern whites thought that Negroes were only capable of doing field or menial labor, the Negro only did field or menial jobs. He did not make an issue; he yielded. Thus the Southern whites were apt to boast, "We get along fine with our Negroes," but they looked upon the Negro with affectionate contempt.

The Chinese chose yet another way—that of withdrawal. If the California social and economic climate became unbearable, the Chinese dispersed eastward. If the white man begrudged him a job, he opened a laundry or restaurant or grocery and became his own employer. If the American courts denied him justice, he bypassed them and set up his own organizations to settle differences among his fellows. He kept his contacts with the larger American society to a minimum. He never intruded, but neither did he resign himself to permanent subordinancy. He endured because he had an ultimate goal in mind.

Though his own life in the United States was wretched, he had hopes for the future. If by "serving a term" in the United States he could save enough to buy several parcels of land in China, he would raise himself to the gentry class. His sons would have a chance to get an education that would open doors to other opportunities. If the sons were in this country, they were urged and prodded into getting as much education as possible, for though the occupational outlook for them here was bleak, they could always go to China to practice as doctors, engineers, or scientists.

Because the Chinese chose to withdraw, reaction of the majority group toward the Chinese differed from that directed toward Jews, Japanese, or Negroes. "The Chinaman was a good loser. He has withdrawn from the struggle; he is no longer a significant threat to the standards of white labor. He may now be treated with a high degree of indifference or even amiability. . . ."[8]

World War II brought about a radical social upheaval resulting again in warm, friendly sentiments toward the Chinese. China and the United States were allies in a global war against a common enemy. The image of the brave and suffering Chinese struck a sympathetic

[8] Oliver Cromwell Cox, *Caste, Class and Race* (New York, Monthly Review Press, 1959), p. 419.

chord in American hearts. This coupled with an acute labor shortage forced many business firms to hire Chinese personnel. Once hired, the Chinese proved admirably that they were capable and reliable. In fact, where Chinese have actually been hired, personnel managers seldom hesitate to hire another Chinese again.

A good example is seen in the case of the Federal Telephone and Radio Corporation of New Jersey. Mr. Nelson, the personnel manager, was interviewing Jang Shoon Ong for a position as waiter for the company restaurant, but he desperately needed a skilled worker for wiring and assembling communications equipment. A question elicited the answer that Ong had taken a course in the Essex Vocational School Machine Shop. Jang Shoon Ong was put in the plant. Within a month, 65 Chinese-Americans were working for the company, and later this number swelled to 145.[9]

If World War II opened doors in the United States for Chinese-Americans, it must be remembered that another door had clanged shut for them in China. Being an active battle zone, it was too dangerous to risk going there. Since then, the Communist take-over has completely cut off any thought of going back to China. It was a question now of sink or swim in the United States.

In 1947, Beulah Ong Kwoh's master's thesis presented the personal opinion and experiences of 337 respondents regarding prejudice as it affected their choice of occupation, their application for employment, and their chances for advancement:[10]

Effect of race on *choice* of occupation:
⅔ felt that race was no determinant in their occupational choice;
¼ felt that it did in some way affect their decision;
1/12 felt that their choice was seriously affected by the racial factor.

Effect of race on *application* for employment:
¼ said it had been cause for denial of employment;
½ said no, it had not;
¼ did not know.

[9] "Chinese on the Job," *Nation's Business* (August 1943), p. 94.

[10] Beulah Ong Kwoh, "The Occupational Status of the American-Born Chinese College Graduate," unpublished master's thesis (University of Chicago, 1947), p. 102.

Effect of race on chances for occupational *advancement*:

½ felt that race was no obstacle. Sometimes racial factor can be a spur to greater and more concentrated effort or it can be an insurmountable handicap and shackle;

⅓ felt that it had hindered them somewhat;

1/10 did not know, as they had not encountered the problem yet.

From personal observation and knowledge, I would say that as late as 1950, the Chinese in the United States had a hard time finding suitable employment. I attended several meetings at the China Institute in New York City where students whose funds from China had been abruptly cut off and who were faced with an urgent and immediate need to support themselves had come to the China Institute for help. Happily, I am in contact with many of these students today, and I can truly say that I have witnessed a remarkable transition.

I knew a young man with a Ph.D. degree in economics who was forced to take a job as hat-check boy in the Plaza Hotel in 1951. Today, he is an official of a large Wall Street Bank. Another economics graduate could find employment only in a Chinese restaurant as a waiter. He is now vice-president of a local branch bank. An engineer friend worked as a dishwasher. Not long ago he supervised the installation of heating and ventilating systems of several new buildings that went up at the J. F. Kennedy International Airport in New York.

Again in the early 1950's I was witness to an example of flagrant discrimination in a government agency. A position of section head in this agency dealing with Far Eastern affairs had been vacant for a long time. In offhand conversation with the division chief, I had made casual reference to this fact and inquired as to the reason why.

He replied, "We just haven't been able to find an American with the necessary Far Eastern background."

"Why, what's the matter with N———?" I said, referring to a colleague of Oriental ancestry. "He's lived and studied in the Far East. He is a graduate of the University of California. And he is an American-born citizen."

"Oh, you know what I mean," said the chief sheepishly. "I mean an American-American."

Fortunately in that very same government agency today, several persons of Chinese ancestry hold administrative and policy-making positions.

In 1956, an aeronautical engineer came to the United States under the Refugee Relief Act. Prior to his arrival, he had represented China on the War Reparations Mission in Japan, supervising the dismantling of Japanese plants for shipment to China. His admittance to the United States was sponsored by a ball-bearing firm that gave him a job as draftsman. This could be interpreted as an insult to the man's experience and former high offices in the government in China. But three years later, having fortified himself with a few refresher courses in aerodynamics and having acquainted himself with his surroundings and the personnel market, he sought and obtained an excellent position with an aircraft manufacturing company on Long Island, New York.

Shortly thereafter, the company suffered reverses, and a severe cutback forced out many engineers with as many as twelve years' seniority. When the Chinese engineer offered to resign, the company, recognizing his potential worth, even offered him inducements to stay.

The Chinese have distinguished themselves in professions and in jobs beyond the circumscribed traditional occupations once relegated to them (see Chapter 16), but one cannot generalize if isolated individuals manage to gain recognition here and there. To get an inkling of how widely the Chinese are represented in American industry, I wrote to the personnel department of the International Business Machines Corporation, certainly one of the giants of American industry. Its manufacturing and research operations are nationwide, distributed in 17 plants and 21 laboratories throughout the country. I was referred to Mr. J. W. LaForte, personnel manager of a nearby plant, the IBM Manufacturing Division at Poughkeepsie, New York.

"Sorry," said Mr. LaForte, "I can't answer your question specifically as to how many persons of Chinese ancestry work in the Poughkeepsie plant. Our personnel records do not show national origin. To give you an approximate figure, I would say there are about 65 to 90. To the best of my knowledge, all of them are professionals. None is in a clerical or custodial capacity. Why don't you visit our plant? My assistant, Mr. Edwin Hartmann, will be glad to show you around and arrange for you to talk to some of our Chinese employees."

I was more than happy to accept Mr. LaForte's invitation. After a personal guided tour through the plant, which gave me a glimpse of some of the electronic marvels of automation, I spoke with four men, each of whom performed a vital task in the chain of production of these intelligent machines.

Gim Lee is in product engineering, where he supervises the work of 22 people. He has been with IBM since 1956, and he has worked on the memory or "brains" of every IBM machine put out by the company, including its latest, the 360. Gim was born in Canton, China, but his father, a laundryman in Bloomfield, N. J., came to the United States when Gim was ten years old. When Gim graduated from Rensselaer Polytechnic Institute, he was offered jobs from such leading companies as Ford, Sperry Rand, and Corning Glass. The best offer came from IBM, the one he accepted.

"At IBM," said Gim, "there is no awareness among us of race differences except perhaps on my own part. I have a strong national pride which makes me feel I must uphold the image and reputation of my people."

P. W., who is shy about being named, has been with IBM for six years. His job is to plan new products such as discs, drums, and peripheral tapes used to store information in the IBM machines. P. W. travels a great deal to interview customers and to familiarize himself with their operations so that he can give them a tailor-made product to suit their needs. Born in Shanghai, P. W. came to the United States in 1952. He holds a B.A. degree from Princeton and an M.A. and E.E. from Columbia. With typical Chinese humility, he answered, "If I don't get ahead at IBM, it will be due to my own lack of ability and not because I am Chinese."

Shortly before my visit, Frank Chin had been singled out at IBM to receive an award from the National Aeronautics Space Agency for outstanding contribution to the successful development of the large-capacity memory used in connection with the Gemini space flights.

Mr. Chin has been with IBM for approximately 10 years. Prior to that, he worked for 11 years with the Radio Receptor Company, now known as General Instruments. He is an alumnus of New York University and the RCA Institute.

"My job as a staff officer in quality control involves working more with people than with ideas or with the computers or with the parts," Mr. Chin insisted. "I'm not kept behind the scenes working alone or with a small group. You see, I am responsible for the training of new personnel."

A little older than the two men I spoke with previously, Mr. Chin remembers when the occupational opportunities for anyone of Chinese ancestry were quite limited. When he came from Toishan, China, in 1940, he first worked in his uncle's grocery store and then in a laundry. With memories of former days, Frank Chin is gratified that he has been able, within the span of his own generation, to elevate himself to the position he now holds at IBM.

John Tiao's job title is Manager, Tape Technology. He supervises the work of 40 men who work with the development of tape used to store data in the IBM computers. Born in Tsingtao, China, Mr. Tiao came to the United States as a student in 1947. When he obtained his mechanical engineering degree from the University of Kentucky, an IBM recruiter offered him a job, which he accepted. That was 14 years ago.

Mr. Tiao travels a great deal in connection with his work. "Have you ever been refused service or hotel accommodations?" I inquired.

"Never," he replied.

It is quite understandable for some Chinese who realize that they are members of a visible minority group and who are sensitive about the treatment accorded the Chinese in the past to be edgy and apprehensive about their present status. For instance, I talked at length with Mr. J. M., president of a Chinese young men's organization, immediately after his organization had sponsored a series of three career-guidance seminars. These were aimed at helping Chinese-Americans explore the occupational opportunities open to them and teaching them ways to go about getting the jobs they want. Competent speakers and authorities were invited to address the seminars, and advance publicity was circulated among the Chinese. This is the gist of my conversation with Mr. J. M.:

SUNG: I'm sorry I couldn't attend the seminars, Mr. M., but I do want to know what happened.

J.M.: There's nothing much to tell. I guess they weren't too successful. We had gone to a lot of effort to arrange for prominent speakers from the New York State Employment Service, the New York City Board of Education, and others to come and counsel us, but hardly any Chinese-Americans showed up.

SUNG: Why? How do you account for the low attendance?

J.M.: I don't know myself. I thought the organization was doing a public service for the Chinese community by setting up these seminars. I expected a large turnout. Frankly, I was disappointed.

SUNG: Could it be that getting a good job is no longer a pressing problem facing Chinese-Americans today—in other words, we either have good jobs or can get good jobs readily, so that your seminars held no special attraction?

J.M.: Oh no, quite the contrary. I think that as Chinese, we will always be faced with the problem of racial prejudice, which makes it harder for us to get a job. I felt the Chinese needed the type of career-guidance counseling which we provided in the seminars.

SUNG: Then you do feel that Chinese-Americans face strong occupational prejudice?

J.M.: Oh yes.

SUNG: How many members are there in your organization?

J.M.: Twenty.

SUNG: Are your members mainly native-born or China-born?

J.M.: All are native-born except one.

SUNG: Can you tell me what sort of work your members are engaged in?

J.M.: I have the membership list here. Let me read it to you. We have three men in insurance, three in investments, two lawyers, a foot doctor, a banker, a writer, an assistant dean at

Columbia University, two teachers, an accountant, a chemist, a sales engineer, a business administrator, and a dentist.

SUNG: Wouldn't you say that all your members, without exception, hold upper-echelon jobs? If there was strong occupational prejudice against the Chinese, do you think your members would be holding jobs like these?

J.M.: I never thought about it that way before.

In similar conversations and similar interviews, my impression is that three-fourths of the young men and women under 30 years of age have not known occupational prejudice or discrimination. Their attitude in general is similar to that expressed by Richard Lee at the beginning of this chapter. The others fall into the following categories:

(1) Young women who are housewives and who have never looked for a job so they cannot speak from personal experience.

(2) Persons over thirty years of age, especially if they come from the West Coast or South.

(3) China-borns who are handicapped by a strong accent in speech or who are shy, reticent, and unable to project themselves aggressively or effectively.

(4) People who have dealt through an intermediary such as an employment agency or low-ranking company interviewer. The function of these people is to screen applicants, and they are more apt to apply the color or racial bar. Even if they themselves are not prejudiced and do not wish to discriminate, they are not sure how the person to whom the applicant is to be referred will react. So they stay on the safe side.

(5) A member of the student group. By student I mean one who was born and brought up in China, Taiwan, or Hong Kong and who originally came to the United States for the sole purpose of pursuing his studies. No doubt many of these students came from well-to-do homes because only the well-to-do could afford an education for their children. Most of these students never knew the meaning of work. In China they were the intelligentsia that scorned manual labor. These students expected to return to China, where educated men being few, they anticipated good jobs. It never occurred to them that they would have to compete vigorously on the American labor market, an experi-

ence for which they were totally unequipped—culturally and emotionally.

Though these students may have had no difficulty with the English written word, they lacked the spontaneity, the fluency, and the idiomatic expressions of American speech. As is customary in China they were outwardly humble about their abilities, but they did not know how to "sell" themselves.

Most of these students had excellent academic backgrounds. Though they were full of book-learning, not many had any experience at all in the actual application of their knowledge. Like all college graduates clutching their newly won sheepskins, they imagined themselves mints of worldly wisdom and knowledge, only to have their egos deflated by the time their fifth interview with a personnel officer was completed.

The applicant may have had a master's degree in accounting and presumed that he knew all there was to know about the subject, but in reality, no amount of textbook learning compensates for the day-to-day lessons learned while actually working with the books and coping with the financial problems of a business firm. No employer is likely to offer a young graduate a responsible position unless he has proven himself in the organization by coming in at the bottom.

I have seen Chinese students who were insulted and incensed that they should be offered a position of junior accountant when they boasted an M.A. or an even more advanced degree. And though they may have condescended to accept the job, they seethed with inward hostility and resentment at what they interpret to be prejudice against them. They do not realize that their Caucasian schoolmates undergo the same deflation to their egos without the crutch of social discrimination to rationalize their disappointment. With the passage of time, the large majority of these students are finding their niches and are making noteworthy contributions in their respective fields.

Housing is another broad area where minority groups have felt the sting of discrimination keenly. "It is not surprising that barriers to equal housing opportunity should be among the most rigid which minority groups must face. Housing is more than physical shelter. Where a person lives bespeaks his social status, which broadly, he shares with others who occupy the same neighborhood. . . . To be a neighbor, therefore, is more symbolic of equal status than to be a co-worker, fellow student or fellow organization member."[11]

W. Lloyd Warner and Leo Srole in their book, *The Social Systems of American Ethnic Groups*, also stated that resistance against admitting a member of the minority group as a neighbor is greater than permitting him his choice of job or mobility in employment. It is also quite evident that attainment of occupational status must precede residential status, for those confined to the lower rung jobs cannot afford better housing.

Some discussion of housing restrictions against the Chinese has already been made in Chapter 9 on Chinatowns. We saw how these ethnic enclaves evolved from the Chinese immigrants' seeking protection in numbers among their own kind and how these boundaries became hard and fast so that eventually the Chinese were restricted to these ghettoes—their choice of residence outside of Chinatown severely limited until recent years.

Lately, indications are that progress made by the Chinese-Americans in housing parallels their progress in the occupational sphere. The last publicized case of housing discrimination against a Chinese occurred in 1952, when Sheng Sing purchased a home in Southwoods, California, a little town of about 400 families. When some of the neighbors learned that a Chinese family was moving in, they protested. A firm believer in democracy and its workings, Sheng Sing boldly suggested a vote. He agreed to abide by the outcome.

When the vote was counted, Sheng Sing was stunned. Only 202 residents voted, but 174 voted against him. When news of the incident leaked out, however, the public was infuriated. Church leaders denounced the vote of the residents of Southwood; veterans of the Korean War protested. And the press spread its front pages with editorials of condemnation. Within two days, Sheng Sing received thirty offers to sell him a home in other suburban neighborhoods of San Francisco where he would be welcomed.

Two weeks after the Sheng Sing incident, Freddie Wing, a cook in a Swiss restaurant, bought a home in Sonoma, fifty miles north of San Francisco. There was no Chinese living in the area, and if

[11] *Where Shall We Live?* Report of the Commission on Race and Housing (Berkeley, University of California Press, 1958), p. 3.

Freddie moved in, he would be the first Oriental there. The Sheng Sing affair was still very much in the news, and Freddie was a bit uneasy, but he went ahead with his plans for a housewarming.

Invitations were sent out. Freddie barbecued a whole pig, set up a cocktail bar in the garage, and awaited developments. The developments came in the form of an uproarious welcome for Freddie and his family. Both the Sheng Sing incident and Freddie Wing's housewarming occurred within a few weeks and within a short distance of each other. Yet in one instance there was rejection and unpleasantness, while in the other, a hearty welcome.

Many years have lapsed since the Sheng Sing affair. Today's generation of Chinese homeowners scarcely know or have forgotten that once there were Alien Land Acts prohibiting their ownership of land or that restrictive covenants once limited their residence to within the prescribed boundaries of Chinatowns.

I worked for a short while in a neighborhood real-estate office. The broker had insisted upon my helping him out. His office is located in the northern part of Queens County, a good middle-class suburb of New York City. As many Chinese had been buying property in the area, the broker felt that a salesperson of Chinese ancestry would attract these customers to his office. With anti-discrimination laws in New York State, a broker is happiest when racial minorities do not come through his door. When he actively solicits such customers in a good neighborhood, the significance of this fact is apparent.

One day, a Filipino customer came in to rent an apartment. I showed her an attractive apartment in a very desirable building. She liked the place, but I could sense a little reservation. Finally she ventured to ask me, "Do you think they would mind Filipinos?"

I tried to reassure her by saying, "Of course not. I have a Chinese friend living in the building, and there are many Chinese in the neighborhood."

"Oh, that's different," she countered; "the Chinese get into the best places."

On another occasion a builder came into the office. "Tell me," he inquired, "is there a Chinese newspaper in New York? I want to place an ad for my houses."

If anyone can speak with authority on minority groups and housing, it is Professor Davis McEntire of the University of California, who directed an exhaustive three-year study on this subject for the Commission on Race and Housing under a grant from the Fund for the Republic. He found that:

"All white neighborhoods in San Francisco are accepting Negroes, Chinese-Americans and members of other minorities without fuss or bother. There is no particular antagonism to the new neighbors, nor is there any particular sympathy for them. They tend to be treated in the same anonymous or impersonal way as any other newcomers in a big city neighborhood."[12]

Christopher Rand wrote in the *New Yorker* of November 1957:

"Asians in San Francisco can now settle anywhere. The San Francisco Council for Civic Unity said that land values are no longer affected by proximity of Asians because the white Californians have simply stopped caring about the matter. The West Coast public is getting used to Asians. . . . Actually anti-Oriental prejudice in this region is at an all-time low."[13]

To some extent, occupational status determines residential status, and both determine social status, but social status is more than a combination of the first two. Vance Packard in *The Status Seekers* listed these determinants of social status: source of income, amount of income, education, occupation, address, type of home, behavior, friends, social clubs, recency of arrival in locality, nationality, race, and religion.

The average Chinese is not interested in seeking social status to the extent of becoming a society leader, of being admitted to an exclusive golf club, or of keeping up with the Joneses in a show of conspicuous consumption. He just wants to be on a friendly, cordial basis with his co-workers and neighbors. In his daily contacts, he is content if he is accepted as an equal or treated without discrimination. His occupational and residential status are so newly won, he is not ready to assault the barriers of snobbery and social exclusiveness. In fact,

[12] "West Coast Whites Accept Other Races," *The New York Times* (Dec. 13, 1954).

[13] Christopher Rand, "A Reporter at Large," *New Yorker* (Nov. 16, 1957), pp. 113–114.

"Society," elite clubs, being seen in the right places with the right people, and ostentatious display of wealth are somewhat alien to Chinese culture. To the Chinese mind, these symbols of social status have not as yet supplanted the prestige that comes from scholarship, official position, and an illustrious family.

The Chinese in this country get along very well with their fellow Americans. Personal relations between them are extremely warm and friendly. Observers have often commented on the similarities in temperament between the two peoples. Their same down-to-earth qualities, their humorous nature, tend to make them think along the same lines and see things in the same light. In reality, there is a genuine affection for the Chinese, who were never so belligerent or pushy as to challenge the white majority's position, nor so submissive and servile as to invite contempt.

The Chinese have always been highly respected even when they were persecuted—for their strong moral qualities, for their industry and perseverance, for their honor, and for their low criminal and juvenile delinquency rates. In recent years, this respect has deepened and broadened because of the large number of Chinese in the professions of medicine, science, engineering, and teaching, all prestige jobs.

In 1961, a survey by the Chinese Embassy showed that more than 1,300 persons of Chinese extraction were on the faculties of 88 American institutions of higher learning. Of these Chinese, 30 were heads of departments, 130 were full professors, and 300 or more had the rank of associate professor. At America's three ranking Ivy League universities—Harvard, Princeton, and Yale—there was a combined total of 98 Chinese on their distinguished faculties.

Vance Packard's job prestige scale of 200 occupations shows that physicians rank second and college professors rank seventh. Nuclear physicists rank twentieth. The fact that the professor is Chinese cannot diminish a student's respect to any great degree if the student has respect for the knowledge the professor imparts. Nor can a patient lack respect for his doctor if he wishes to be cured of his malady. In other words, respect is inherent in certain occupations in which large numbers of Chinese are employed.

The Chinese are served in restaurants and admitted to movies, hotels, schools, bathing pools, and other public places. Only in isolated cases has segregation been imposed upon the Chinese. For a brief period in Mississippi, schools were segregated into those for whites, those for Negroes, and those for Chinese. The small number of Chinese students made this setup unfeasible. Shortly thereafter, the Chinese pupils were accepted into the white schools.

Prejudice against the Chinese is more often presumed than real. In *The Nature of Prejudice*, Professor Gordon Allport related an experiment which proved that "actual discrimination is low compared to verbal rejection of the Chinese."

A social worker accompanied a Chinese couple traveling to all sections of the United States. They stopped at 66 sleeping places and 184 eating places. They were refused service only once. Afterwards, the proprietors of these places received questionnaires through the mail asking if they would take Chinese guests in their establishments. Over 92 percent of the places stated they would *not* serve Chinese people. A control group of places not visited gave the same results. These proprietors undoubtedly had an abstract and unfavorable preconceived idea about Chinese. When confronted with Chinese in the flesh, their notions were modified.

From this, we see that there is a wide variance between popularly held ideas and attitudes and the degree of actual social acceptance of the Chinese in our midst. Again, this is clearly evident in the extent of intermarriage between Chinese and whites in the United States.

The worst fear that one race has for another is loss of identity through mixed marriage or a more disparaging term, miscegenation. Fear on both sides of the fence is equally intense. And the ultimate in acceptance or rejection of a group is determined by the attitude toward marriage with a member of the out-group. Marriage and its attendant physical intimacy play upon the emotions. While a person may have no objection to sitting in the same restaurant, working in the same office, or living next door to a person of different coloring or different beliefs and background, marriage results in union and fusion with the marriage partner. Issue from the union will bear the stamp of both the parents, with the characteristics and blood of both parents in their veins. The blood of the lineal descendants will be forever altered, never to run pure again.

Against such stupendous considerations, intermarriage, therefore, becomes a major determinant of prejudice and discrimination. Where the Alien Land Acts have been invalidated, where the exclusion acts have been repealed, where discrimination in housing, in employment, in social contacts have been battered down, there still exists, in twelve states, laws which expressly forbid marriage between whites and persons of the Mongolian race.* These states are Arizona, Georgia, Idaho, Louisiana, Mississippi, Missouri, Nebraska, Nevada, South Dakota, Utah, Virginia, and Wyoming. Each state words its laws differently, some naming the Chinese outright, others referring to the Mongolian race or non-Caucasic race. The following chart shows the states which have had miscegenation laws affecting the Chinese:

TABLE 14–1

State Miscegenation Laws Against Chinese

State	*Law*	*Penalty*
Arizona	Marriage between white person and persons of Negro, Mongolian, Malayan, or Hindu blood null and void.	—
California	Miscegenation law held unconstitutional in 1948.	
Georgia	It is unlawful for a white person to marry any other than a white person. Such marriages void.	Guilty of felony and shall be punished by imprisonment for not less than 2 yrs. and not more than 5 yrs.
Idaho	Marriage between white person and person of Mongolian, Negro, or mulatto blood is illegal.	—
Louisiana	Marriage between white person and person of color is forbidden, null and void.	Penalty imposed for solemnizing such marriages.
Mississippi	Marriage between white person and any other person having ⅛ Negro, mulatto, or Mongolian blood is unlawful and void.	Fine of $500 or imprisonment in State Penitentiary for 10 yrs. or both.

*On June 12, 1967 the Supreme Court ruled that states cannot outlaw marriages between whites and nonwhites.

State	*Law*	*Penalty*
Missouri	Marriage between white person and person with ⅛ Negro or Mongolian blood is prohibited and void.	Imprisonment in penitentiary for 2 yrs. and not less than $100 fine or imprisonment in county jail for 3 mos. or both fine and imprisonment.
Montana	Miscegenation law repealed in 1953.	
Nebraska	Marriage between white person and any other with ⅛ or more Negro, Japanese, or Chinese blood is void.	—
Nevada	Mixed marriages between Caucasian and Ethiopian or black race, Malayan or brown race, and Mongolian or yellow race is unlawful.	Penalty for solemnizing such marriages. Penalty for contracting parties, fine not exc. $500 and not less than 6 mos. and not more than 1 yr. or both.
Oregon	Miscegenation law repealed in 1951.	
S. Dakota	Mixed race marriages void from beginning between white person and any other person belonging to African, Korean, Malayan, or Mongolian race.	Guilty of misdemeanor. Fine not exc. $1000. Imprisonment in State Penitentiary not exc. 10 yrs. or both.
Utah	Marriage between white person and Negro, Mongolian, Malayan, mulatto, prohibited and void.	Penalty for solemnizing such marriages and for issuing licenses for such marriages.
Virginia	Unlawful for white person to marry any other save a white person with no trace whatsoever of any blood except Caucasian, but persons with 1/16 American Indian blood and no other but Caucasic blood shall be deemed to be white.	Penalty for solemnizing such marriages. Punishment by confinement in Penitentiary for not less than 1 yr. and not more than 5 yrs.

State Miscegenation Laws Against Chinese

State	*Law*	*Penalty*
Wyoming	Marriage between white person and persons of Negro, mulatto, Mongolian, or Malayan blood shall be illegal and void.	Penalty for solemnizing such marriages. Fine not less than $100 and not more than $1000 and imprisonment of not less than 1 yr. and not more than 5 yrs. or both.

SOURCE: *States' Laws on Race and Color*. Compiled and edited by Pauli Murray. Cincinnati, Ohio: Woman's Division of Christian Service, Board of Missions of The Methodist Church Service Center, 1950.

States' Laws on Race and Color and Appendices. Compiled and edited by Verge Lake, LL.B., and Pauli Murray, LL.B., LL.M., Cincinnati, Ohio: Woman's Division of Christian Service, Board of Missions of The Methodist Church Service Center, 1955 Supplement.

In his book, *People Who Intermarry*, Milton Barron gives the results of a survey conducted among high school students in 1942, asking them to list the order of the racial, religious, or national groups whom they would *least* like to marry. Each group had strong antagonism against intermarriage with other groups. For all four groups of students, the second strongest aversion was intermarriage with a Chinese (See Table 14–2).

Judging from talks with the Chinese themselves, it is difficult to determine whether the Chinese or non-Chinese are more averse to intermarriage. This is the one fear uppermost in the minds of Chinese parents. They pay more attention to bringing their children into contact with other Chinese children, even to the extent of trying to arrange in-marriages for them, than they do to helping their children along in their careers. When their children do intermarry, they are more distressed than, say, if the offspring were hurt in an automobile accident. Some comments go to extremes:

"He's better off dead."

"She's no daughter of mine."

Pastors and marriage counselors are unanimous in their advice against intermarriage. Although the parties to the marriage may feel they are able to surmount the personal difficulties of adjustment to

TABLE 14-2

Order of Least Desirable Marriage Partner of Different Faith or Race

Protestant Students:		*Catholic Students:*	
Negroes	91.6%	Negroes	92.8%
Chinese	71.9	Chinese	75.5
Jews	51.6	Jews	58.8
Catholics	19.9	Protestants	25.2
Swedes	7.7	Swedes	9.3
Irish	4.7	Irish	2.8

Jewish Students:		*Negro Students:*	
Negroes	95.0%	Jews	57.8%
Chinese	80.0	Chinese	54.1
Catholics	28.8	Swedes	45.0
Protestants	26.3	Irish	42.2
Swedes	26.3	Catholics	29.4
Irish	23.8	Protestants	22.0

SOURCE: Milton L. Barron, *People Who Intermarry* (Syracuse, N.Y., Syracuse University Press, 1946), p. 258.

each other, still they must face the hostile reactions of their respective families, their friends, their own group, and public opinion in general.

If a Chinese man takes a non-Chinese wife, he loses a certain amount of social standing and respect among his relatives and friends. The non-Chinese wife never becomes a member of the in-group. The other wives shun her; the men are uneasy in her presence. They may even ignore her altogether. She is looked upon with curiosity and made to feel uncomfortable. If the husband has no family or close kin, the wife does not feel the ostracism so acutely, for then she will turn her husband toward her own group, and the husband, in turn, suffers the feeling of not completely belonging.

Even pure outsiders with no interest whatsoever in a mixed marriage can cause a lot of unpleasantness. I recall an incident that took place in church. A beautiful white woman who came in to worship arrived arm-in-arm with her husband, a very dark but handsome Negro. Intuitively, all eyes turned from the altar of God and became transfixed upon this couple. Unperturbed, the couple took their seats and followed the service while loaded looks and knowing glances shot back and forth between the worshippers. Immediately after the service, a steady hum of nasty remarks began:

"Did you see that?"

"He's so dark, too."

"With her looks, she could have done better than that."

The worshippers could not even wait to get out of church to voice their catty remarks.

In spite of the miscegenation laws, in spite of the unequivocal aversion to marriage with a Chinese as expressed by the students, in spite of the intense opposition of the Chinese themselves, and in spite of the personal and social hurdles of intermarriage, Milton Barron found that in Los Angeles, of 97 marriages involving Chinese in the decade from 1924 to 1933, 23.7 percent were interracial marriages.

In New York State, exclusive of New York City, for the same period, of 650 marriages involving Chinese, 150 or 23 percent were contracted with a marriage partner who was non-Chinese. In comparison, again for the same period, Negroes in Los Angeles had an intermarriage rate of 1.1 percent. Of 595 marriages involving Japanese, only 6.3 percent were mixed marriages.[14]

Jewish leaders have voiced consternation at the rising rate of intermarriage among Jews. In a study by sociologist Erich Rosenthal published in 1964, it was found that 13.1 out of every 100 marriages involving a Jewish person in Greater Washington, D.C., was not with a partner of the Jewish faith. Yet the rate is only half of that for the Chinese.

The fact that one out of every four marriages involving a Chinese is interracial is substantiated by two other independent studies. Homer Loh's study of 81 Chinese families in Philadelphia revealed that 22 were mixed marriages. Sixteen of the non-Chinese mates were white, five were Negro, and one other was not specified.

Shepard Schwartz found that of 254 marriages among Chinese males in New York City from 1931 to 1938, 26 percent were with

[14] *Ibid.*, pp. 116–119.

non-Chinese females. There was no case of a Chinese female marrying outside of her national group. The 254 grooms took 186 Chinese brides, 53 white brides, and 15 Negro brides. Although Mr. Schwartz thought the 26 percent rate was comparatively high, he discovered that it was a significant drop from former years. From 1908 to 1924, one out of every two marriages involving a Chinese was a mixed marriage.[15]

In the absence of more recent surveys, I would speculate that the rate of intermarriage is lower, especially now that there are more Chinese women and the immigration restrictions have been relaxed. Yet a few summers back it suddenly dawned upon me, as I was wrapping up another wedding gift, that this was the sixth Chinese girl friend or relative who had married a Caucasian husband within the relatively short period of three months. I mentioned this fact to a girl friend who did not share my surprise in the revelation at all. Of eight brothers and sisters in her family, she was the only one married to a Chinese.

What is the significance of this high rate of intermarriage in the face of such powerful deterrents? Of course the scarcity of Chinese women in the United States was in large part responsible. The exclusion acts made it impossible for most men to return to China where they could set up even a mutilated family (the man living in the United States while his family remains in China). But what explains the willingness of non-Chinese to accept a Chinese in marriage in spite of professed objections? Can it be another substantiation of Professor Allport's contention that "actual discrimination is low compared to verbal rejection of the Chinese"? With the prevalence of intermarriage, will the physical characteristics setting the Chinese apart gradually become obscure in the future?

A Chinese-American may count five generations of his ancestors in the United States. He may be perfectly Americanized in speech, mannerisms, habit, and loyalty. He may feel more at ease among American friends than among Chinese. Yet he will always be identified as Chinese and therefore as foreign and alien. Visibility of his

[15] Shepard Schwartz, "Mate Selection Among New York City's Chinese Males," *American Journal of Sociology* (May 1951), pp. 562–568.

physical features is the one barrier that will prevent total elimination of prejudice against the Chinese.

The arch example of this was the internment of both *Issei* (first generation or foreign-born) and *Nisei* (second generation or native-born) Japanese during World War II. When the third or fourth generation Japanese were released from the camps and permitted to come East, they still suffered abuse, harsh stares, and resentment by the public, while German and Italian aliens walked the streets free from similar molestation or maltreatment.

The Chinese have already passed through a complete cycle of being welcomed with open arms, to being rejected and persecuted, back to friendly acceptance again. What happens if the American economy takes a nose dive? Will history repeat itself? What does the future portend?

Circumstances are different today, but the Chinese themselves should take some steps to counter any backslides. So far, they have coasted along with the mood of the times. When times were bad, they withdrew into themselves and adapted their outlook accordingly, but they did nothing positive to alleviate their situation. When times were good, they rode the crest of good will and enjoyed the gains from their improved status. They have no comparable organization such as the Anti-Defamation League or the NAACP.

Any constructive action to combat prejudice or discrimination was done singly. The individual worked for a better education to give himself a better economic base. He worked harder in his career or business to compensate for his minority status. He conducted himself in a manner that would be inoffensive and above reproach. These are commendable means, but collective effort utilizing the hypotheses culled from studies on the nature of prejudice can further consolidate the gains made by the Chinese.

Professor Francis L. K. Hsu, chairman of the Department of Anthropology at Northwestern University, contends that there is a need created by the American ideal of rugged individualism for prejudice in spite of what the various minority groups do or do not do. This does not mean that the different minority groups are equally subject to prejudice. There are other factors involved. But overriding the separate factors is the fundamental American need for prejudice as a defense mechanism against inferiority on the part of the individual who finds that he has very little human support with any kind of permanency.[16]

One must accept the fact that prejudice is a noneradicable human trait. Our environment shapes our irrational preferences and dislikes. Self-interest dominates our actions. Even where prejudice is nonexistent, someone will always cry foul. It is fairly common knowledge that the New York City Police Department is predominantly Irish. The police chief's and the mayor's forebears were Irish. Because the rank and file in the department opposed the mayor's and police chief's move to set up a civilian review board, they screamed, "Mayor discriminates against the Irish in police promotions." What precipitated the cries of outrage was the appointment of three non-Irish persons to higher positions.

Much to their credit, the Chinese view prejudice with a very healthy attitude. They were never overly bitter. They have gone into occupations which command respect and which lessen conflict from competition. The Chinese are not concentrated entirely in one section of the country. More dispersion away from the vortexes of San Francisco and New York should be encouraged. This ought to be a long-range goal of the Chinese because distribution reduces the degree of visibility.

The Chinese are not as clannish as they used to be. Former Chinatown organizations such as the family associations, the *tongs*, and the benevolent associations have lost their hold on the younger generations. More Chinese now live outside the boundaries of Chinatowns. They are sprinkled among American communities where they have been socially accepted and are highly regarded. The Chinese are more acculturated to the American way of living. Intermarriage is blurring some of the physical features. For these reasons, the majority groups may be less prone to turn against a people who think and act as they do.

With these racial tensions reduced, the most menacing cloud threatening the status of the Chinese in this country is the strained relations between China and the United States. If Sino-American

[16] Francis L. K. Hsu. "Rugged Individualism Reconsidered," *The Colorado Quarterly,* Vol. IX, No. 2 (Autumn, 1960).

relations continue to deteriorate, will the Chinese-Americans be caught in the cross fire?

I hope this book has given evidence that the Chinese have transferred their allegiance and loyalty to the United States. The former sojourners who have been reunited with their families here now feel that at last their roots can take hold in American soil. Their sons and daughters will call this land home. They know no other. They belong and they are accepted. There is no need to look to another land for economic opportunity or for a haven from persecution or discrimination.

The wave of newcomers are in large part refugees from Communist rule. Severance of their physical ties to China was a final and irrevocable decision. Their reception and treatment in this country have firmly convinced them that their decision was sound. They certainly do not subscribe to Communist beliefs, but the emotional ties to their ancestral homeland are difficult to shake. However, the China they love is no longer the China they knew. The newcomers are a more educated, more sophisticated, more somber group, who seek more than gold in the United States. They also expect fulfillment of their ideals.

15

Joining the Mainstream

"STOP calling me Chinese," retorted Lila Huey of Golden, Colorado. "I'm American. My father happened to be born in China, but he's been here for more than thirty years. My mother was born in this country, and we're citizens of the United States.

"I have no interest in China, and it always rubs me the wrong way when strangers ask me if I'm Chinese or Japanese. I answer by asking them if they are Italian or Greek or whatever."

Lila was brought up in Golden, Colorado, where her father ran a grocery store. Rarely was Chinese spoken at home, and when it was, it was a scattered word or phrase sandwiched in between the English. The few Chinese families in Golden lived far apart, and though the parents visited back and forth, Lila and her brother and sister found their friends and schoolmates in the neighborhood. The family grocery store was a popular gathering place for the people in the neighborhood, and when customers came in, they not only bought but stopped to chat and gossip with Lila's parents.

Lila's father and mother liked Chinese food, but the ingredients had to be ordered from San Francisco. Besides, it was so much simpler to prepare American food. However, on the Chinese New Year, Lila's father personally saw to it that authentic Chinese dishes were prepared. Lila recalled with fond memories those Chinese New Years' dinners.

All three Huey children graduated from the University of Washington. Lila majored in biology and was a member of the cheering squad. She had no difficulty getting a job after graduation as a laboratory technician for a brewery company. In college, Lila dated Chinese boys, and for the first time in her life, realized that she was not entirely Americanized.

"I would like to marry a man of my own race," confessed Lila, "but gosh, the boys from Seattle and Portland that I knew in college were more than 'squares.' We didn't even speak the same language."

Harry Dear doesn't mind being called Chinese. "I'm a Chinese-American and I'm proud of my people and my heritage. I came to the United States as a little boy and I was raised in New York's Chinatown. I didn't speak English until I went to public school.

"My mother was a widow. She raised me by sewing in a clothing factory. She didn't speak of a word of English—she still doesn't. All my friends in Chinatown spoke chop-suey Chinese-English. I never got better than a 'C' in English until I got to college. At Dartmouth, I got quite a few laughs in my freshman year when this chop-suey speech unconsciously came out of my mouth in class."

Harry Dear is now chief engineer for a management consultant firm. More than fifty men work under him. His job as an engineering trouble-shooter calls for writing voluminous reports, but you won't find many chop-suey phrases in them now.

Harry owns his own home, a substantial solid brick house on Long Island. The Dears have two children and the widowed mother lives with the family. Harry belongs to the company bowling team and is an avid Yankee fan, but the Dears also belong to several Chinese young people's social and civic organizations.

It is apparent that Harry is beginning to spread a little around the waist. This is his explanation:

"At lunchtime, I have to entertain clients, so I take them out to a fancy restaurant and have a drink or two before the appetizer. Personally, I don't care for this cocktail routine, but I have to keep the clients happy. I'm glad I married a Chinatown girl who can cook a decent bowl of rice and brew a fragrant pot of tea. A solid hunk of meat and raw vegetables is not my idea of civilized eating."

Raymond Eng is a travel agent, a licensed insurance broker, real-estate agent, income tax consultant, confidential letter writer, official court interpreter, and candidate for president of the Chinese Six Companies. All these activities are conducted under one roof on Grant Avenue in San Francisco's Chinatown.

A graduate of Sun Yat Sen University in Kwangtung, China, Raymond was sent to this country in 1937 to work on the *Young China* newspaper, an official organ of the Kuomintang. His job was to sustain the loyalty of the Chinese in the United States to the Kuomintang or Nationalist Party of China.

As a reporter, he circulated among the people and got to know the Chinatown leaders and intricacies of their politics. As a man of higher Chinese learning, he commanded great respect and found himself in demand as an arbiter, confidant, letter writer, and counselor. These roles led naturally into the multifarious jobs where Raymond's clientele is mainly, if not solely, Chinese. He gave up his job as reporter long ago. Real estate and insurance are much more lucrative now that the Chinese are no longer remitting their money home.

Tze-chun, Raymond's wife, took the name Gloria because no one could pronounce her Chinese name correctly. She came to the United States as a graduate student. After Red China's take-over on the mainland, she sought permission to stay in the United States. Now she teaches Chinese at the Hip Wo High School.

The Engs live in the Ping Yuen housing project, a group of modern apartment houses on the periphery of San Francisco's Chinatown. The professional, business, and social life of the Engs revolve entirely around their own people and remain within this limited sphere. Both husband and wife have become American citizens. Yet, on Double-Ten, China's Independence Day, Raymond can deliver an emotion-laden speech about driving the Communists out of "our beloved Motherland." (The habit is hard to break.)

In a few months, Man Fook Liu will be fifty-nine years old. Forty years of his life have been spent in the United States—twenty-five of them in the same laundry in Boston, Mass.

Ever since he could remember, Man Fook knew that he would come to the United States, for his father was a "guest of the Mountain of Gold" and could arrange for his entry to the promised land. In his castle-building moments, Man Fook dreamed of how he would work hard, save his pennies, and return to China with his pockets laden with gold.

Before he left, however, the family made sure that he had married and had properly presented them with a male descendant.

Man Fook came to the United States in the early 1920's. True to his vow, he worked hard and looked to the day when he could accumulate enough to call it quits and go home. But somehow that day never arrived. Life was dull and monotonous. His only day off was Sundays, and the only place he headed for was Chinatown. A few cronies would gather around the fan-tan table and even small bets, after a few hours, left a considerable dent in the week's earnings.

"When I make a big killing I'll go home," Man Fook rationalized to himself, but as the weeks went by, year after year, Lady Luck eluded him. Then there were world events like the Sino-Japanese War, World War II, and the Communist take-over of mainland China, which somehow made it inconvenient or unsafe for him to go home.

When Man Fook had money, he sent some home, but the big pile never materialized. From Monday morning to Saturday night, Man Fook seldom left his laundry. He subscribed to the Chinese newspapers from New York and occasionally went to a movie. His main recreation was to go to Chinatown, where he first stocked up on the week's groceries and then headed for the fan-tan tables. If he won, he treated himself and others to a special dinner. If he lost, the winner treated him.

Forty years of this kind of existence has left Man Fook in a semistupor. Besides having hard luck at the fan-tan tables, Man Fook lost track of his son, who went into interior China during the Japanese War; his wife died long ago. Only one thing in Man Fook's outlook has changed. He isn't sure he wants to go back to China any more. In fact he doesn't know what he wants to do. He works from mere habit. The future to him promises only old age without the solace of work.

Each of these four people—Lila Huey, Harry Dear, Raymond Eng, and Man Fook Liu—represent segments of the Chinese population in the United States in the four major stages of acculturation. It must be recognized that this group is no longer homogeneous. There are native-borns and China-borns. There are newcomers and old immigrants, southerners and northerners, political refugees and those who came for economic reasons. Because their backgrounds are different and because the time and conditions of their arrival are not the same, it is impossible to generalize about the Chinese as a whole.

Lila is *converted* totally. She identifies herself completely with the United States because she was physically removed from her ethnic group and fully accepted by those among whom she lived.

Harry has successfully *emerged* from his exclusively Chinese surroundings to the larger American society. He reveals his upbringing and background by his likes and preferences, but he is perfectly adaptable to American ways when the occasion demands.

Raymond is *bound* to his own group. Though he is a liaison between majority and minority, he is entirely dependent upon his own people for a livelihood, for social life, and for recognition.

Man Fook is a *sojourner*. Though he has spent a lifetime in the United States, his mind and soul never left China.

Converted, emerged, bound, and sojourner were terms developed or used by Kian Moon Kwan in his dissertation written at the University of California on "Assimilation of the Chinese in the United States."

The term "assimilation," in referring to the Chinese, is not as applicable as "acculturation." Assimilation means that the immigrant group not only loses the modes of behavior previously acquired in another society and gradually takes on the ways of the new society, but that the group no longer thinks of itself as distinctly different and in turn is not treated in a special category apart from the rest of society.

In other words, assimilation is a three-way process: letting go of the old, taking on the new, and being fully accepted into the dominant society. But the Chinese, as Lila Huey persistently found to her annoyance, are never wholly considered American. Their physical differences set them apart and immediately stamp them as "foreign."

Acculturation is more restricted in meaning. It is a process of accommodation to the cultural norms of the new society. It does not necessarily mean giving up entirely the behavior and attitudes of one's own ethnic group and substituting for these American mannerisms and American ways of thinking. The test is whether both old and new can be modified and blended so that no conflict results. This is exemplified by Harry Dear's preference for tea, but willingness to take cocktails because he recognizes that the social drink in the United States is the cocktail and not tea.

The usual process of assimilation may be compared with the course of a river. The water flows down the mountains, through the plains, and out into the sea. But if an impediment such as a dam blocks the flow, the water backwashes. For the Chinese in the United States, the unalterable factor of physical differentiation is the impediment to the normal process of assimilation.

Still the waters cannot climb back up the mountains toward their sources, nor can the Chinese ignore the fact that they have spanned the Pacific and made their homes in the United States. The degree to which they have acquired the cultural norms of their new environment is determined in each case by birth, residence, age, and the individual's own personal experiences.

Birth refers to whether a person is native-born or an immigrant. As a native-born, he possesses American citizenship. He does not have first-hand experience with Chinese traditions and customs. They have only been handed down to him secondhand and are, of course, diluted by American ways.

C. C. Wu, in a doctoral dissertation entitled "Chinatowns," states:

> Native-born Chinese are Americanized to such an extent that Chinese from China are just as strange in their eyes as the Africans are in the eyes of the American Negro. . . .
>
> Of course the influence of the old culture is never entirely absent even with the native-born. But the force of it is getting weaker and weaker. The younger Chinese are drifting away gradually from the Chinese cultural influence and adopting the American traditions and customs. If the old world traits are a barrier to the assimilation of the Chinese, they no longer function effectively in the case of the native-born.[1]

In Chinese-American lingo, the native-borns are derisively labeled *jook-sing*, meaning the hollow part of a bamboo pole. In other words, they are empty of the cultural traditions of China. In retort, China-borns are labeled *jook-kock*, literally, a bamboo joint which is stiff, impervious, and unadaptable.

Taking the Chinese in the United States as a group, the ratio of

[1] C. C. Wu, "Chinatowns, A Study of Symbiosis and Assimilation," unpublished Ph.D. Dissertation (University of Chicago, 1928), p. 284.

foreign-born to native-born has shifted from a preponderance of foreign-borns (90 percent in 1900) to a clear majority of native-borns (61 percent in 1960). Each decennial census recorded a decided increase in the number of native-borns. Then, too, the base has been laid for a geometric increase in numbers of native-borns by the large influx of female immigrants over the past fifteen years. Table 15–1 below shows the percentage of foreign-born to native-born Chinese in the United States by decades, 1900 to 1960.

TABLE 15–1

Nativity of the Chinese by Decades
1900–1960

Year and Nativity	*Numbers*	*Percent*
1900: Native-born	9,010	10
Foreign-born	80,853	90
1910: Native-born	14,935	21
Foreign-born	56,596	79
1920: Native-born	18,532	30
Foreign-born	43,107	70
1930: Native-born	30,868	41
Foreign-born	44,086	59
1940: Native-born	40,262	52
Foreign-born	37,242	48
1950: Native-born	62,090	53
Foreign-born	55,050	47
1960: Native-born	142,796	61
Foreign-born	93,288	39

SOURCE: U.S. Censuses

The increasing number of native-borns means that a large proportion of Chinese fall within the converted or emerged stages of acculturation.

Place of residence is equally important in determining the pace of acculturation. If the person lives among or near his own people where Chinese ways are practiced and perpetuated, he retains or is influenced by Chinese traditions and attitudes. Thus, if a person lives within the radius of a Chinatown, or if he lives in a state or city with a large Chinese population, he is more inclined to turn inward toward his own people. Even if the economic opportunities within his own group are too limited, and his job, of necessity, must be outside the group, at least he may find a wholesome social life among his own people.

One woman, born and raised in New York's Chinatown, lived an outmoded, almost ancient, Chinese way of life under her parents' roof. Chinese came more naturally to her than English although her speech was peppered with American terms. Only Chinese food was served in the home and Chinese formalities were rigidly observed. Once married, she and her husband bought a home in the suburbs. Now she finds it difficult to express herself in Chinese, and her speech is English peppered with Chinese terms. She smokes, drives a car, throws cocktail parties, wears slacks or shorts most of the time, dances the lindy, and considers herself 90 percent if not 100 percent Americanized.

Although the Chinese are moving out of Chinatowns, they are still clustered around three major vortexes: California, Hawaii, and New York. According to the 1960 census, the four cities of San Francisco, Oakland, Honolulu, and New York, contain more than half of the Chinese in this country.

This concentration, of course, retards acculturation. At the same time that more members of an ethnic minority are grouped together so that their physical presence becomes obtrusive, the majority becomes less inclined to receive them into the mainstream of American life. Yet, these considerations must be counterbalanced by the greater emotional security and satisfaction that the Chinese derive from ready social intercourse when they live in proximity.

Age is a major determinant in rendering an individual more pliable or resistant to change and adaptation. Like old shoes, habits and values acquired over a long period of time fit easily and are more comfortable, while those recently acquired are dismissed with ease.

By and large, the Chinese population in the United States is a young one and will tend to become younger in future years because of the large influx of female immigrants. According to the 1960 census, one out of every ten Chinese is under five years of age and one out of every three is under nineteen. Immigrants arriving in this country before their teens are soon like native-borns in every respect.

However, most immigrants are full-grown men or women. These will always retain a large measure of their Chinese upbringing depending upon where they live and the extent of their exposure to American ways.

The opportunities for economic advancement given to a minority group and the measure of social recognition and status accorded to it determine to a large extent whether the group members will withdraw into their shells and perpetuate their ways or commingle with the larger society, fusing and being fused with the dominant culture.

Those who have been rebuffed or hurt, withdraw or limp back to their own group to salvage their pride or lick their wounds. Their process of acculturation is arrested. Those who have emerged successful, socially and occupationally, will look for their place in the larger American society. In recent years, the gates of economic and social advancement have been opened to the Chinese. Whether these gates stay open or whether they will clang shut when economic or political conditions worsen is a barometer that will be carefully watched and that will determine whether the Chinese progress or retreat along the road of acculturation.

The above four factors are those which influence the *degree* of Americanization, but there are *areas* of human activity that tend to give ground easily, while others are clung to more tenaciously. Mr. David Te Chao Cheng, in his study of the Chinese in Philadelphia, concludes there is a tendency toward predominance of American traits over the Chinese ones.[2] This is the result of the compulsion of American public opinion toward conformity. In areas where nonconformity would be obvious and obtrusive, the Chinese have adjusted their ways, especially along the lines of material traits. In their dress, their homes, their furnishings, appliances, gadgets, cars, and possessions, the Chinese have adopted the American standards.

It would be simple to state that material traits are easily acquired because there is no emotional involvement in the exchange of one

[2] Cheng, David Te Chao, "Acculturation of the Chinese in the U.S., a Philadelphia Study," Fukien University Press, 1948.

set of traits for the other. This is not a completely valid assumption. Let me explain. The average American, in his way of thinking, strives for a nice home, decent furnishings, a sleek car, a fancy wardrobe, and other outward symbols of success. He may live beyond his income and go into debt to provide these material luxuries, often not so much for the sake of the utilitarian value of these goods, but as badges of success.

On the other hand, buying a house has another significance for the average Chinese-American besides material possession. It means that he intends to make this country his home. The popularity of investing in a home in the United States is rather recent. Ownership of a house means permanency, the putting down of roots.

In buying a car, a new appliance, or plaything, the Chinese has to overcome public censure instead of public admiration. He was taught that such trivialities are unnecessary extravagances, and a person who spent freely was wasteful and hence not to be trusted or respected. That many Chinese families today are not without their cars, their appliances, their television sets, air conditioners, cameras, projectors and the like indicates a shift away from Chinese attitudes and thinking.

In the areas of thought, attitudes and character traits, there are strong streaks of Chinese culture evident in the fiber of the Chinese-American personality. For instance, family unity, respect for elders, respect for authority, personal discipline, and individuality are traits deeply imbedded in the Chinese. A young fellow, according to C. C. Wu,[3] revealed how he was at first obsessed by American ideas of equality. He could not accommodate this equality to the Chinese teachings of respect and obedience to one's elders. As he matured, he began to see the merits of the Chinese system of respect and reverence for parents and the aged, and he admitted that the Chinese system was, in fact, superior.

Sometimes there is a blending of cultural traits. For example, the Chinese-American, unlike his compatriots in China, is forthright in his manner of speech and action. In his readiness to help those beyond his immediate family, in his generosity to charitable and worthy

[3] Wu, *op. cit.*, pp. 258–259.

causes, and in his democratic outlook toward those financially and socially above him and below him, he exhibits traits that show strong American influence.

Not all Chinese traits are good ones. A very exasperating one is disregard for punctuality. At Chinese affairs, it would be making good time to begin an hour late. Another equally exasperating trait is the inability of Chinese in the older generation to cooperate and work together toward a common goal. In club projects, in civic undertakings, in joint ventures, leaders are frustrated at every turn by the apathetic and individualistic attitude of their members. Coming from a country where it was often safer and saner to say nothing and participate in as few activities outside of the family as possible, this trait has carried over to the United States where leaders find it difficult to direct and organize the Chinese into a cohesive unit.

In Chapter 13, dealing with the impact of the Christian Church among the Chinese, it was brought out that there is no predominant religion among the southern Chinese who migrated to this country. As their concept of religion allows a wide margin of tolerance, Christianity, for all practical purposes, has been adopted in form by the Chinese-Americans.

As for recreational activities, mah-jong and fan-tan are favorite games, but the great literatures and philosophies of China are beyond the grasp of the average Chinese-American with his meager knowledge of the written language. Nor is the best of its music, opera, and theater available. As a consequence, the Chinese have accepted American movies, television, sports, picnics, and dances for their leisure-time activities. Folk festivals and Chinese holidays are relegated to secondary status, while fun and relaxation are sought along American lines.

Speech is an important index of acculturation. That their principal medium of communication today is English indicates that the Chinese have made rapid strides toward Americanization. Twenty-five years ago, a native-born who could not converse in Chinese found himself at a distinct disadvantage because he *had* to deal with his own people. There was no place outside of the Chinese community for him. At the same time, a China-born could reside in this country for twenty or thirty years without feeling an acute need for learning more than a few perfunctory words in English. His needs were satisfied within his own group.

Consequently, it was almost imperative for the Chinese-American child to have the rudiments of a Chinese education. This schooling followed regular classes in American public schools. Instruction was given two hours daily on weekdays and Saturday mornings. By the time the child finished six years of Chinese school, he had a reading knowledge of the language and an acquaintance with Chinese history and culture.

Yu Chen Liu, in her survey among the Chinese in Portland, Oregon, found that eighty percent of those interviewed spoke "much Chinese." Twenty-nine percent of the males reported that their comprehension of Chinese was good and fifty-one percent could read a little.[4] This is a high percentage considering the difficulty of the Chinese language, the trying circumstances under which it is taught and learned, and its total dissimilarity to the English language.

As a national group, the Chinese have retained more knowledge of their mother tongue than other groups. At one time, the United States government urgently needed a corps of Chinese and Japanese translators. The country was combed for qualified personnel. There were ample numbers of Chinese translators, but competent Japanese translators were impossible to find. In the end, the government had to send to Japan to recruit alien personnel.

Americans are apt to view the retention of a mother tongue with suspicion and derision. Yet, in America's role of world leader, the demand for persons skilled in the art of speech and language has brought out the fallacies of her past attitude. Just as scientists and technical personnel are vitally necessary for supremacy in the armaments field, so linguists are equally important in the field of international relations and diplomacy.

The Chinese language is admittedly a very complicated and difficult language even for a Chinese. China has a unified written language, but there are numerous local dialects in the spoken language. The

[4] Yu Chen Liu, "Interactions Within Chinese-American Families of Portland, Oregon, Resulting from Cultural Differences," unpublished Ph.D. Dissertation (Oregon State University, 1951).

two major ones are Mandarin (the common dialect) and Cantonese. Others commonly used by the Chinese in the United States are the Toishan dialect, the Shanghai dialect, the Amoy, Fukien, Swatow, Hakka, and a number of others. Persons with a foundation in this complex language will naturally find the learning of Chinese an easier task than those without any acquaintance with the language. That is why Chinese-Americans should be encouraged to study and retain their mother tongue as an invaluable asset and natural resource.

However, because acculturation is proceeding so rapidly, the Chinese language, like Chinese dress, religion, and leisure-time activities, is being discarded by the Chinese-Americans. Though a child's first words may be in Chinese and though he may know no other until school age, he immediately discards his original tongue upon entering school. To the chagrin and dismay of his parents, he may never regain his speech or knowledge of Chinese unless a determined effort is made to pound some of it back into an unreceptive head.

But Chinese parents can be very determined and relentless when it comes to instilling their offspring with some knowledge of the Chinese language. Personally, I know of many American-born Chinese mothers who want to send their children to Chinese school though they may never have attended Chinese school themselves. And they go to great inconveniences and expend a lot of time and energy to give their children this opportunity. For instance, a group of young mothers on Long Island, New York, formed a club to sponsor a Chinese school in Hempstead. These mothers run the school, teach the classes, and shoulder the finances. Every Saturday morning, they converge upon Hempstead from within a radius of twenty miles. The classes are elementary and small, but the mothers feel that their children are at least getting some of the fundamentals of their ancestral tongue.

Retention of the mother language means the written as well as the spoken word. The foreign language press in the United States has been accused, at times, of retarding assimilation and perpetuating the mother culture. Yet, without these papers and periodicals, the newly arrived immigrant would be lost in an abyss of bewilderment and confusion. Unable to read English, he would be totally ignorant of world events affecting him. If government regulations were passed concerning him, he would be completely in the dark. His ties with the mother country would be severed by one blow, setting him adrift before he had time to cast anchor on other shores. The foreign language press cannot be accused of disservice because it performs a very useful function in helping the immigrant bridge the transition from the old culture to the new.

Presently, there are eleven Chinese language newspapers in the United States—three in San Francisco, five in New York, one in Chicago, and two in Honolulu. The names and circulation figures of these newspapers are given below:

TABLE 15–2

Chinese Language Newspapers in the United States

	CIRCULATION*
San Francisco†	
Chinese Times	9,600
Chinese World	5,000
Young China	4,500
New York†	
Chinese Journal	7,000
United Journal	6,250
China Tribune	5,000
China Daily News	400
Min Chih Daily	5,000
Chicago	
San Min	4,000
Honolulu	
New China Daily	4,000
United Chinese Press	4,000

SOURCE: China News Service, New York City

* Circulation figures given in *Ayers Directory of Newspapers and Periodicals* seemed much too high.

† The *Chinese Post* of San Francisco and the *Chinese Nationalist Daily* of New York are now defunct.

The *Chinese World* is the only bilingual paper among the eleven. It is an independent paper built up by its late editor-in-chief, Dai-Ming Lee. The oldest and most respected paper in San Francisco is the *Chinese Times* founded by Walter Lum in 1926 and published by the Chinese American Citizens Alliance. This organization is a civic and fraternal lodge whose membership consists of outstanding native-born Chinese. As such, the paper is more in tune with the problems and needs of Chinese-Americans. On the East Coast, the *Chinese Journal* and the *United Journal* are the most widely read. These papers are not confined to the city in which they are published, but are mailed to subscribers throughout the country. The editor of the *Chinese Journal* said that a good proportion of his newspapers go to Central and South America, where there are no locally published Chinese newspapers.

Because of the limited circulation, meager budgets, lack of space, and manifold handicaps under which a foreign language newspaper operates, they cannot be compared with American dailies. Merely the bare essentials of world events, news from China and the home villages, and other items of interest on the American scene are given. There is little space for more expanded coverage because the papers run only from four to sixteen pages, and more than half of the space is given to advertising. For these reasons, the papers are neither equipped nor prone to crusade for worthy causes.

Seldom is the news gathered first-hand, but merely translated from American newspapers or wire services. A number of these newspapers were originally financed by the Nationalist Party, which has always concerned itself with the retention of the loyalty and support of the overseas Chinese.

The faithful readers of Chinese newspapers are still those of the first generation. The native-born Chinese does not depend upon Chinese newspapers for news. English is easier for him to read and scan. And since there are few articles of interest to him in the Chinese newspapers, there is little incentive for him to peruse or subscribe. However, to cater to his interest in items of news and gossip that pertain to him and his group, there are monthly or quarterly sheets printed in English that serve this purpose. An excellent example is the *Chinese American Times* of New York, edited and published by William Yukon Chang.

The Chinese language newspaper, like the Chinese language school and customs and habits, is traveling down the same road. Their readership, their influence, their roles are rapidly diminishing, due for eventual extinction. When the Chinese learn to read English, when they become citizens, and when they become an integral part of the American community, they drop their subscription to the Chinese papers and buy the American papers. They listen to the radio and watch television for the latest news bulletins. They are no longer dependent upon their own language newspapers for news and information.

In the past, the Chinese tended to shy away from American political activity or from exercising their right to vote. They figured, "What's the use? My lone vote or a handful of votes is insignificant. There'll never be a Chinese to represent us in elective office, and candidates for office can't pay much attention to single votes. A drop in the river can't make much of a splash."

This is a commonly employed rationalization popular with many people who shirk their duty as citizens in a democracy, but the Chinese are gradually beginning to realize the fallacy of their thinking. The *Chinese American Times* reported that registration for the New York Chinatown area rose 90 percent between the presidential elections of 1952 and 1956.

Mr. James Typond, president of the New York Democratic Club in Chinatown, reported that there is increasing political activity and an awareness of the effectiveness of voicing one's vote at the polls. He said, "One would think that it would be the younger generations, the native-born Chinese-Americans who were brought up in the traditions of a democracy to be the more active in this respect, but it is the older ones, the businessmen, those who remember bygone days when the Chinese did not enjoy the status they now have, who are wielding their votes. The young ones have had it easy," he explained. "Times have been good and jobs have been easy to get. Wisdom and maturity, through experience, will teach them eventually that the vote is a priceless heritage in a country where the government is by the people."

A few weeks before the election of November, 1956, New York's Chinatown was the scene of increased political activity. Sound trucks were blaring, band wagons were playing, and ladies were handing out handbills. An onlooker commented: "I can't remember a livelier election year. Maybe it's because our young people are growing up and are taking their places in the democratic pattern. They're living and working in America. It's a good thing."[5]

I spent an evening observing the voting at P.S. 23, polling place for the Chinatown district in New York City in the 1964 presidential election. I was curious to see if many Chinese voted and most of all to see what type of people exercised their vote. I observed the expression on their faces and saw the activity that went on at the polls. I had not anticipated the endless stream of Chinese who came in to vote from 6 P.M. to 10 P.M. The voting district at P.S. 23 is not exclusively Chinese. It has large Italian and Jewish populations as well, but by and large, the voters were Chinese. Energetic party workers brought them in by the carloads and they voted with deadly seriousness. I asked Mr. Typond, who has been active in Democratic Party ranks for many years, "Do you think there are enough Chinese votes, if organized, to swing the election of a candidate for office, one way or the other?"

"No," was the reply, "but what's more important, local candidates would know that we can be an effective group and they would listen to our opinions."

That the Chinese can be elected to high office was proven by Mr. Wing F. Ong, who was elected to the Arizona legislature in 1946. Nor did Mr. Ong depend upon a large number of Chinese votes to put him in office. Only thirteen voters in his constituency were members of his own race, and he won by a plurality of 1,500 out of a total 5,000 votes. Mr. Ong served from 1947 to 1951.

In Providence, R. I., Wing Wu ran as Republican candidate for the House of Representatives in 1960. The Democrats swept the state so Wu lost out, but Wu noted philosophically that he got more votes than most of his fourteen fellow Republican candidates who ran on the same ticket with him.

A successful contender in March, 1962, for a position in the City Council of Seattle, Washington, was Wing Luke. He became the first person of Chinese ancestry to win a public election in the Pacific Northwest. Commenting on this precedent, Mr. Luke said, "It places

[5] *Chinese American Times* (Nov. 1956), p. 1.

a tremendous responsibility on me. I am humbly aware of its historic significance."[6]

The Chinese-American who holds the highest elective office is Hiram L. Fong, Senator of the United States from the state of Hawaii. Senator Fong epitomizes the Horatio Alger legend of American opportunity. His story will be recounted in Chapter 16.

Without a doubt, the Chinese are emerging and participating more fully in American life, mainly because the economic and social bars against them have been lowered and secondly because they no longer consider their lives in this country a sojourn or temporary interlude.

A standard greeting among Chinese in the old days was, "When are you going back to China?" This was the day for which they hoped. This was their purpose. This was the epitome of their dreams. They could have afforded material comforts in this country—a home, a car, fancy clothes, a few luxuries. But these were nothing compared to the intense desire of the Chinese to go home, so they worked hard and spent sparingly for their singular purpose.

As a young child, I remembered that adult conversation invariably revolved around going back to China. I gained a deep impression that China must be some sort of fairyland paradise. Whenever my mother and her best friend got together, my ears were filled with lamentations about "going home."

Nowadays, when I go to visit my mother's good friend, I hear no more talk about going back to China. This woman's children are grown and married, living in their own homes near her. Her life, her roots are deeply imbedded in American soil. Strange as it may seem, her daily life is almost the same as it was thirty years ago. She is residing at the same address. She and her husband operate the same hand laundry. She barely speaks a word of English, but her mind is now oriented to the thought that she is going to spend the rest of her days in the United States.

Table 4 in Chapter 6 gives the number of emigrants going back to China for the years 1944 to 1958. From a peak of 2,238 Chinese who went back to China in 1948, the number of emigrants plunged

[6] *Ibid.*, April 1962, p. 1.

to a mere 2 in 1958. (The Immigration and Naturalization Service gives no figures for Chinese emigration after 1958.)

This change of mind about going back to China is one of the most profound changes to come over the Chinese in the United States. It means that the Chinese are going to spend their money here, to invest their savings in America, and to give their undivided loyalty to the United States.

Consider what the Chinese used to remit to China. Since China was opened to trade with the Western world, she exported little and imported much. There was a tremendous demand for the scientific and mechanical marvels that the foreigners produced, while the raw materials that China had to offer in return brought little in the world market. Yet, year after year, China could pay for her purchases and balance her foreign trade debit thanks to one looming item—overseas Chinese remittances.

In 1942, Liu Wei-chih, Minister of Overseas Affairs, stated that for the twenty or thirty years prior to the outbreak of the Sino-Japanese War, the annual cash remittances to China from the overseas Chinese had averaged $300,000,000 Chinese national currency—an amount far exceeding the country's unfavorable trade balance. The *China Handbook* of 1950 gives the following breakdown of remittances by country of origin for the years 1938 to 1947:

TABLE 15–3

Remittances to China by City or Country of Origin
1938 to 1947

From	*Amount*
London	12 million pounds
Hong Kong	5 million Hong Kong dollars
Malaya	57 million Malayan dollars
Burma	7 million rupees
Philippines	7 million pesos
East Indies	8 million guilders
Indo-China	4 million piasters
Siam	5 million bahts
United States	70 million United States dollars

SOURCE: *China Handbook*, 1950

For 1946 to 1952, the *China Handbook* of 1954–1958 presents overseas Chinese remittances by type of currency remitted. This data is given in Table 15–4.

TABLE 15–4

Overseas Chinese Remittances, 1946–1952

Year	*Chinese Currency*	*U.S. Dollars*	*Sterling*
1946	61,162,002,000		
1947	292,223,761,000		
1948		7,145,607	
1949	12,843	601,018	
1950		551,956	2,237
1951		756,687	49,009
1952		1,550,429	121,495

Year	*HK Dollars*	*Straits Dollars*	*Phillip. Pesos*
1946			
1947		22,945,133	
1948		15,422,846	
1949		4,726,135	193,411
1950	1,186,399	20,358,915	
1951	8,501,721	35,306,255	
1952	7,055,170		

SOURCE: *China Handbook*, 1954–1955

No matter how you look at these figures, the amount staggers the imagination. From the years 1938 to 1947, an average of seven million dollars per year was remitted to China from the United States. This vast sum was sent for the living expenses of family members residing in China, for investment in land and real estate, and for contributions to the war effort.

By and large, remittances from the United States overshadowed those from any other area, especially because other currencies except for the British pound were much cheaper than the United States dollar. This staggering sum was sent by only a few thousand Chinese in the United States as compared with the millions of overseas Chinese residing in the Southeast Asian countries. It is no wonder that the United States was known as the Mountain of Gold!

When the Communists assumed control of mainland China in 1949, we can see that remittances dropped off sharply. By 1951, with the outbreak of the Korean War, the United States invoked the Trading with the Enemy Act, forbidding remittances of American currency to mainland China. Another potent factor damming the flow of remittances back to the homeland was the uniting of families in the United States, made possible by the repeal of the exclusion acts. Money formerly sent home for the support of family members must of necessity now be spent here. Chinatown real estate in New York, once almost wholly owned by non-Chinese, is now almost completely held by Chinese. A laundry proprietor who rented his place of business for forty years finally changed his mind and bought the building. Insurance agents as well as stock brokers are doing a land-office business with the Chinese. By according the Chinese better treatment and encouraging them to integrate, the United States profits. For money earned in this country is now being spent and invested here to fertilize and multiply America's economy instead of being siphoned off.

The political allegiance of the Chinese-American is beclouded on many sides. There is a tendency on the part of Caucasic Americans to classify all Chinese as "foreign" and to suspect their allegiance. According to the Constitution of the United States, persons born in the United States or its territories are automatically American citizens. Hence, all native-born Chinese are American citizens. This basis for conferring citizenship is known as *jus sol.*

American citizenship is also derived through naturalization proceedings. From 1944 to 1964, over 37,000 Chinese were granted citizenship through naturalization.

Traditionally, however, Chinese governments have conferred citizenship on the basis of *jus sanguine*. In other words, all persons with Chinese blood and born of Chinese parents are automatically Chinese citizens. This citizenship cannot be renounced unless the individual is of age and puts in a personal appearance before an authorized representative of the Chinese government to make a formal declaration of renunciation.[7] The prerequisite of appearing before an authorized representative of the Chinese government must be met, otherwise any renunciation is invalid. As few Chinese-Americans go through these formalities, it is obvious that they are clothed with dual nationality.

This is not a situation peculiar to the Chinese alone, for many countries recognize citizenship on the basis of *jus sanguine*, and the American government has formulated rules governing dual nationality.

Taking on American ways, manners, and attitudes, and transferring their loyalty and allegiance to the United States does not imply that the Chinese have divested themselves of all interest in and sentimental attachment to China. As Carl Wittke wrote of the Irish in America, "It is natural for nationality groups in a cosmopolitan country like the United States to follow with sentimental interest the progress of events in their fatherland, to sympathize with the aspirations of friends and relatives at home and find pleasure in their progress."[8]

Thus the Irish-Americans have their St. Patrick's Day and the wearing of the green. The fierce sentimental attachment of American Irishmen to Ireland is expressed in this ditty:

> Columbia the free is the land of my birth
> And my paths have been all on American earth.
> But my blood is as Irish as any can be,
> And my heart is with Erin far o'er the sea.[9]

Italian-Americans have their Knights of Columbus parades, and the Jews have their Zionist movement and United Jewish Appeal. Few people would ever attempt to shake an English immigrant's indomitable faith in the British Empire, yet American nationalism and patriotism have never been found wanting among the diverse races and nationalities in the United States.

So, too, the Chinese in the United States will always keep a warm

[7] Chinese Nationality Law of 1909.
[8] Carl Wittke, *The Irish in America* (Baton Rouge, Louisiana State University Press, 1956), p. 150.
[9] *Ibid.*

spot in their hearts for their ancestral land. This should not be confused with disloyalty or lack of patriotism. For, to the degree that economic and social opportunities are accorded them, Chinese-Americans are joining the mainstream of American life.

16

Distinguished Company

Ernst P. Rawlings was in a hurry. He had to get down to the plant early that morning. The boss was bringing in a consultant on that F-1 engine, for a critical problem had developed in the third stage of the engine's design. This was the largest engine in the world with 7.5 million pounds of thrust. It was being built for the Apollo program to send a man to the moon. Testing had revealed that high turbulence in the engine would cause it to disintegrate before it could achieve its target.

The company had combed the country for the best aerospace minds to tackle the difficulty. The foremost authority in the field was called in and given a team of aeronautical experts. They poured over vast amounts of technical literature on the subject. One name—Ju Chin Chu—kept cropping up.

Who was Mr. Chu? A check through *American Men of Science, Who's Who in Engineering, Who's Who in New York, Who's Who in Atoms, Chemical Who's Who, Who's Who in the East, Who's Who in American Education, Leaders in American Science*, and *Who's Who in Commerce and Industry* revealed that he was a professor of chemical engineering at the Polytechnic Institute of Brooklyn. From 1956 to 1957 he served as Technical Director in charge of Research, Development and Process Engineering for the Chemical Construction Corporation, a company with chemical plants all over the world with an aggregate value well over one billion dollars. In 1961 and 1963, he represented the United States at the NATO Conference on Propulsion. With extensive experience in chemical, petroleum, and aerospace industries, he has served as consultant in the past 20 years to numerous giant corporations and government agencies such as Sun

Oil, American Cyanamid, Union Carbide, IBM, Argonne National Laboratories, Rohm & Haas, North American Aviation, Space Technology Labs of Thompson-Ramo-Wooldridge, the Aircraft Nuclear Propulsion Department of General Electric, Rocketdyne, Grumman Aircraft, Aerospace Corporation, and others.

More than 70 research papers, patents, and patent disclosures have been published to his credit in the diversified fields of propulsion, process technology, distillation, petro-chemicals, heat and mass transfer, fluidization, drying, extraction, fuel cells, engineering application of thermodynamics and kinetics, nuclear technology, system optimization and transient kinetics, and radiation effect on processes.

The honors and awards that had been heaped upon Professor Chu were equally impressive.

"Get Mr. Chu on the phone," roared the boss. "We have a multi-million-dollar contract tied up with this thing. We have a deadline coming up."

A person-to-person call found Professor Chu teaching his class at Brooklyn Polytech. He called back and agreed to fly out to the plant. He was due that morning.

Rawlings gulped down the last of his coffee and grabbed his brief case, but before he could get out of the door, Mrs. Rawlings sweetly handed him a bundle of soiled shirts.

"Drop these off at Chew's Laundry on your way, won't you, dear?"

Rawlings opened his mouth to explain that he was in a special hurry that morning, but his wife's goodbye kiss smothered his words, and he found himself running down the front walk with the bundle of shirts clasped in his arms.

Chew's Laundry was in town. Rawlings double parked and left his motor running. He dashed into the store, dumped the shirts on the counter, and grabbed the ticket from Chew's hand. "Ready by Friday, Charlie?" he asked as he rushed back out to the car.

When Rawlings had more time, he stopped occasionally to talk to Chew, whose first name was not really Charlie. They would exchange greetings, and Rawlings would inquire about the Chew children, but the conversation was rather limited because it seemed that Chew had difficulty expressing himself in English. Nevertheless, Rawlings liked to talk to Chew because Chew always smiled, nodded his head vigorously, and said, "Yes, yes" to everything Rawlings said. Likable chap, mused Rawlings as he drove through the plant gates.

As soon as he got to his office, Rawlings received a message: Please come to the boss' office. The others were waiting for him. Rawlings dropped his hat on his desk and went down the hall. The boss introduced him, "Mr. Rawlings, meet Professor Ju Chin Chu."

Rawlings swallowed hard and extended his hand to the man who looked almost like Chew in the laundry.

"Chew, sir?" he inquired as he fought desperately to clear up his mind. "Do you spell it C-H-E-W?"

"No, Mr. Rawlings. It's probably the same surname in Chinese, but I spell it C-H-U. It's pronounced the same though."

"It must be something I ate for breakfast," thought Rawlings. "My eyes and ears are playing tricks on me." For the Professor Chu who stood before him was about the same age and height with similar features to the Charlie Chew he had just left in the laundry.

"Well, Rawlings," intoned the boss. "Will you introduce Professor Chu to the fellows and go over the plans with him? And bring him back to my office for lunch."

Mechanically, Rawlings went through the motions of explaining, but his mind could not close the gap between Chew the laundryman and Chu the aerospace consultant. He was using highly technical vocabulary, and the physics principles involved were complex and abstract. Rawlings stole a glance at Professor Chu's face. It was unexpressive. "Am I making myself clear? Do you understand what I am saying?" Rawlings hesitantly inquired.

"Oh yes, yes. Yes, yes," replied the professor. He nodded his head vigorously and smiled because in his mind, a solution to the problem was already apparent. Within weeks, the difficulty was ironed out. The F-1 engine was built, and one was exhibited at the entrance to the NASA (National Aeronautical and Space Agency) exhibit at the New York World's Fair.

Grudgingly, Rawlings conceded Professor Chu's genius. However, a mental block continued to interfere with the recasting of the stereotyped image he had about the Chinese in the United States. He had met only a few Chinese such as Chew, and though he was friendly and amiable toward Chew, his concept of the group as a whole was based in part upon ignorance, in part upon hearsay, stereotypes, and misconceptions, and in part upon his limited contacts. It just never occurred to him that the Chinese might also be men of science, technology, or the arts.

Like the first wave of all immigrant groups, the Chinese began at the bottom of the social and economic ladder. They were forced to remain longer at the bottom because they could not rise above the barrier of racial prejudice created by their physical features. But rapid social changes sparked by the last global war released the discriminatory forces that held them down. Unobtrusively, the Chinese are bettering their economic and social status so that a few distinguished ones are found near the top in many fields. Yet the image of the first-generation immigrant persists and predominates in the popular mind. The eminent ones are few, but in proportion to the size of the Chinese population in the United States they are significant, and their ranks increase with each passing year. Especially noteworthy is the diversity of their fields of achievement.

POLITICS

Hiram L. Fong sits in the august chambers of the U.S. Senate. His election in 1959 to one of the highest elective offices in the land has several distinctions. He is the first American of Asian ancestry to be elected to the U.S. Senate, and he is Hawaii's first senator to the national legislature after that state's admission to the Union. His personal popularity with his constituents is so great that he was elected as a Republican from a predominantly Democratic state. In his re-election to the Senate in 1964, he received an overwhelming vote of confidence in spite of a Democratic landslide. When Lyndon B. Johnson swept Hawaii with 78.8 percent of the votes cast for President, Senator Fong's election set an all-time record in Senatorial elections. Running 31.8 percent ahead of his party's candidate for President, Senator Fong broke the previous record held by Harry F. Byrd of Virginia, who ran 30.4 percent ahead of Democratic Presidential candidate Adlai Stevenson in 1952.

Senator Fong's ascent from the slums of Kaliki exemplifies the American success story. Born in 1907, he was the seventh of eleven children, his parents having migrated to Hawaii to work on the sugar plantations. When he was four years old, he and his brothers and sisters were picking algarroba (mesquite) beans to be sold as cattle feed. A thirty-pound bag netted the children ten cents. By age seven, young Hiram had already branched out into shining shoes, selling newspapers, catching and selling fish and crabs, delivering poi, and caddying.

Neither poverty nor hardship deterred Hiram Fong from satisfying his quest for an education. It was three years after his graduation from high school before he had accumulated sufficient funds to attend the University of Hawaii. But he completed four years' work in three years with honors and graduated with a Phi Beta Kappa key. While at the University, he served as editor of the school paper and associate editor of the yearbook. He also managed to distinguish himself on the debating, volleyball, and rifle teams.

This ambitious young man's sights were set on a degree from the Harvard Law School and a career in law. Lack of funds held him back only temporarily. At one time he held jobs simultaneously as a collector of overdue bills, as a college correspondent for the *Honolulu Advertiser*, and as a guide for tourists visiting Oriental temples. Two more years lapsed before he had saved up $2,000 to resume his education. He had to borrow another $3,000 before he completed his degree in 1935. When he landed back in Honolulu, he had exactly ten cents in his pocket.

With a Japanese, a Korean, and a Caucasian-Hawaiian, Hiram Fong founded the law firm of Fong, Miho, Choy and Robinson. As his law practice grew, Fong began investing in real estate, insurance companies, shopping centers, a banana plantation, finance companies, and innumerable other business interests. Senator Fong is now a wealthy man with personal assets of several million dollars.

His first position in public service was as Deputy Attorney for the City and County of Honolulu. He was elected to the Legislature of the Territory of Hawaii in 1938 and served continuously for fourteen years. Four years after he entered the Legislature, he became Vice-Speaker of the House of Representatives. He served in this capacity from 1944 to 1948, until he was elevated to Speaker of the House. In this position, he served for another six years. As Vice-President of the Hawaii State Constitutional Convention, he was instrumental in obtaining statehood for Hawaii.

Wing F. Ong was the first Chinese to sit in the councils of a state legislature. In many respects, Ong's life story is similar to that of Hiram L. Fong except that Ong was born in Hoi Ping, China, and did not come to the United States until 1921, when he was thirteen years old.

Lánding in San Francisco, Ong sought out relatives who offered him work in a laundry, but Ong wanted to learn English and go to school. His eagerness to study was not applauded. His relatives accused him of wanting to "eat easy," but this did not deter him from attending classes in a Baptist mission school where he studied from the Bible and was taught a few basic English phrases.

When he heard that opportunities were better for the Chinese in Arizona, Ong borrowed $20 and set out for Phoenix. He found a job in a grocery store and registered in public school starting at the kindergarten level. His embarrassment at being in the same class with five- and six-year-olds did not last long. Within two years, Ong had completed grade school all the while working, sleeping in the storage room, and subsisting on one cold meal a day.

Ong wanted to go to high school, but his employer felt that the boy had had enough schooling and that he should work full time. Ong held true to his course. He quit the grocery and went to work as a houseboy for ex-Governor and Mrs. Tom Campbell. The kindly Campbells taught him an awareness of world affairs and politics and encouraged him in his studies. Within two years he had completed high school, during which time he won a state-wide essay contest. In the essay, he urged the United States to participate in the League of Nations. He also predicted the inevitability of World War II unless the United States supported the League.

By selling insurance, Ong earned his keep and his means of attending junior college. With astute business sense, he bought a bankrupt grocery store for $300 which was grossing $8 a day. Within two years he had raised the daily gross to $150. He sold the grocery for $3,500 —a profit of more than ten times his original investment.

When he was 21 years old, Ong received a picture of a girl from an elder in China who decided that it was time Ong took a wife. One look at the picture and Ong agreed. In time, Ong and his picture bride, Rose, became the proud parents of two sons and four daughters.

During the Great Depression, when the entire country was hard hit by adversity, Ong and his wife came through the ordeal with a savings account of $4,500. The formula for their success was ingenuity and hard work. Instead of waiting for business to come to him in his grocery store, Ong went out and aggressively peddled his wares. Husband and wife picked cantaloupes in an abandoned field for nothing and sold them for fifteen cents a dozen. Rose Ong said, "We were poor, but we had confidence. We knew nothing could go wrong with America, and we still feel the same way."

Ong's fellow countrymen sneered when he announced that he was running for the Arizona State Legislature in 1940. "Look at your face," they gibed. "It's yellow, not white. Do you think anyone's going to vote for a Chinaman?"

Ong lost by a mere 17 votes, but he did not blame his race or pay any attention to his taunters. Instead, he decided to qualify himself further. "Before a man should expect to make laws, he should know something about law-making," he concluded. At age 32, he went back to school, enrolling in the law school at the University of Arizona. As usual he undertook an accelerated program, graduating with the highest honors in 1943.

Now Ong felt qualified. When he ran for the Legislature in 1946, he was elected. In 1948 he was easily re-elected. Ong's political philosophy is that legislation should be of the greatest benefit for the most people. He advocated and voted for increased real-estate taxes although he was a large property owner himself. He worked hard on behalf of the Chinese lobbying in Washington to prevail upon the Immigration and Naturalization Service to desist from their harassment of Chinese immigrants.

For many years, Ong's election to public office was unique among the Chinese on the U.S. mainland. With increasing frequency in recent years, Chinese names are cropping up on voting ballots from councilmen to judge to mayor. In March, 1962, Wing Luke won a seat in the Seattle City Council at the age of 36. He served as president pro tempore and sometimes as acting mayor in the absence of that city's highest elective officer. Tom Tang was sworn into office on

January 7, 1963, as Superior Court Judge of Maricopa County, Arizona. Previously, Judge Tang had already established his political reputation as city councilman and vice-mayor of Phoenix.

In the East, Wing Wu ran as Republican candidate for the state House of Representatives from the 11th District of Providence, Rhode Island, in 1960. It was a Democratic sweep, as it was when Edward Hong ran as Republican candidate for New York state assemblyman in 1965. In their defeat, both men attached greater significance to the fact that they had been privileged to run for elective office.

William D. Soo Hoo of Oxnard, California, is reputedly the first person of Chinese ancestry to be elected to the office of mayor in the United States.[1] Immediately after Soo Hoo's election in April, 1966, Pat Brown, governor of the State of California, paid the new mayor the unprecedented honor of going to Oxnard to congratulate him in person.

The city of Oxnard, situated 60 miles north of Los Angeles, is a community of 64,000 people, among whom are only 60 Chinese. It is one of the fastest growing cities in southern California. Soo Hoo was born and brought up in Oxnard. He attended third grade in the same room where he now wields the gavel.

The people of Oxnard do not think of Soo Hoo as Chinese. The issue never came up in his campaign. To the townspeople, Soo Hoo is a native son, a local boy of whom they are proud, for he had already built himself a solid reputation by his splendid record as city councilman. His right to the highest elective office in Oxnard was assured by the largest popular vote in the city's history. He garnered the most votes in 11 out of 21 precincts.

The mayor is a registered Democrat, but an examination of the returns from all the precincts showed that Soo Hoo had wide public support from both political parties and people at all levels and from all walks of life.

Mayor Soo Hoo won the respect of his colleagues and his constituents by his ability to get things done. As councilman, he not only tried to deal with the day-to-day problems at hand, but he also gave

[1] John Wing claims that he is the first U.S. mayor of Chinese ancestry. He was elected mayor of Jonestown, Mississippi, in 1965. Perhaps there are others who have attained public eminence, but whose achievement was not publicized.

forethought to the future. Oxnard's economy, still basically an agricultural one, has wide fluctuations in employment and income. One of the mayor's major programs is to attract industries that will balance the city's economy.

When queried about the secret of his success, Mayor Soo Hoo replied as Lincoln did when asked the same question: "All that I am or ever hope to be, I owe to my angel mother." Unfortunately, his mother, who settled with her husband in Oxnard nearly fifty years ago and who reared their five children by operating a restaurant, died a year before William D. Soo Hoo took his oath of office as mayor.

PHYSICS

The names Chen Ning Yang and Tsung Dao Lee will go down in history and be listed with such famous men of science as Newton, Edison, Einstein, and Fermi.

On January 15, 1957, the Department of Physics of Columbia University announced in *The New York Times* what it described as "the most important development in physics in the past ten years." William L. Laurence of the *Times* called it "a development which, indeed, may lead to the removal of at least two, and possibly three, of the seemingly insurmountable obstacles that have stood in the way of man's efforts to probe into the mysteries of the fundamental structure and constitution of the cosmos. In fact, physicists are confident that the new findings may lead to the conception of a new order and harmony in the universe.

"This discovery, by removing the major roadblock that stood in the way of understanding the meaning of the newest particles in the atomic nucleus, promises at last to clear a straight road into the open out of the present atomic 'jungle.' It may be likened to the final realization that the earth was not flat, which opened the way to the understanding of the motions of planets, the stars and the galaxies and to the laws of motion in general, which led directly to the Machine Age, as well as to the age of electricity, radio, television and earth satellites. The fruits of the new discovery may not ripen for another quarter century or more, but scientists are now confident that they are at last on the right road to a better understanding of the forces that govern our universe, and very likely to their better utilization for the benefit of mankind."

Yang and Lee were the two men responsible for this astounding discovery. They had shattered a universally accepted "inviolate" law of nature—the Principle of the Conservation of Parity. Recognizing the tremendous impact of Yang's and Lee's contribution to science and moving with unprecedented speed, the Swedish Academy immediately bestowed the Nobel Physics Prize for 1957 on the two Chinese physicists.

At that time, Yang was a member of the Institute for Advanced Study at Princeton. He was 34 years old. Lee was a professor of physics at Columbia University. He was 30 years old and the youngest full professor on the faculty. A third collaborator, also Chinese and a professor of physics at Columbia University, Dr. Chien Shiung Wu, carried out the difficult experiments which Drs. Lee and Yang suggested. Dr. Wu is considered the world's foremost woman physicist.

It is hard to imagine Tsung Dao Lee as a full professor. He could easily be mistaken for a teen-age student on the Columbia campus. Shy and self-effacing, he does not like to talk about himself. His complexion has a porcelain-like quality, smooth and unfurrowed by the world-shaking ideas that have emanated from his brain.

Lee was born November 24, 1926, in Shanghai, China, the third of six children. His father was a well-to-do businessman. Dr. Lee attended the National Southwest Associated University in Kunming, where Chen Ning Yang was also studying, although the two never met and did not know each other in China.

Before he had finished his undergraduate work, Lee was awarded a Chinese government fellowship in 1946, enabling him to come to the United States for advanced study. He chose the University of Chicago, which permitted him to take graduate courses at the undergraduate level. There his path crossed that of Chen Ning Yang, who was also working for his Ph.D. degree in physics. Both were students of Enrico Fermi, father of the atomic bomb. It was during their Chicago years that Yang and Lee learned to think and work together as a team.

Lee was awarded his Ph.D. degree in 1950 and was immediately offered a fellowship at the Institute for Advanced Study. This is a place where the most brilliant minds in the country are brought together at Princeton to think. Two years later, when Lee left the Institute to accept an appointment at Columbia, Dr. Robert Oppenheimer, the director, said, "We saw him . . . leave with great regret. He is one of the most brilliant theoretical physicists we have known. His work in statistical mechanics and in nuclear and subnuclear physics has brought him world-wide renown, and justly. He has solved some problems of long standing of great difficulty. His work has shown a remarkable freshness, versatility, and style."

Chen Ning Yang was born September 22, 1922, the eldest of five Yang children. He grew up on the campus of Tsing Hua University in Peking, China, where his father was a professor of mathematics. Yang had a carefree childhood, surrounded by books and scholars. He, too, attended National Southwest Associated University, from which he was graduated in 1942. In 1945 he received a scholarship to study at the University of Chicago under the great Enrico Fermi.

Yang completed his doctorate in physics in 1948. Early recognition of his genius came the following year, when he was named a member of the Institute for Advanced Study. When Lee was accorded this honor in 1951, the two men had ample opportunity to be together, to think, to converse, and to exchange ideas. When Lee went to Columbia in 1953, they would meet in a Chinese restaurant near the University. There, after a delectable meal, they would sit over a pot of tea and talk and argue, long and loud and loud and long. Onlookers sometimes thought the two men were at odds.

It was in May, 1956, after an especially good lunch at the restaurant that Yang and Lee decided to challenge the Conservation of Parity Law itself. According to this principle, elementary particles in nature are always symmetrical—there is no way of telling which is the left and which is the right side, and there is no way of telling which is the actual and which is the mirror image of a given set of actions, for they would obey the same laws of nature.

For most observed phenomena, the law of parity held true, but experiments conducted in recent years seemed to contradict this universally accepted principle. Instead of questioning the law, most scientists tried to make all observations fit it, never doubting that there might be instances where parity did not hold.

Yang and Lee were courageous enough to challenge the law itself, but not without justifiable reason. They, too, had been taught that parity was inviolate, but once having decided to attack the law, they were able to suggest within a month's time a set of experiments which would prove or disprove whether parity would be conserved in the realm of weak interactions.

To conduct their experiments, they turned to a compatriot, Dr. Chien Shiung Wu, also a professor of physics at Columbia University. When, in the spring of 1958, Princeton awarded Dr. Wu the first honorary doctorate in science that it had ever bestowed upon a woman, the president of the university declared that she had "richly earned the right to be called the world's foremost female experimental physicist."

Dr. Wu came to the United States in 1936 to pursue her graduate studies under Dr. Ernst Lawrence, Nobel Prize laureate and director of the radiation laboratory at the University of California. At the time of her arrival in this country, Miss Wu had already received her B.S. from the National Central University in Nanking, China. At the University of California, Miss Wu met a fellow graduate-student of physics, Luke Chia Liu Yuan, whom she married. Luke Yuan is an eminent physicist in his own right and is presently connected with the Brookhaven Laboratory on Long Island, New York. The Yuans have a son.

Looking back to her childhood days in China, Miss Wu recalls that she was a happy little girl who lived in Liu Ho, a small town near Shanghai. Her father, Wu Zong Yee, was the principal of a school. It was he who instilled in his daughter and two sons an everlasting love of learning. A man who was farsighted and ahead of his time, he educated his daughter as well as his sons.

Miss Wu received her doctorate in physics in 1940. By 1943 she had demonstrated such rare qualities that Princeton University asked her, a young woman of twenty-seven, to teach nuclear physics to its men students.

Dr. Wu accepted the Princeton offer, but before she had had time to get used to her new job, she was called to work on the Manhattan

Project at Columbia. This project, as most people know, is the one that developed the atomic bomb.

In 1956, when Dr. Wu agreed to undertake the experiment suggested by Yang and Lee, she asked for collaboration from the National Bureau of Standard's Low Temperature Physics Group and the Atomic Energy Commission. With a team of distinguished radiation specialists, she began one of the most intricate experiments posed by modern physics. Six months later, Dr. Wu was able to announce to an astonished world that a weak interaction and its mirror image are not always the same. Left can be distinguished from right. Particles now had to be identified by their handedness. The Law of Conservation of Parity was shattered.

Although Drs. Yang, Lee, and Wu are sons and daughter of China, they found in the United States the unmatchable opportunities and the fertile soil in which to utilize their brilliant minds. They were privileged to study under the most gifted teachers of our time. Their genius was quickly recognized and as quickly used to advantage in the furtherance of man's understanding and his quest toward the ultimate truth.

BIOCHEMISTRY

Another very likely Chinese-American candidate for a Nobel Prize, this one in biochemistry, is Dr. Choh Hao Li. In 1962, he was named winner of the Albert Lasker Medical Research Award. The award, one of the highest recognitions in basic medical research in this country, was presented to Dr. Li by Mrs. Lyndon Johnson along with a $10,000 honorarium and a statue of the Winged Victory of Samothrace representing victory over death. Since the Albert Lasker Award was established in 1955, twelve of its recipients later went on to win Nobel Prizes.

Dr. Li's achievements have been considerable. Since 1950, he has been Professor of Biochemistry and Experimental Endocrinology, and director of the Hormone Research Laboratory at the University of California. He is the world's foremost authority on the pituitary gland, the walnut-sized master gland which lies at the base of the brain. The pituitary is called the master gland because its secretions regulate the growth and functions of the other glands.

Dr. Li is concerned primarily with the anterior lobe or the front part of the pituitary, which determines body growth, reproduction, thinness or fatness, lactation, and skin coloring. He has isolated in pure form six of its hormones, including ACTH, and HGH or the human growth hormone.

In addition, Dr. Li performed the difficult feat of determining the composition and structure of ACTH and HGH molecules, thereby making possible the synthesis of these powerful hormones. ACTH has been used successfully for more than a decade in the treatment of rheumatoid arthritis and rheumatic fever. HGH is used in the treatment of dwarfism. Unfortunately, the amount of these hormones derived from natural sources is minute. Extracts from 5,000 human pituitaries obtained at autopsies yield only about a sixth of an ounce. Synthesis enables the scientist to produce these hormones in laboratories at will.

The profound importance of Dr. Li's discoveries is reflected in the honors accorded him over the years. In 1947 he received the Ciba Award in Endocrinology. In 1948 he was a John Simon Guggenheim Memorial Foundation Fellow. He was the first to receive the American Chemical Society's California Section Medal in 1951. The Francis Emory Septennial Prize of the American Academy of Arts and Sciences went to Dr. Li in 1955. The Chinese government in Taiwan honored him with a gold metal in 1958. The Chinese American Citizens Alliance and the Chinese Institute of Engineers honored him respectively in 1961 and 1965. The Catholic University of Chile conferred upon him an honorary Doctor of Medicine degree in 1962. That same year he won the Albert Lasker Award and was appointed Faculty Research Lecturer at the University of California San Francisco Medical Center, one of the highest honors that the university faculty can confer on one of its members.

Dr. Li does not rest on his laurels. In 1963 he reported the synthesis of a 19 amino-acid fragment of the ACTH molecule. This fragment exercises a number of the biological functions of the natural ACTH molecule, which consists of 39 amino acids. In 1966 he reported that the complete chemical structure of HGH had been determined.

Choh Hao Li, born in Canton, China, on April 21, 1913, came to the United States as a graduate student in 1935. He has spent most of his life in this country and in the same university where he obtained his Ph.D. degree. At California, he was privileged to sit at the feet of a great teacher, Herbert McClean Evans, a pioneer in the study of the pituitary gland. Li followed in his teacher's footsteps. He has spent almost thirty years probing into the mysteries of that life-giving gland.

Li is one of four sons of a Canton industrialist. His family's affluence enabled him to complete his requirements for a B.S. degree at the University of Nanking and to go abroad for advanced study. He found his purpose and his life's work at the University of California.

Citing both public and private support for his research projects, Dr. Li said, "The United States is one of the very few places in the world where programs like ours could have been carried out." After twenty years in this country, he became an American citizen in 1955.

Dr. Li's three brothers are also in this country. Leafing through the 10th edition of *American Men of Science*, I found the names of all four brothers. Dr. Choh Ming Li was Professor of Business Administration at the University of California. Presently he is vice-chancellor of the Chinese University of Hong Kong. Dr. Choh Luh Li is a neurosurgeon at the National Institutes of Health in Bethesda, Maryland. Dr. Choh Hsien Li is Director of Metallurgical Research at the Minneapolis-Honeywell Corporation. Each is distinguished in his own right.

ART

In the realm of contemporary art, Dong Kingman has attained international recognition as one of America's major artists. In the medium of watercolor, he is a leading master. His paintings hang in the permanent collections of more than forty major museums and art galleries in the United States including the Metropolitan Museum of Art; the Whitney Museum of Modern Art, New York; the Brooklyn Museum; the Museum of Fine Arts, Boston; the American Academy of Arts and Letters; the Art Institute of Chicago; the San Francisco Museum of Art; the Toledo Museum of Art; and others too numerous to list here.

Private collecting of his paintings is even more widespread. Since 1935, Dong Kingman has painted on the average of 50 pictures a year. Every one of them is sold, including a few which have not been painted as yet. One could say that Dong Kingman does not have a Kingman to his name.

Kingman is well known to the American public. His very first exhibition in San Francisco back in the 1930's excited a great deal of interest in the art world and marked him as a promising young artist. By 1940, the Metropolitan Museum of Art had already acquired its first Kingman painting. Millions have been introduced to Kingman through the pages of *Life* magazine, which has done five illustrated stories on him. He is also a favorite biographical subject for the *American Artist, Design*, the *New Yorker*, and other magazines. A book titled *The Water Colors of Dong Kingman and How the Artist Works* by Alan Gruskin, director of New York's Midtown Galleries, is an illustrated account of Kingman's unique watercolor methods. Three film demonstrations of how Dong Kingman creates a picture have been made. One shot by James Wong Howe has been shown around the world as an educational film.

Kingman was very popular with his students of art at Hunter College and Columbia University. Presently on the faculty of the Famous Artists School at Westport, Connecticut, he is in great demand as a lecturer, and it distresses him greatly when he must turn down many invitations to speak.

In 1954 the State Department asked him to represent the United States as a cultural envoy to the Orient. His trip was so successful that his tour was expanded to take him around the world. At each stop on his itinerary, he exhibited his paintings and gave speeches and demonstrations. Everywhere he was received with acclaim and affection, and he established for himself an international reputation.

When he returned from his trip, he posed a problem for the staid and conventional State Department personnel. Instead of filing a written report of his trip, he presented the State Department with a forty-foot scroll highlighting his trip in pictograph form. The idea was so novel and the pictures so delightful that the scroll was reproduced in *Life* magazine and enjoyed by its millions of readers. When asked about his unique report, Dong Kingman made the wry comment: "I know it was kind of hard for them to file away, and I didn't make a carbon copy."

Dong Kingman is one of the least pretentious, friendliest, and most humorous people that I have ever met.[2] This humor is very much in evidence in all of his paintings. Alan Gruskin calls it "gentle satire." In his street scenes, one-way signs have arrows pointing in both directions. Along with his characteristic flock of sea gulls a chicken will be found soaring overhead. The sandwich man's plaque reads "Don't Eat at Joe's." Kingman would think nothing of hanging a clothes line across the Manhattan Bridge.

Every cell in Kingman's body reveals the artist in him. Every movement, every waking moment of his life, is absorbed in his art. Wherever he goes a sketch pad goes with him, and his fingers are constantly at work recording his impressions and his thoughts. He sees what others can never see, and it is his gift and talent to be able to transmit through the inanimate media of paper and paint the blinking of a neon sign, the clackety-clack of an overhead train, the buoyancy of a child at play, or the tranquillity of a lazy floating cloud.

Kingman even sketches when he is at the movies in a darkened theater. His eyes may be transfixed upon the screen, but his fingers are busily drawing on an open pad in his lap. When asked why he does this, he answers with characteristic modesty, "To practice drawing."

Dong Kingman was born in Oakland, California, in 1911, the second of eight children. Dong's father operated a not-too-successful laundry, so that by the time Dong was five years old, the family decided to return to Hong Kong. There in that bustling port of the Orient, young Kingman grew up. His father opened and ran a successful merchandise store, but it was from his mother that Dong inherited his talent.

Dong attended the Hong Kong branch of Lingnan University, where he learned about Chinese painting and where he practiced his brush strokes day after day by copying the old Chinese masters. A well-known Chinese painter, Sze-to Wai, recognized the talent in his young pupil and took a special interest in him. But Sze-to Wai was not strictly a Chinese painter of the old school. He had studied in Paris and had brought back with him many reproductions of the

[2] See the sketch of him in the *New Yorker* (March 12, 1960), p. 44.

great European moderns, particularly ones by Van Gogh, Cézanne, and Matisse. Kingman was much affected by these exciting approaches to art.

In 1929 when he was eighteen years old, Dong returned to the land of his birth. The year was not a very auspicious one to start an art career or even earn food and lodging. Young Kingman went through the gamut of traditional occupations open to the Chinese. He worked for two years in his brother's overalls factory. He bought a restaurant, but it failed when he was found more often in the back painting than in the front serving his customers. His next job was as a houseboy for an American family. In 1936, the WPA (Works Progress Administration) program gave him the chance to paint and to eat. With the troublesome problem of survival taken care of, Kingman was able to devote himself to serious painting. Art critics at his first showing were very enthusiastic. Kingman's career and reputation have been on the rise ever since.

A work of art knows no national boundaries, but his Oriental ancestry and his American upbringing subject Dong Kingman to the perpetual question of whether his paintings reflect more of his Chinese or Western background. "I'm in the middle," says Dong Kingman with characteristic forthrightness, but he qualifies this statement by elaborating:

"My early study when I was a youth in China has unquestionably affected my approach to painting, and my thoughts, technique, and composition are often based on Chinese art and poetry. Yet today, after all my years of painting in this country, I feel that my work has little obvious Chinese influence. Developments in Western art over the past fifty years or more have affected my art considerably, and Western influences undoubtedly are now predominant."[3]

Indeed, Dong Kingman is the embodiment par excellence of an East-West blend. Even his name reflects the compromise between Chinese and American tradition. Actually, Kingman's surname is Dong, because in China the family name comes first. Since Americans assume that the last name is the surname, they mistook his name to be Kingman. To the Chinese he is Mr. Dong, and to Americans he is

[3] Alan Gruskin, *The Water Colors of Dong Kingman and How the Artist Works* (New York, Thomas Y. Crowell, 1958), pp. 115–116.

Mr. Kingman, but even as he signs his name Kingman in Arabic letters, the brush strokes are the calligraphic Chinese style.

CINEMATOGRAPHY

Q.: When does a Hollywood cameraman get star billing on theater marques with his name ablaze in neon lights?

A.: When his name is James Wong Howe.

Q.: Why does he rate such distinction?

A.: Obviously because his name, like the names of movie stars, attracts movie-goers.

According to *Current Biography*, "James Wong Howe is not only supposed to be the highest paid cameraman on the lots, he is also considered among the ten best. Some critics have even called him the finest cameraman in the world."

Newsweek (January 11, 1960) stated: "Among movie cameramen, none ranks higher than Jimmy Howe, a Chinese-American veteran of 42 years. Hollywood films director John Sturges, for whom Howe did "The Old Man and the Sea," says flatly, 'He is the greatest stylist in the business.' "

Aaron Sussman, in his classic *Amateur Photographer's Handbook*, wrote: "Watch especially for those [films] photographed by that amazing Chinese genius, James Wong Howe. He has made motion picture photography a great art."

Movie stars fight over him. Greta Garbo would be photographed by no other. In "The Story on Page One," his job was to make Rita Hayworth appear ugly. Assignments like these call for the highest skills not only in cinematography but also in diplomacy.

The name James Wong Howe is well known, but few among the general public realize that he is Chinese-American. In the reverse order of surnames, Howe's real family name—Wong—got shunted to the middle instead of the front as in Dong Kingman's case. Howe, which sounds more British than Chinese, is James' father's given name.

James was born into the Wong family near Canton, China, some time before the turn of the century. The family emigrated to Pasco, Washington, where Mr. Wong became quite prosperous as the owner of two restaurants, a grocery store, a hardware store, and good amount of real estate.

Young Jimmy was a scrappy little boy who learned early how to use his fists. Being short of stature—he is less than five feet tall—he had to be fast on his feet and quick with his hands. When Jimmy discovered that fast footwork and swift punches compensated more than adequately for his height, he decided that he wanted to become a professional prize fighter. As the only Chinese pugilist in the United States, he gained a certain amount of popularity, but there were times when he did not duck fast enough or when the other fellow had more punch behind a swift blow than he had. Jimmy quickly lost interest in his first-chosen career.

Wandering around the Plaza of Los Angeles one day, Howe came upon the filming of a Mack Sennett comedy in the park. He was fascinated. A friend of his told him that being a cameraman was a soft job, only twelve hours a day at $10 a week. Howe decided to become a cameraman. He pestered the studios until Lasky's gave him a job—picking up the camera and moving it from place to place.

Howe became very curious about the camera that he carted around. Besides, the man who turned the crank in the camera earned a lot more than the one who moved it around. By scrimping and saving, Howe bought himself a camera and experimented with lights and lenses.

One day he walked up to the then-famous actress Mary Miles Minter and asked her to pose for him. She graciously consented. When she saw the prints, she was astounded. Never had she been photographed so magnificently before. When she found out that he could do the same thing with a movie camera, she demanded that Howe be made her cameraman.

The road ahead was not a smooth one. Because he was Chinese, "he was supposed to stick in the background and accept a certain number of insults." He was also given the worst equipment on the lot, but Jimmy was used to being picked on, and he knew that to compensate for racial prejudice, he had to be better than the others. When the producers saw what miracles he produced with the wreck of a camera they gave him, they quickly signed him to a contract.

Since then, James Wong Howe has written his own ticket in the motion picture industry. He has worked for Fox Studios, MGM, London Films, Warner Brothers, Selznick, Columbia Pictures, and RKO. He formed his own company in 1948 and has the pick of the best film scripts.

James Wong Howe's latest accolade was an Oscar for "Hud" in 1964. What possibly might have been a modern western with a shallow plot was heightened and transformed into a powerful film by the panoramic sweeps of James Wong Howe's camera. His shots of the wide-open country of Texan landscape created a raw-boned atmosphere of land and environment lying between nature and cheap urbanity. The superb effect was achieved with black-and-white photography.

"Come Back Little Sheba," "The Last Angry Man," "The Old Man and the Sea," and "The Rose Tattoo" are a few of the recent outstanding pictures filmed by James Wong Howe. For the latter, he won another Oscar for cinematography in 1955.

When this book goes to press, James Wong Howe will have completed fifty years in one of the most highly competitive, volatile, and demanding industries in the world. He has remained at the top of his profession for more than half of this time—a mighty enduring record for a champion. He has not earned this distinction without hard work. Whenever there is a new discovery in motion picture photography, James Wong Howe is the first to try it out. The scrappy little fighter in him still feels that he has got to be better—much better—than the man who does not have one strike against him.

ARCHITECTURE

Ieoh Ming Pei's face broke into a broad grin at a press conference called by the Kennedy family in December, 1964. He had every reason to be smiling. The architectural plum of the half-century had just been awarded him. As *Time* magazine said, "It was a commission that any architect would have sold his ancestral home to get." The commission: To design the John F. Kennedy Memorial Library as a shrine to the memory of one of America's most beloved Presidents.

In her inimitable way, Jacqueline Kennedy tried to tell why Pei (pronounced *pay* or more accurately *bay* in Chinese) was chosen above a select group of eighteen internationally famous architects. "We wanted the memorial to my husband to be designed by an American architect," explained Mrs. Kennedy, "and Pei—why he just loves things to be beautiful."

Not only was Pei Mrs. Kennedy's first choice, he was the unanimous choice of the Kennedy clan and a subcommittee of an international advisory committee of architects. He is the man who everybody believes will create a monument that will embody the living spirit of John F. Kennedy.

In spite of the unanimity of decision, the announcement came as a surprise to the profession and most of all to Pei himself. "A commission like this," he said with disarming candor, "usually doesn't come my way."

I. M. Pei is very much aware of the heavy mantle that has been placed upon his shoulders. This building, like no other, will be built upon the hearts of the American people. A year after President Kennedy was cut down by an assassin's bullet, 800,000 letters of sympathy and condolence had poured into P. O. Box 2500, Boston, Mass. A large number enclosed sums from a few pennies to a few dollars for the Kennedy Library. Millions of pennies collected by children from all over the country have been presented to the Kennedy Memorial Library Fund. Gifts and donations have also poured in from foreign governments and people from every corner of the globe. John F. Kennedy was universally admired and universally loved. His monument could not reflect less.

"My own inclination is that it should be thought-provoking rather than awe-inspiring," says Pei. "We all agree that it should be something that people will use—a living memorial."

The Library will be a national institution with facilities available to students and scholars from all over the world. It will consist of four components: a memorial, a library, a museum, and an institute for advanced political study which will be operated in conjunction with Harvard University. Pei felt that the two-acre site originally set aside by the Kennedy family in Boston for the Library was much too small and inadequate. His first concern was to find another site which would be easily accessible by rapid and public transportation. This is typical of the way Pei operates. He approaches the problem from the point of view of the visitor and the user; for each year, millions will make the pilgrimage to this shrine.

Confidence in Pei stems from the imprint he has already left upon the urban landscape of almost every major city throughout the United States and upon a score of metropolises spanning the globe from Montreal to Taipei to Tel Aviv. More than any other architect, Pei is engaged in a vast revamping of the American cityscape. Some of his award-winning projects are Denver's Mile High Center, Honolulu's Pan Pacific Center, Pittsburgh's Washington Plaza Apartments, New York City's Kips Bay Plaza, Philadelphia's Society Hill Development, Chicago's University Gardens Hyde Park Redevelopment, Syracuse University's School of Journalism, and the National Airlines terminal at New York's Kennedy International Airport.

Pei is rejuvenating 160 acres of Cleveland, is master planner with vast authority of a $200 million reconstruction project in Boston, and is involved in downtown redevelopment projects in Los Angeles, Oklahoma City, and Washington, D.C. A Pei-designed control tower will soon be built in 25 U.S. airports.

This man, who is putting his stamp on American cities, was born in Canton, China, on April 26, 1917, the son of Tsu Yee Pei, a banking magnate. As most scions of well-to-do families in China were wont to do in those days, Ieoh Ming went abroad for his higher education. His father wanted him to go to England, but I. M. decided to come to the United States. He enrolled at the University of Pennsylvania in 1935 for a degree in architecture, but decided that he could not draw as well as his fellow classmates. He gave up architecture and went to MIT to study architectural engineering. At MIT he was persuaded to go back to architecture, but he played safe by graduating with degrees in both fields in 1940.

His professors considered him one of the brightest architectural students to emerge in some time. He was awarded an MIT traveling fellowship which enabled him to visit many American cities, most of which he considered aesthetically unattractive. It was then that he decided to focus his attention on slum clearance and urban rejuvenation.

Pei's first desire was to return to China to aid in the reconstruction of his homeland, but his own country was torn asunder by war and

Japanese occupation. He accepted a position at Harvard, where he taught from 1945 to 1948, at the same time earning his degree of Master of Architecture. At Harvard, he caught the eye of William Zeckendorf, a New York realtor who juggled multi-million dollar real-estate parcels as if they were rubber balls. Zeckendorf invited Pei to be his chief architect. During their association, Pei designed for his boss a circular penthouse office which is a landmark on New York's Madison Avenue.

With Communist rule established in Mainland China in 1949, Pei cut his political allegiance to the land of his birth and applied for U.S. citizenship. He received his naturalization papers in 1954. Four years later, I. M. Pei set up his own architectural firm with headquarters in New York.

Pei says his Chinese ancestry has never made it hard for him to attract customers. Quite the opposite, it helps. "If I make a mistake, people think I must mean something else." Nor does Pei's work reveal any Oriental or Chinese influence. Of Chinatowns in the United States, Pei merely grimaces in horror.

In planning his prize project, Pei meets frequently with Mrs. Kennedy, who has devoted her time and energy almost exclusively to the Library. It will not be a reality until 1970, but it will perpetuate the legacy that John F. Kennedy left to his people: That one man can make a difference and that every man should try.

LITERATURE

In the literary field, the Chinese in the United States are well represented by Lin Yutang. Rare is the American library that does not contain several volumes of Lin Yutang's works, for few writers have been as prolific as he. Ever since his publication of *My Country and My People* in 1935, Lin has given the American public on the average of a book a year. His latest and thirty-first book, the *Flight of the Innocents*, was published in 1965.

No writer, barring Pearl Buck, has written so extensively, so intimately, so charmingly, and so humorously about China—its people, its traditions, and its beliefs. Lin Yutang is one of the best interpreters of the Chinese mind to the American people, and to his critics who disagree with his interpretations, one can only say that there are few who are as perceptive and as lucid as he. His enduring contribution is that he aroused a warm and receptive interest in China, bringing that vast and mysterious land down to the common denominator of human experience, so that West could relate to East.

The charm of Lin Yutang's writing is in its earthliness and humor. Reflecting his Oriental background, he had an aversion for the abstract and a penchant for the concrete that made his philosophy so personal and so appealing. On happiness, for instance, he wrote in his *Importance of Living* that man is an animal and that happiness lies in being natural. One of the great achievements of science, he feels, is in making it clear that we are more like monkeys than like angels.

Lin Yutang was always at his best when he was philosophizing or discoursing on the small pleasures of life. Many gems for meditation are found in his Wisdom series: The *Wisdom of Confucius, Wisdom of China and India, Wisdom of Laotse*, and *On the Wisdom of America*. In the latter book, he turned the tables on his reading public by leading his readers to an introspection of their own philosophy of life as reflected in the writings of their own leaders and thinkers.

Lin Yutang's first novel, *Moment in Peking*, was a monumental work of 815 pages. Clifton Fadiman in the *New Yorker* called it a remarkable panorama which you must allow to flow past your eyes. "The book is so full, so explicit, that in the end, if we read slowly enough and soak ourselves in its atmosphere, the Chinese way of life—at any rate the way of life of the cultivated *bourgeoisie*—becomes so real to us that it ceases entirely to have the shallow values of mere oddity and becomes as understandable and precious as our own."

Mary Ross, reviewer for *Booklist*, captured the total essence of Lin Yutang's writings when she wrote: "*Moment in Peking* is painted on a large canvas with a glowing brush. One can feel the author's joy and pride in the cities and mountains of which he writes so lovingly, in the allusions to art and literature and customs which he makes so understandable to those who are of other traditions. . . . It is the great fortune of the West that someone not of it has been able to look at China objectively and to show its virtues and weaknesses, its beauties and on occasion its sordidness and tragedies as Lin Yutang [has]."

Lin was born on October 10, 1895, in Fukien, China. His father was a Christian pastor. His mother, according to Lin, was a simple, guileless soul, adored by her brood of six boys and two girls. As part of a mission family, Lin grew up with a great deal of exposure to Western civilization. It was not until he had graduated from St. John's University in Shanghai and had gone to teach at Tsing Hua University in Peking that he discovered he knew very little about his own cultural heritage and that he had cut himself off from a veritable treasure house of philosophy and folklore.

The emptiness of this huge void led Lin to furiously make up for lost time, and the vacuum's pull on him was powerful. In a way the West has become the benefactor in this curious twist of circumstance because Lin was forced to look at his own country and his own cultural heritage as an outsider. Because he was not totally steeped in its traditions and customs as a youngster, he was more detached and able to view Chinese life more objectively when he was older. This, I feel, explains in part Lin's extraordinary ability to translate and convey the mind and wisdom of China's past to a Western audience. Lin must have grappled with the interpretation himself and had successfully resolved it in his own mind.

The beginning of Lin's long sojourn in the United States began in 1919, when he came with his young bride to Harvard University for a graduate degree in philology. The following year he departed for Germany and the Universities of Jena and Leipzig. The year 1923 found him back in China teaching at the National Peking University, where he became known as a radical and independent thinker. He left the academic world in 1927 for a brief fling in government service, but he found himself turning more and more to writing, both in Chinese and English. He founded the *Analects Fortnightly*, a humorous magazine, and two literary fortnightlies, the *Cosmic Wind* and *This Human World*. He wrote, in addition, for two English language journals, *The China Critic* and *T'ien Hsia Monthly*.

My Country and My People, published in 1935, established Lin Yutang's stature in the literary field. With the outbreak of the Sino-

Japanese War, Lin returned to the United States, and over the span of a quarter of a century, New York City was his home base although he made his residence abroad at times in Europe, Singapore, and Taiwan. Most of his writing was done in his apartment on East 79th Street, where he and Mrs. Lin brought up their three daughters, who have become literary figures in their own right.

In 1965, Lin Yutang celebrated his seventieth birthday with the decision that he would retire to Taiwan. He has taken temporary leave of this country, but I cannot help feeling that Lin Yutang will not be gone for long. For beneath that long flowing Mandarin gown which Lin prefers to Western-style suits, I suspect there is a man who is more American in make-up and outlook than many of us.

FINANCE

A persistent question making the rounds of Wall Street is: "What's Jerry Tsai doing?" People are not inquiring into his personal affairs; they are wondering how he is investing the more than $400 million of the Manhattan Fund. He calls the shots on additional hundreds of millions of the Fidelity Mutual Funds, for which Tsai is the management consultant.

Gerald Tsai, Jr. (pronounced *sigh*) made Wall Street history when in February, 1966, on the strength and reputation of his name alone, 150,000 investors bought a total of 42 million shares of the new Manhattan Fund, amounting to $270 million. Tsai is its founder and president. He is the hottest money manager to hit Wall Street in many a year, and Wall Street has never lacked for flamboyant personalities.

What was originally to have been a $25 to $75 million offering was oversubscribed within a matter of days. The total was raised to $100 million, then to $250 million, and finally to $270 million. A record was set when $19 million worth of shares was sold in a single day. Wall Street regulars, long accustomed to astronomical figures in finance, were flabbergasted. Even the prestigious name of Lehman drew less than $200 million from the public when he set up his One William Street Fund.

The man who attracted this enormous sum was a 37-year-old Chinese-American. Born of a well-to-do family in Shanghai, China, on March 10, 1928, he came to the United States when he was 18 years old and became a naturalized citizen in 1957. Tsai attended Boston University, earning a B.A. and M.A. in economics almost concurrently. He worked briefly for a textile firm and then joined Bache & Co. as a junior analyst at $50 a week. Fourteen years later, at the closing of the Manhattan Fund offering, it was Mr. Harold L. Bache himself who handed Gerald Tsai a check for $247,050,000. "This is the biggest check I have ever signed," Mr. Bache remarked happily. After all, he had just pocketed a $22,950,000 commission as underwriter of the new mutual fund.

Tsai learned his trade and made his reputation at the Fidelity Fund of Boston, which he joined in 1952 when it was a small outfit. Moving in and out of stocks with cool, calm detachment and trading in large blocks, Tsai established himself as an aggressive investment manager. His sense of market timing was uncannily precise. He accurately called the turns on two major companies, which led to an extended upswing in the market. Any stock in his portfolio that did not move was ruthlessly weeded out. He parleyed the Fidelity Capital Fund from scratch in 1954 to net assets of $240 million in 1965. In the latter year alone, Fidelity Capital shares soared 47 percent in value while the Dow Jones industrial average rose 11 percent. His boss, Edward C. Johnson, II, recognized his ability and gave him a free hand. He also recognized his worth and allowed him to buy 20 percent of the capital shares.

Tsai's methods were unorthodox, but he was successful. He began to set the pace. Any news that Tsai was buying or selling was apt to send the stock moving sharply. Corporate management, conscious of Tsai's power to move big blocks of stock, felt obliged to consult him in any contemplation of financing. He is on easy, informal terms with some of the top men in U.S. industry.

In contradiction to the rule of diversification, Tsai believes in concentrating his attention and his money in a narrow list of select stocks. He shoots for a 25 percent gain and relies heavily on technical analysis. He buys and sells with steel-cool courage. As *Business Week* said, "He played yo-yo with Communications Satellite Corp.," piling up a total of 1.9 million in paper profits on both the ups and downs.

Three months after the sensational offering, the first stockholders' meeting of the Manhattan Fund was held. Eight-hundred shareholders crowded into New York's Americana hotel to catch a glimpse of the Wall Street prodigy. In the front and center rows sat some of the most prestigious magnates of finance eagerly watching the performance of the youthful newcomer.

Tsai handled himself with aplomb. Five-feet seven inches tall, he is a handsome, impeccably dressed man with an air of self-assurance. His speech is deliberate and sprinkled with a keen sense of humor. His Bostonian accent marks him more as an aristocratic Yankee than as a Chinese immigrant. Septuagenarians rose on the floor to question him about his handling of the Fund, and they sat down expressing their confidence in him.

Beaming in the audience sat his proud parents, Mr. and Mrs. Gerald Tsai, Sr. Junior no doubt acquired a great deal of his financial acumen from Daddy, who is a graduate of the University of Michigan and a textile industrialist.

There are some areas of economic life which are more difficult than others for members of distinct minorities to penetrate. Finance is one of them. And the pinnacles of Wall Street are generally beyond reach. When asked to comment on his spectacular climb in a tightly restricted field, Tsai said, "I encountered no barriers. If I can buy American Motors for you at $100 and sell it for you at a profit of $50, does it matter if my skin is white or yellow?"

One can dispute this point, but in Tsai's case it did not matter. He feels that opportunities for the Chinese in the United States are excellent by pointing out that there are a large number of Chinese account executives or brokers who are doing very well for their clients. In Tsai, however, I think I detect the notes of distinction.

He exudes self-confidence without being vain. His actions are backed by homework, conviction, and forethought, so that when he moves, he knows he has made the best decision on the basis of his facts. He accepts his due as his right, which is more important for success than is customarily thought. And he thinks big. Take an example: At the shareholders' meeting, Tsai asked for authorization to increase the Fund's shares from 27 million to 300 million—enough shares to total a three billion dollar fund! Why such an enormous increase? Why not do it gradually? Tsai's answer was simply stated:

He did not want to come back to the shareholders each year for an increase. The shareholders voted him what he wanted.

The hardest task facing Tsai is that he must fill his own shoes and fulfill his own legend. He is a very young man, and there are many years ahead of him.

The people whose stories I have related here are a select few whose accomplishments have been exceptional. Some were born in the United States. Some emigrated from China. All are U.S. citizens and may be properly labeled Chinese-Americans.

Those like Senator Hiram Fong, state assemblyman Wing Ong, artist Dong Kingman, and author/philosopher Lin Yutang came from humble homes and had far to climb on their way up. Others like architect I. M. Pei, biochemist C. H. Li, and finance wizard Gerald Tsai, Jr., started many notches above their compatriots by virtue of better family circumstances. But the success of each in his own field did not come without extraordinary talent or ability and hard work.

The list is not exhausted. There are more. The work of some Chinese-Americans in the sciences, the arts, or technology may have profound repercussions in our lives. For example, mere mention of The Pill seems sufficient to identify it. A recent survey revealed that between 3.5 to 4.1 million married women under age 45 are using this oral contraceptive. This constitutes over 15.5 percent of the total number of American women in this group. Effects of universal use of The Pill may be even more far-reaching. The Pill may launch one of the most sweeping socio-medical revolutions in history. Yet how many people realize that of the three men who perfected this pill, one is Dr. M. C. Chang, a Chinese biologist connected with the Worcester Foundation in Massachusetts?

Or take Dr. M. C. Li of the Mineola Hospital in New York. His work in cancer research has shown exceptional promise. Would men like Ernst P. Rawlings (a fictitious name of an actual person mentioned at the beginning of this chapter) believe that the second highest income in the State of California for the year 1939 belonged to Joe Shoong, a Chinese immigrant who founded the merchandising chain, the National Dollar Stores, and the National Shoe Company on the Western seaboard?

The Chinese have always been reticent about publicizing their grievances or their accomplishments. Instead of vigorously protesting the inequities of the immigration laws specifically passed against them, the Chinese bore the injustice with stoicism, alleviating their own frustrations by backdoor tactics. Instead of dealing with the issues that confronted them in their daily lives in this country, they sustained themselves by looking to China as an inner sanctum and a place to which they could retreat. Their accomplishments and their contributions went unnoticed and unappreciated.

Withdrawal and humility are cultural inclinations of the Chinese people, but they are also cultural lags more suited to the times and circumstances of a bygone China.

China is no longer an avenue of escape. Native-borns, old-timers, and newcomers alike accept the United States as their permanent home, and they are grateful to be here. Riding the crest of the Civil Rights Movement and the change in social attitudes toward minority groups, the Chinese have been able to utilize their abilities in this country to their fullest extent.

Could Drs. Lee and Yang have disproved the Principle of Parity without the education par excellence they received at the University of Chicago and the resources placed at their disposal at the Institute for Advanced Study and Columbia University? Very unlikely.

Could Dr. Wu have carried out her experiments without the elaborate equipment and professional assistance made available to her at the National Bureau of Standards? Hardly.

Could Dr. Li have carried out his research on the pituitary gland, synthesized ACTH, and determined the structure of the human growth hormone without the foundation laid by his teacher and the Hormone Research Laboratory at the University of California? Dr. Li himself questions it.

Could I. M. Pei have wielded such tremendous architectural impact on the urban landscape of Chinese cities if he were in China instead of the United States? I doubt it.

Without Hollywood, could James Wong Howe's genius in cinematography found expression? Possibly, but not likely.

Looking back over a little more than a hundred years since the first Chinese set foot on American soil, we see the tremendous change in the position of the Chinese in the United States. The past is history. Today, the Chinese are in very favorable circumstances. The opportunities are unparalleled, and the Chinese have much to offer.

Appendix

TABLE A-1

Chinese Immigrants Admitted by Sex
Years Ending June 30, 1945 to 1965

Year	*Male*	*%*	*Female*	*%*	*Total (100%)*
1945	45	41	64	59	109
1946	71	31	162	69	233
1947	142	13	986	87	1,128
1948	257	8	3,317	92	3,574
1949	242	10	2,248	90	2,490
1950	110	8	1,179	92	1,289
1951	126	11	957	89	1,083
1952	118	10	1,034	90	1,152
1953	203	19	890	81	1,093
1954	1,511	55	1,236	45	2,747
1955	1,261	48	1,367	52	2,628
1956	2,007	45	2,443	55	4,450
1957	2,487	49	2,636	51	5,123
1958	1,396	44	1,799	56	3,195
1959	2,846	47	3,185	53	6,031
1960	1,873	51	1,799	49	3,672
1961	1,418	40	2,099	60	3,517
1962	1,916	41	2,753	59	4,669
1963	2,297	43	3,073	57	5,370
1964	2,597	46	3,051	54	5,684
1965	2,242	47	2,527	53	4,769

SOURCE: *Annual Reports,* Immigration and Naturalization Service, 1945–1961, Table 10; 1962–1965, Table 9.

TABLE A–2

Chinese Immigrants Admitted, by Sex and Age Groups
Years Ending June 30, 1956 to 1961

FEMALES

Age Group	*1956*	*1957*	*1958*	*1959*	*1960*	*1961*	*Total (6 Years)*
Under 5	110	103	43	188	119	155	718
5–9	225	228	86	268	94	89	990
10–14	107	133	54	220	125	143	782
15–19	226	206	101	216	123	175	1,047
20–24	379	420	328	484	342	427	2,380
25–29	355	438	318	439	248	292	2,090
30–34	287	298	202	362	173	210	1,532
35–39	214	262	156	240	117	103	1,092
40–44	162	171	110	211	104	110	868
45–49	114	146	121	191	121	121	814
50–54	84	84	84	133	103	99	588
55–59	70	58	74	115	61	77	455
60–64	48	45	53	59	36	48	289
65–69	36	23	27	39	21	32	178
70–74	18	9	24	9	7	12	79
75–79	5	6	10	6	3	5	35
80 and Over	3	5	8	5	1	1	23

TABLE A-2 (*continued*)

MALES

Age Group	*1956*	*1957*	*1958*	*1959*	*1960*	*1961*	*Total (6 Years)*
Under 5	123	114	48	190	109	105	689
5–9	242	217	105	314	101	139	1,118
10–14	138	145	59	285	188	193	1,008
15–19	139	127	55	173	84	65	643
20–24	161	178	105	153	79	75	751
25–29	199	236	205	239	98	85	1,062
30–34	239	325	224	255	117	86	1,246
35–39	243	375	175	276	155	88	1,312
40–44	183	236	91	190	126	72	898
45–49	114	154	75	155	140	77	715
50–54	105	155	106	167	137	91	761
55–59	69	133	72	159	183	95	711
60–64	29	54	44	153	166	100	546
65–69	14	27	21	91	125	93	371
70–74	2	8	9	32	43	36	130
75–79	4	–	1	9	17	9	40
80 and Over	1	2	–	5	4	8	20

SOURCE: *Annual Reports*, Immigration and Naturalization Service, 1956–1961, Table 10.

TABLE A-3

Chinese in the United States
Sex and Sex Ratio
1860–1960

Year	*Male*	*Female*	*Sex Ratio*
1960	135,549	101,743	133.1
1950	77,008	40,621	189.6
1940	57,389	20,115	285.3
1930	59,802	15,152	394.7
1920	53,891	7,748	695.5
1910	66,856	4,675	1430.1
1900	85,341	4,522	1887.2
1890	103,620	3,868	2678.9
1880	100,686	4,779	2106.8
1870	58,633	4,566	1284.1
1860	33,149	1,784	1858.1

SOURCE: U.S. Censuses, *Nonwhite Population by Race.*

TABLE A-4

Marital Status of the Chinese
20 Years and Over
1960

Marital Status	*Male*	*Percent*	*Female*	*Percent*
Total, 20 yrs and over	88,455	100.0	57,935	100.0
Single	26,239	29.7	7,840	13.5
Married	55,403	62.6	44,204	76.3
Spouse present	44,293	50.1	42,402	73.2
Spouse absent	11,110	12.5	1,802	3.1
Separated	1,940	2.2	348	0.6
Widowed	3,455	3.9	4,527	7.8
Divorced	1,408	1.6	1,016	1.8

SOURCE: U.S. Census, 1960, *Nonwhite Population by Race*, p. 66

TABLE A-5

Occupation of the Chinese in the United States
Total, by Sex and Percent Distribution, 1960

	Total	*Per-cent*	*Male*	*Per-cent*	*Female*	*Per-cent*
Total	98,784	100.0	71,435	100.0	27,349	100.0
Prof. tech. & kind. workers	17,713	17.9	13,125	18.4	4,588	16.8
Farmers & farm managers	602	.6	523	.7	79	.3
Managers, officials and proprietors	12,531	12.7	11,042	15.4	1,489	5.4
Clerical & kindred workers	13,680	13.8	5,458	7.6	8,222	30.1
Sales workers	6,512	6.6	4,313	6.0	2,199	8.0
Crafts, foremen & kind. wkrs.	5,120	5.2	4,892	6.8	228	.8
Operatives & kind. wkrs.	14,821	15.0	8,996	12.6	5,825	21.3
Private household wkrs.	1,035	1.0	608	.9	427	1.5
Service wkrs. except household	18,582	18.8	16,215	22.7	2,367	8.6

TABLE A – 5 *(continued)*

	Total	*Per-cent*	*Male*	*Per-cent*	*Female*	*Per-cent*
Farm laborers & foremen	421	.4	310	.4	111	.4
Laborers, except farm & mine	1,317	1.3	1,222	1.7	95	.3
Not reported	6,450	6.5	4,731	6.6	1,719	6.3

SOURCE: U.S. Census, 1960, *Nonwhite Population by Race,* p. 111

TABLE A – 6

Family Income of the Chinese and Percentage Comparison with Total United States
1959

Income Group	*Number Chinese*	PERCENT *Chinese*	PERCENT *U.S.*
Under $1,000	1,609	3.3	5.6
$ 1,000–$ 2,999	6,179	12.7	15.8
$ 3,000–$ 4,999	10,478	21.5	20.5
$ 5,000–$ 6,999	10,153	20.8	23.0
$ 7,000–$ 9,999	9,833	20.1	20.1
$10,000–$14,999	7,041	14.4	10.5
$15,000 and over	3,497	7.2	4.6
Median Family Income:			
Chinese: $6,207			
U.S.: $5,660			

SOURCE: U.S. Census, 1960

Bibliography

BOOKS

Adamic, Louis. *Laughing in the Jungle*. New York and London, Harper Bros., 1932.

——— *The Native's Return*. New York, Harper Bros., 1934.

Adams, R. *Interracial Marriages in Hawaii*. New York, The Macmillan Company, 1937.

Allport, Gordon W. *The Nature of Prejudice*. Reading, Mass., Addison-Wesley Publishing Co., 1954.

Auerbach, Frank L. *Immigration Laws of the United States*. Indianapolis, Bobbs-Merrill Co., 1955.

Ayscough, Florence. *Chinese Women, Yesterday and Today*. Boston, Houghton Mifflin Co., 1937.

Bancroft, H. H. *History of California, 1884–1890*. San Francisco History Co., Vol. VII.

Barron, Milton L. *People Who Intermarry*. Syracuse, N.Y., Syracuse University Press, 1946.

Barth, Gunther. *Bitter Strength: A History of the Chinese in the United States, 1850–1870*. Cambridge, Mass., Harvard University Press, 1964.

Bennett, Marion. *American Immigration Policies—A History*. Washington, D.C., Public Affairs Press, 1963.

Bolton, Sarah. *Famous Men of Science*. New York, Thomas Y. Crowell Co., 1960.

Brown, Francis J. and Joseph S. Roucek, eds. *One America*, 3rd ed. Englewood Cliffs, N.J., Prentice-Hall, 1952.

Bruce, J. Campbell. *The Golden Door*. New York, Random House, 1954.

Bryce, James. *The American Commonwealth*. New York, The Macmillan Co., 1927.

Buck, Pearl S. *Of Men and Women*. New York, John Day Co., 1941.

Cattell, Jacques, ed. *American Men of Science*, 10th ed. Tempe, Ariz., Jacques Cattell Press, 1960.

Cayton, H. R. and A. O. Lively. "The Chinese in the United States and the Chinese Christian Churches." New York, National Council of Churches of Christ, 1955.

Chan, Sou. *House of Chan Cook Book*. New York, Doubleday, 1952.

Chen, Ju-Chou. *Handbook of Chinese in America*. New York, 1946. (In Chinese.)

Chen, Ta. *Emigrant Communities in South China* (A study of overseas Chinese migration and its influence on standard of living and social change).

Cheng, David Te Chao. *Acculturation of the Chinese in the United States: A Philadelphia Study*. China, Fukien University Press, 1948.

Child, Irvin I. *Italian or American? The Second Generation in Conflict*. New Haven, Conn., Yale University Press, 1943.

China Handbook, 1950, 1952–1953, 1954–1955.

Chinese Year Book, 1946.

Clappe, Louise. *The Shirley Letters from the California Mines*. New York, Alfred A. Knopf, 1961.

Coleman, Elizabeth. *Chinatown, U.S.A*. New York, John Day Co., 1946.

Conwell, Russell H. *Why and How the Chinese Emigrate*. Boston, Mass., Lee & Shephard, 1871.

Coolidge, Mary R. *Chinese Immigration*. New York, Henry Holt & Co., 1909.

Cox, Oliver Cromwell. *Caste, Class and Race*. New York, Monthly Review Press, 1959.

Davy, Charles, ed. *Footnotes to the Film*. New York, Oxford University Press, 1937. (re James Wong Howe)

Dictionary of Chinese Place Names. National Peking Research Institute, 1920. (In Chinese.)

Dillon, Richard H. *The Hatchetmen: Tong Wars in San Francisco*. New York, Coward McCann, 1962.

Dobie, Charles. *San Francisco's Chinatown*. New York and London, D. Appleton-Century Co., 1936.

Dulles, Foster R. *China and America—Foreign Relations Since 1784*. Princeton, N.J., Princeton University Press, 1946.

Dunbar, Seymour. *A History of Travel in America*. Indianapolis, Ind., Bobbs-Merrill Co., 1915.

Eberhard, Wolfram. *Chinese Festivals*. New York, Henry Schuman, 1952.

Elegant, Robert. *The Dragon's Seed*. New York, St. Martin's Press, 1959.

Ellenwood, James Lee. *One Generation After Another*. New York, Charles Scribner & Sons, 1953.

Feldman, Herman. *Racial Factors in American Industry*. New York, Harper Bros., 1931.

Feng, Doreen Yen Hung. *The Joy of Chinese Cooking*. New York, Greenberg Publishers, 1954.

Fields, Harold. *The Refugee in the United States*. New York, Oxford University Press, 1938.

Fisk University. *Orientals and Their Cultural Adjustment*. Nashville, Tenn., 1946.

Galloyway, J. D. *The First Transcontinental Railroad—Central Pacific and Union Pacific*. New York, Simmons-Boardman, 1950.

Gittler, Joseph. *Understanding Minority Groups.* New York, John Wiley & Sons, 1955.

Griswold, A. Whitney. *Far Eastern Policy of the United States.* New York, Harcourt, Brace & World, 1938.

Gruskin, Alan. *The Water Colors of Dong Kingman and How the Artist Works.* New York, Thomas Y. Crowell, 1958.

Handbook of Chinese in America. The People's Foreign Relations Association of China, 1946. (In Chinese.)

Handlin, Oscar. *Adventure in Freedom.* New York, McGraw-Hill, 1954. (History and adaptation of Jews in America.)

——— *Immigration as a Factor in American History.* Englewood Cliffs, N.J., Prentice-Hall, 1959.

——— *The Newcomers: Negroes and Puerto Ricans in a Changing Metropolis.* Garden City, N.Y., Doubleday Anchor Books, 1962.

——— *Race and Nationality in American Life.* Boston, Little Brown & Co., 1957.

Hendrickson, Robert C. with Fred J. Cook. *Youth in Danger.* New York, Harcourt, Brace & World, 1956.

Historical Statistics of the United States. U.S. Census Bureau.

Hsu, Francis L. K. *Americans and Chinese—Two Ways of Life.* New York, Henry Schuman, 1953.

——— *Under the Ancestor's Shadow.* New York, Columbia University Press, 1948.

Hwuy, Ung. *A Chinaman's Opinion of Us and of His Own People.* New York, Frederick A. Stokes & Co., 1927.

International Motion Picture Almanac, 1966.

Jaffe, Bernard. *Men of Science in America.* New York, Simon and Schuster, 1958.

Javits, Jacob. *Discrimination—U.S.A.* New York, Harcourt, Brace & World, 1960.

Joy, C. Turner (Admiral). *How Communists Negotiate.* New York, The Macmillan Co., 1955.

Konvitz, Milton R. *The Alien and the Asiatic in American Law.* Ithaca, N.Y., Cornell University Press, 1946.

Kung, S. W. *Chinese in American Life.* Seattle, Wash., University of Washington Press, 1962.

Kuo, Ping Chia. *China, New Age and New Outlook.* New York, Alfred A. Knopf, 1956.

LaFargue, Thomas Edward. *China's First Hundred.* Pullman, Wash., State College of Washington, 1942.

Lasker, Bruno. *Asia on the Move.* New York, Henry Holt & Co., 1945.

Lee, Calvin. *Chinatown, U.S.A., a History and Guide.* Garden City, N.Y., Doubleday, 1965.

Lee, Rose Hum. *The Chinese in the United States of America*. Hong Kong, Hong Kong University Press, 1960.

Levi, Werner. *Modern China's Foreign Policy*. Minneapolis, Minn., University of Minnesota Press, 1953.

Lewis, Oscar. *The Big Four*. New York, Alfred A. Knopf, 1938.

Lin, Yueh-Hwa. *The Golden Wing: A Sociological Study of Chinese Familism*. New York, Oxford University Press, 1947.

Lind, Andrew. *Hawaii's People*. Honolulu, University of Hawaii Press, 1955.

Lindsay, Michael. *China and the Cold War*. Melbourne, Melbourne University Press, 1955.

Liu, Ling. *Chinese in North America*. 1949. (In Chinese.)

Lowe, Pardee. *Father and Glorious Descendant*. Boston, Little Brown & Co., 1943.

McEntire, Davis. *Residence and Race*. Berkeley, Calif., University of California Press, 1960.

McWilliams, Carey. *Brothers Under the Skin*. Boston, Little Brown & Co., 1951.

——— *California, the Great Exception*. New York, Current Books, Inc., 1949.

Marden, Charles F. *Minorities in American Society*. New York, American Book Co., 1952.

Margo, Elizabeth. *Taming the Forty-Niner*. New York, Rinehart & Co., 1955.

Markham, Edwin. *California, the Wonderful*. New York, Hearst's International, 1914.

Maurice, Davie. *World Immigration*. New York, The Macmillan Co., 1936.

Mears, Eliot Grinnell. *Resident Orientals on the American Pacific Coast*. Chicago, University of Chicago Press, 1928.

New York City Guide. American Guide Series. New York, Random House, 1939.

Norton, Henry K. *The Story of California*. Chicago, A. C. McClurg & Co., 1913.

Palmer, A. W. *Chinatown: Orientals in American Life*. New York, Friendship Press, 1934.

Panunzio, Constantine. *The Soul of an Immigrant*. New York, The Macmillan Co., 1921.

Park, No Yong. *Chinaman's Chance*. Boston, Meador Press, 1940.

——— *An Oriental View of American Civilization*. Boston and New York, Hale, Cushman and Flint, 1934.

Phelps, Harold and David Henderson. *Population in Its Human Aspects*. Appleton-Century-Crofts, 1958.

Poats, Rutherford. *Decision in Korea*. New York, McBride Co., 1954.

Pruitt, Ida. *The Daughter of Han.* New Haven, Conn., Yale University Press, 1945.

Purcell, Victor. *The Chinese in Southeast Asia.* London, Oxford University Press, 1951.

Remer, C. F. *A Study of Chinese Boycotts.* Baltimore, Johns Hopkins Press, 1933.

Report on World Population Migrations. Washington, D.C., George Washington University, 1956.

Riggs, F. W. *Pressures on Congress: A Study of the Repeal of Chinese Exclusion.* New York, King's Crown Press, 1950.

Ritter, Edward, Helen Ritter and Stanley Spector. *Americans All, Our Oriental Americans.* New York, McGraw-Hill, 1965.

Rose, Arnold and Caroline Rose. *America Divided.* New York, Alfred A. Knopf, 1953.

Reischauer, Edwin O. *Wanted: An Asian Policy.* New York, Alfred A. Knopf, 1955.

Ross, Edward A. *The Changing Chinese, the Conflict of Oriental and Western Cultures in China.* New York, Century Co., 1911.

——— *Standing Room Only.* New York, Century Co., 1927.

Sabin, Edwin L. *Building the Pacific Railway.* Philadelphia, J. B. Lippincott Co., 1919.

Sih, Paul K. T. *Decision for China.* Chicago, Henry Regnery Co., 1959.

——— *From Confucius to Christ.* New York, Sheed and Ward, 1952.

Skinner, G. William. *Leadership and Power in the Chinese Community of Thailand.* Ithaca, N.Y., Cornell University Press, 1958.

Smith, Bradford. *Americans from Japan.* Philadelphia, J. B. Lippincott Co., 1948.

Smith, William C. *Americans in Process.* Ann Arbor, Mich., J. W. Edwards, 1937.

Sone, Monica. *Nisei Daughter.* Boston, Little Brown & Co., 1953.

States' Laws on Race and Color. Compiled and edited by Pauli Murray. Cincinnati, Ohio: Woman's Division of Christian Service, Board of Missions of The Methodist Church Service Center, 1950.

States' Laws on Race and Color and Appendices. Compiled and edited by Verge Laki, LL.B., and Pauli Murray, LL.B., LL.M. Cincinnati, Ohio: Woman's Division of Christian Service, Board of Missions of The Methodist Church Service Center, 1955 Supplement.

Statusz-Hupe, Robert, ed. *American-Asian Tensions.* Foreign Policy Research Institute Series No. 3. New York, Frederick A. Praeger, 1956.

Taylor, Bayard. *Eldorado.* New York, Alfred A. Knopf, 1949.

Thompson, Warren. *Plenty of People.* New York, Ronald Press, 1948.

——— *Population Problems.* New York, McGraw-Hill, 1942.

U.S. Census of Population, 1950 and 1960, Non-White Population by Race. U.S. Dept. of Commerce, Bureau of the Census.

Vital Statistics of the United States. U.S. Dept. of Health, Education and Welfare, Public Health Service.

Waln, Nora. *House of Exile*. New York, Blue Ribbon Books, 1933.

Wang, Gung Hsing. *The Chinese Mind*. New York, John Day Co., 1946.

Warner, W. Lloyd and Leo Srole. *The Social Systems of American Ethnic Groups*. New Haven, Conn., Yale University Press, 1949.

Where Shall We Live. Report of the Commission on Race and Housing. Berkeley, University of California Press, 1958.

Wittke, Carl. *The Irish in America*. Baton Rouge, Louisiana State University Press, 1956.

——— *We Who Built America*. Englewood Cliffs, N.J., Prentice-Hall, 1940.

Wong, Jade Snow. *Fifth Chinese Daughter*. New York, Harper Bros., 1950.

Yang, C. K. *The Chinese Family in the Communist Revolution*. Cambridge, Mass., MIT Press, 1959.

Yost, Edna. *Women of Modern Science*. New York, Dodd Mead & Co., 1959.

Young, Donald R. *American Minority Peoples*. New York, Harper Bros., 1932.

Yung Wing. *My Life in China and America*. New York, Henry Holt, 1909.

Yutang, Lin. *Chinatown Family*. New York, John Day Co., 1948.

——— *My Country and My People*. New York, John Day Co., 1935.

——— *Wisdom of Confucius*. New York, Carlton House, 1938.

ARTICLES AND PAMPHLETS

"Admission of Wives of American Citizens of Oriental Ancestry," U.S. Immigration and Naturalization Service.

"America, Asia and the Future." *Colliers* (Oct. 9, 1943), p. 82.

Asbury, H. "Doyer Street." *American Mercury* (June, 1926), pp. 228–236.

Bassal, H. "Chinese on the Job." *National Business* (Aug., 1943), p. 94.

Bennett, J. E. "Chinese Tong Wars in San Francisco." *Harper's Weekly*, 44 (1900), p. 747.

Bellox, F. "Great American Scientists." *Fortune* (Mar., 1960), pp. 236–242.

Berquist, Laura. "Jacqueline Kennedy Goes Public." *Look* (Mar. 22, 1966), p. 46. (re I. M. Pei)

Braun, Marcus. "How Can We Enforce Our Exclusion Laws?" *Annals of American Academy of Political and Social Sciences*, 34 (Sept., 1909), 140.

Burma, John H. "Research Note on the Measurement of Interracial Marriage." *American Journal of Sociology* (Nov., 1951), p. 587.

"Career for Young Americans." *Nation* (Sept. 3, 1960), p. 102.

Chang, Francis. "An Accommodation Program for Second Generation Chinese." *Sociology and Social Research*, XVIV (July-Aug., 1934), pp. 541–583.

"Changing Scene in United States Chinatowns." *National Council Organization*, 5 (April, 1955), p. 13.

Chen, Ta. "Chinese Migration with Special Reference to Labor Conditions." *U.S. Bureau of Labor Statistics Bulletin*, No. 340 (1923), pp. 5–11.

Chinese American Times. Edited by William Yukon Chang, 165 Park Row, New York City. A monthly newspaper.

"Chinese and Japanese in America." *Annals of American Academy of Political and Social Sciences,* 34 (Sept., 1909), p. 68.

"Chinese Body Chemistry Different from Caucasian." *Science Newsletter* (Aug. 6, 1955), p. 88.

"The Chinese in America." *Encyclopedia Americana.*

"Chinese and Japanese Immigration to Pacific Coast." *California Historical Society Quarterly* (Dec., 1949), p. 343.

"Chinese Exclusion." *New Republic*, 109 (Sept. 6, 1943), p. 323.

"Chinese in Boston." *Economic Geography*, 28 (July, 1952), p. 245.

"The Chinese in Colorado." *Colorado Magazine,* 29 (Oct., 1952), p. 273.

"Chinese in New York's Chinatown." Remarks by Arthur Klein submitted to House prepared by *New York Post*. 83rd Congress. Appendix *Congressional Record* (Aug. 2, 1955), pp. A5668–72.

Chong, Janet. "Sorry But You're Chinese." *Asia* (Feb., 1944), p. 69.

Choy, W. Wong Yan. "Survey Needs of Christian Chinese." *Christian Century*, 72 (June 15, 1955), p. 712.

"Congress Debates Chinese Exclusion Laws." *Scholastic*, 43 (Nov. 8, 1943), pp. 6–7.

Conniff, J. C. G. "Our Amazing Chinese Kids." *Coronet* (Dec., 1955), pp. 31–36.

Cooper, C. R. "Dope Dynasty." *American Magazine,* 126 (Nov., 1938), p. 37.

Coolidge, Mary Robert. "Chinese Labor Competition on the Pacific Coast." *Annals of the American Academy of Political and Social Sciences,* 34 (Sept., 1909), pp. 120–121.

Corbally, John. "Orientals in Seattle Schools." *Sociology and Social Research,* XVI (Sept.-Oct., 1931), pp. 61–67.

Current Biography:
Hiram Fong—1960.
James Wong Howe—1943.
Dong Kingman—1962.

Choh Hao Li—1963.
Lin Yutang—1940.
C. N. Yang and T. D. Lee—1958.

Ecclesine, Margaret. "The Church in Chinatown, U.S.A." *Catholic Digest* (Aug., 1960), pp. 57–62.

Ettenbery, Eugene M. "The Intimate World of Dong Kingman." *American Artist* (Sept., 1961), p. 24.

"Facts About Chinese Tongs." *Good Housekeeping* (Jan., 1959), p. 97.

"Filmfacts" (May 30, 1963). (re James Wong Howe)

Fong Man Hee. "Drop of Chinese Blood." *Asia* (Feb., 1945), p. 120.

Foster, J. W. "The Chinese Boycott." *Atlantic Monthly*, 97 (Jan., 1906), pp. 122–123.

"Fresh Face in Money Management." *Business Week* (Feb. 20, 1965), p. 54.

"Friends of China, Seattle's China Club." *Time*, 67 (Feb. 27, 1956), p. 26.

Gault, K. M. "Chinatown's Boswell." *Christian Science Monitor Magazine* (Dec. 21, 1946), p. 7.

Glick, Carl. "Year of the Monkey." *Colliers* (June 19, 1937), pp. 49–54.

Glick, Clarence. "Relation Between the Position and Status in the Assimilation of Chinese in Hawaii." *American Journal of Sociology*, XLVII (Mar., 1942), pp. 667–679.

Gong, E. "I Want to Marry an American Girl." *American Magazine*, 160 (Sept., 1955), pp. 15–17.

"Hard Work at Hip Wo School in San Francisco." *Life*, 38 (Apr. 25, 1955), pp. 71–72.

Haynor, Norman and Charles Reynold. "Chinese Family Life in America." *American Sociological Review*, 2 (Oct. 1937), pp. 630–637.

"How America Lives, Americans All." *Ladies Home Journal*, 60 (Dec., 1943), pp. 103–105.

Hoy, William. "The Chinese Six Companies," 1942. (pamphlet in Library of Congress)

——— "Tales of California Chinese." (unpublished radio talk) San Francisco, Sept. 16, 1940.

Hsu, L. K. Francis. "What Americans Need to Know About China." *Asia*, 45 (Mar., 1945), pp. 129–132.

——— "Rugged Individualism Reconsidered." *The Colorado Quarterly*, IX, No. 2, (Autumn, 1960).

Huang, Lucy. "Dating and Courtship Innovations of Chinese Students in America." *Marriage and Family Living* (Feb., 1956), pp. 25–30.

"I. M. Pei." *Time* (Dec. 25, 1964), p. 40.

Immigration and Naturalization Service, *Annual Reports*, 1944–1965.

"Immigration and Naturalization Systems of the United States." *Senate Report* No. 1515, 81st Congress, 2nd Sess. Washington, 1950.

"Inscrutable Mr. Tsai." *Newsweek* (May 9, 1966), p. 84.

"James Wong Howe." *Newsweek* (June 11, 1960), pp. 90–91.

Kong, W. "Name Calling: Thoughtless Social Errors Create Barrier Between Chinese and Americans." *Survey Geographic*, 33 (June, 1944), p. 296.

Kwoh, Beulah Ong. "The Occupational Status of American-born Chinese Male College Graduates." *American Journal of Sociology*, 53 (Nov., 1947), pp. 192–200.

Lai, Kum Pui. "Attitudes of the Chinese in Hawaii Toward Their Language Schools." *Sociology and Social Research*, 20 (Nov.-Dec., 1935), p. 140.

Laurenti, Luigi. "Property Values and Race." University of California Press, 1960.

Lee, Chingwah. "The Second Generation of the Chinese." *Hospital Social Service*, XXI (Mar., 1930), pp. 192–197.

Lee, Rose Hum. "Chinese Immigration and Population Changes Since 1940." *Sociology and Social Research*, 41 (Jan., 1957), pp. 195–202.

——— "Chinese in the United States Today." *Survey Geographic*, 31 (Oct., 1942), p. 419.

——— "Decline of Chinatowns in the United States." *American Journal of Sociology*, 54 (March, 1949), p. 422.

——— "Delinquent, Neglected and Dependent Chinese Boys and Girls of the San Francisco Bay Region." *Journal of Social Psychology*, 36 (Aug. 1952), pp. 15–34.

——— "Established Chinese Families of the San Francisco Bay Area." *Midwest Sociologist*, 20 (Dec. 1957), pp. 19–26.

——— "Recent Immigrant Families in San Francisco-Oakland Area." *Marriage and Family Living*, XVIII (1956), pp. 14–24.

Lee, T. H. "Six Months Since Repeal." *Asia*, 44 (July, 1944), p. 322.

Lee, W. J. "Chinese Studies in America." *Free China Review* (Oct., 1966), pp. 31–38.

Lew, Chew. "The Biography of a Chinaman." *Independent*, 55 (1903), p. 420.

Li, Han Hun. "Districts of Kwangtung Province." Sept., 1940. (In Chinese.)

Liu, Chiang. "Chinese Versus American Ideas Concerning the Family." *Journal of Applied Sociology*, 10 (1925–1926), pp. 243–248.

Louis, K. K. "Problems of Second Generation Chinese." *Sociology and Social Research*, XVI (1932), pp. 250–258 and 455–462.

Lowe, Pardee. "Boyhood in East Belleville." *Yale Review*, ns 30 (June, 1941), pp. 766–783.

Lung, C. F. "A Chinese Student and Western Culture." *Sociology and Social Research*, 16 (Nov., 1931), pp. 23–38.

McKenzie, R. D. "The Oriental Finds a Job." *Survey*, LVI (May, 1926), pp. 151–153, 218, 221.

——— "The Oriental Invasion." *Journal of Applied Sociology*, X (Nov.-Dec., 1925), pp. 120–130.

Marshall, J. "Cathay, Hey, Hey." *Colliers*, 109 (Feb. 28, 1942), p. 13.

Murphey, Rhoads. "Boston's Chinatown." *Economic Geography*, 28 (July, 1952), pp. 244–255.

Murphy, T. E. "Portrait of an American Family." *Reader's Digest*, 44 (Mar., 1944), pp. 71–74.

"New Mutual Fund Starts Scramble." *Business Week* (Feb. 12, 1966), p. 126.

"No Chinese-American Juvenile Delinquents." *America*, 93 (July 23, 1955), p. 402.

"Note from the Chinese Minister." Chinese Legation, 1905.

O'Brien, Hubert W. "Status of Chinese in the Mississippi Delta." *Social Force*, 20 (Mar., 1941), pp. 386–390.

O'Meara, J. "The Chinese in Early Days." *Overland Monthly*, n.s.v. 3 (1884).

Page, P. "Chinatown, Not East, Not West." *The New York Times Magazine* (Dec. 15, 1946), p. 24.
See rebuttal—Wong, D. *The New York Times Magazine* (Jan. 12, 1947), p. 24.

Park, Robert E. "A Race Relations Study of Oriental Population of the Pacific Coast." *Journal of Applied Sociology*, 8 (Mar., 1924), pp. 195–205.

Patterson, R. "Tongs in San Francisco." *American Mercury*, 74 (Feb., 1952), pp. 93–99.

"Peking's Constitution and Overseas Chinese." (Their rights and duties) *Far Eastern Economic Review*, 17 (Aug. 5, 1954), pp. 161–164.

Purwin, L. "Chinese Daughters of Uncle Sam." *Independent Woman*, 23 (Nov., 1944), pp. 336–337.

"Racial Ban Cited in Jobs on Coast." *The New York Times*, Aug. 3, 1958.

"Raising Chop Suey on Long Island." *Literary Digest*, 102 (Sept. 14, 1929), pp. 70–74.

Rand, Christopher. "A Reporter at Large." *New Yorker* (Nov. 16, 1957), pp. 113–114.

Reed, R. B. "Career Girl, Chinese Style." *Independent Woman*, 21 (Sept., 1942), pp. 259–260.

"Repeal of the Chinese Exclusion Act." Congressional Hearings, 78th Cong., Sess. 1 and 2.

"Repeal of the Chinese Exclusion Acts." *Monthly Labor Review* (Feb., 1944), pp. 367–368.

"Research on Intermarriage." *American Journal of Sociology* (Nov., 1951), p. 249.

Ripkin, Rona. Unpublished research paper on Chinese community in New York's Chinatown.

Ritchie, R. W. "The Wars of the Tongs." *Harper's Weekly*, 54 (Aug. 27, 1910), pp. 8–10.

Schwartz, S. "Mate Selection Among New York City's Chinese Males, 1931–1938." *American Journal of Sociology*, 56 (May, 1951), pp. 562–568.

Sifakis, C. "Last Great Tong War." *Coronet* (Mar., 1958), pp. 60–64.

Slater, L. "Success Story." *McCalls* (Sept., 1961), p. 12. (re Kingman)

Smith, William. "The Second Generation Oriental American." *Journal of Applied Sociology,* 10 (Nov.-Dec., 1925), p. 160.

Smod, S. H. "San Francisco's Chinatown." *Holiday* (Aug., 1954), p. 98.

"Social Process in Hawaii." No. 18. Sociology Club of U. of Hawaii.

Spinks, Nelson. "Repeal Chinese Exclusion." *Asia and the Americas*, 42 (Feb., 1942), pp. 92–94.

"Text: Repeal of Chinese Exclusion Acts." Immigration and Naturalization Laws and Regulations (Mar., 1944), pp. 126–127.

"Toward a Living Memorial." *Look* (Nov. 17, 1964), pp. M10–16.

"Treaty, Laws and Regulations Governing the Admission of Chinese." Dept. of Commerce and Labor, Bureau of Immigration and Naturalization, Jan. 10, 1911.

Villard, O. G. "Justice for the Chinese." *Christian Century,* 60 (May 26, 1943), pp. 633–634.

Walsh, R. J. "Repeal Chinese Exclusion Now." *Asia*, 43 (Oct., 1943), p. 564.

"We Should End the Affront to China." *Saturday Evening Post*, 216 (Oct. 23, 1943), p. 112.

"West Coast Whites Accept Other Races." *The New York Times,* Dec. 13, 1954.

Whiteside, T. "Wet Wash Chinatown." *New Republic*, 115 (Dec. 23, 1946), pp. 872–874.

"Why No Chinese-American Delinquent." *Saturday Evening Post*, 227 (Apr. 30, 1955), p. 12.

Yeung, K. T. "The Intelligence of Chinese Children." *Journal of Applied Psychology*, V (1922), pp. 267–274.

Yieh, T. K. "Adjustment Problems of Chinese Students." (Pamphlet, New York City Public Library), p.v. 489.

Young, Kimball. "Social Psychology of Oriental-Occidental Prejudices." (Pamphlet, New York City Public Library, 1929), p.v. 401.

THESES AND DISSERTATIONS

Barnett, Milton L. "Alcohol and Culture: A Study of Drinking in a Chinese-American Community." Ph.D. Cornell, 1953.

Bingham, Edwin R. "The Saga of the Los Angeles Chinese." M.A. Occidental College, 1942.

Chen, Wen-hui. "Changing Socio-cultural Patterns of the Chinese Community in Los Angeles." Ph.D. University of Southern California, 1952.

Chinn, F. M. "Religious Education of the Chinese Community of San Francisco." M.A. University of Chicago, 1920.

Chu, Louis H. "The Chinese Restaurant in New York City." M.A. New York University, 1939.

Divine, Robert A. "American Immigration Policy, 1924–1952." Ph.D. Yale, 1953–1954.

Fan, Tin Chiu. "Chinese Residents in Chicago." M.A. University of Chicago, 1925.

Heyer, Virginia. "Patterns of Social Organization in New York City's Chinatown." Ph.D. Columbia, 1953–1954.

Holmes, Maybel M. "A Source Book of Chinese Food Habits." Ph.D. Cornell, 1948.

King, Haitung, "An Analysis of Selected Demographic Aspects of the Chinese-American Population." Ph.D. Louisiana University, 1951.

Kung, S. S. "Personal and Professional Problems of Chinese Students and Former Students in the New York Metropolitan Area." Ph.D. Columbia, 1955.

Kwan, Kian Moon. "Assimilation of the Chinese in the United States." Ph.D. University of California, 1957–1958.

Kwoh, Beulah Ong. "The Occupational Status of the American-born College Graduates." M.A. University of Chicago, 1947.

Lasker, Gabriel Ward. "Physical Characteristics of the Chinese: A Study of Physical Differences and Development Among Chinese at Home and Abroad." Ph.D. Harvard, 1945.

Liang, Yuan. "The Chinese Family in Chicago." M.A. University of Chicago, 1951.

Liu, Ching Ho. "The Influence of Cultural Background on the Moral Judgment of Children." Ph.D. Columbia, 1950.

Liu, Fu-ju. "A Demographic Comparison of Native and Foreign-born Chinese Americans in the United States." Ph.D. Michigan State, 1953.

Liu, Yu Chen. "Interactions Within Chinese-American Families of Portland, Oregon, Resulting from Cultural Differences." Ph.D. Oregon State College, 1951.

Loh, Homer. "Americans of Chinese Ancestry in Philadelphia." Ph.D. University of Pennsylvania, 1944.

Meldrum, George W. "The History of the Treatment of Foreign and Minority Groups in California, 1830–1860." Ph.D. Stanford, 1949.

Shen, Yun Kung. "American Official Attitudes Toward the Government in China, 1898–1947." Ph.D. University of Wisconsin, 1948.

Siu, Paul C. P. "The Chinese Laundryman: A Study of Social Isolation." Ph.D. University of Chicago, 1953–1954.

Wu, C. C. "Chinatowns, A Study of Symbiosis and Assimilation." Ph.D. University of Chicago, 1928.

Index